Educational Research

Insights and Applications

R. Scott Baldwin
Edinboro University of Pennsylvania

Don T. Basse
Adams State College

Dawn M. Snodgrass
Edinboro University of Pennsylvania

EDINBORO UNIVERSITY PRESS
219 Meadville Street, Edinboro, Pennsylvania 16444

Copyright ©2008
Library of Congress Catalog Card Number:
ISBN: 0972753036
All rights reserved. No part of this publication may be reproduced,
stored in a retrieval system, or transmitted, in any form or by any
means, electronic, mechanical, photocopying recording, or otherwise,
without the prior written permission of the copyright owner.
Printed in the United States of America
10   9   8   7   6   5   4   3   2   1

Table of Contents

Preface iv

About the Authors vi

Unit One: Preparing for Research 1

    Chapter 1:   Structure of Social Science Research 1

    Chapter 2:   Research Topics, Questions, & Statements 12

    Chapter 3:   Review of the Literature 26

Unit Two: Statistics and Quantitative Research Methods 39

    Chapter 4:   Overview of Quantitative Research 39

    Chapter 5:   Descriptive Statistics 47

    Chapter 6:   Correlation 64

    Chapter 7:   Measurement 80

    Chapter 8:   Quantitative Methods 96

    Chapter 9:   Analysis of Variance 113

    Chapter 10: Research Validity 132

Unit Three: Qualitative Research Methods 150

    Chapter 11: Qualitative Research I: Characteristics, Use, & Design 150

    Chapter 12: Qualitative Research II: Data & Analysis 163

    Chapter 13: Multimethod Research 188

References 196

Glossary 199

Appendices 208

    Appendix A: Answers to Self-Tests and Activities 208

    Appendix B: Supplemental Readings 218

 # Preface

In comprehensive institutions of higher education, master's degree programs in education and counseling usually have requirements in the areas of measurement, statistics, and research. Frequently, those requirements are met in a single course with a title something like Introduction to Educational Research.

In our combined 50+ years of experience teaching educational research, we have found that master's students generally find the research course to be the most challenging educational requirement in their programs of study. It has also been our experience that - in the mad rush to be all inclusive – authors of research textbooks attempt to cover so much material that the fundamentals get confused with the more esoteric aspects of research, which master's degree students will never need unless they move on to doctoral study.

We decided to develop a book sufficiently limited in scope to include what we believe master's students need from their one research course – and nothing more. Consequently, the text presents measures of central tendency, variance concepts, and validity. It does not include semi-partial correlation, factor analysis, or Greco-Latin squares designs. *Educational Research* is a readable and coherent introduction to quantitative and qualitative research. Its primary objective is to assist students in becoming intelligent, critical, and confident consumers of research. A second objective of the text is to assist students in designing research, writing research proposals, and conducting real research.

Chapters begin with an anticipation guide, chapter rationale, objectives, and a graphic organizer, which are designed to preview the chapter and establish a purpose for reading. Chapters end with a reaction guide and a self-test, to bring closure to the chapter and to assist in reviewing progress and changes in student thinking. Chapters also include research articles that contextualize chapter content.

The companion website at www.edinboro.edu/press is a multi-faceted resource supporting literature reviews, chapter content, and research activities. The companion website includes:

- Active links to random number generators and statistical programs for computing descriptive statistics, chi square, correlation, t-tests, and ANOVA
- Active links to resources for literature reviews
- Supporting activities for each chapter
- Recommended research readings

Note to Students. Master's students are frequently fearful of a course in educational research because they imagine their math skills will be inadequate. This math phobia is needless! If you can add, subtract, multiply, divide, and push the square root button on a simple hand calculator, you will be able to handle the math required to master the material in this text. The real challenge lies in your willingness to think in new ways.

RSB   DTB   DMS

 # About the Authors

R. Scott Baldwin, PhD, is Dean of the School of Graduate Studies & Research at Edinboro University of Pennsylvania. His professional interests are currently focused on designing Web-based degree programs with virtual environments. Scott's hobbies include trading commodity futures and applying probability theory to games of chance.

Dr. Don T. Basse is Chair and Professor in the CACREP accredited Counseling Department at Adams State College in Alamosa, CO. Don's professional interests are currently focused on the design of Web-based instructional delivery systems for counseling education. He is a motorcycle enthusiast and lives in Alamosa with his wife Laura and their two pugs.

Dr. Dawn M. Snodgrass is a professor in the Department of Professional Studies at Edinboro University of Pennsylvania where she teaches research to master's degree candidates. She has edited two research monographs, published three textbooks, and written numerous professional articles. Dawn enjoys serving in youth ministry at her church and traveling with her husband and son.

1 Structure of Social Science Research

Anticipation Guide

1. Figuring your gas mileage is research.   Agree _____ Disagree _____

2. Research without numbers is not research.   Agree _____ Disagree _____

3. Statistical methods used in education and the behavioral sciences are derived from agricultural research methods.   Agree _____ Disagree _____

4. Girls have stronger bonds with pets than do boys.   Agree _____ Disagree _____

5. Reading research supports strong phonics programs.   Agree _____ Disagree _____

Chapter Rationale

Sometimes a *mob* might *grift* all day without *turning them over*, but this is unlikely except in the case of a *jug mob*, which takes a limited number of *pokes*. Any pick-pocket who has on his person more than one wallet is something of a hazard both to himself and to the mob, for each wallet can count as a separate offense if he should be caught. Therefore, it is safer to have cash only. *Class mobs* usually count the money each time they *skin the pokes*. One *stall* is commonly responsible for all of it, and an accounting in full is made at the end of the day [our italics]. (Maurer, 2003, p. 194)

All groups of people, whether they are pick-pockets, plumbers, lawyers, or computer technicians, have a specialized vocabulary or jargon that allows them to communicate with each other in highly specialized ways. Insiders use this vocabulary freely to gain access to information and to keep outsiders at a disadvantage. We want you to become an insider when it comes to educational research.

The purposes of this chapter are to give you a basic definition of research, establish the value of research in education and counseling, and to give you a sense of what you will learn in the remaining chapters. In addition, we want to introduce you to some of the vocabulary of educational research by having you read a research article. Because we believe it is essential for you to learn the basic jargon of research, the entire text has a strong focus on learning and retaining the relevant vocabulary.

Objectives

As a master's degree candidate you have an obligation to understand your field of study on a deeper and more complex level than would be expected of undergraduate students. You should be able to read original research and make your own judgments about its quality and value to the field. You should also be able to conduct practical research that will assist you in making professional decisions. Therefore, the primary objectives of this chapter are to introduce you to both the fundamental vocabulary and the structure of educational research.

Graphic Organizer

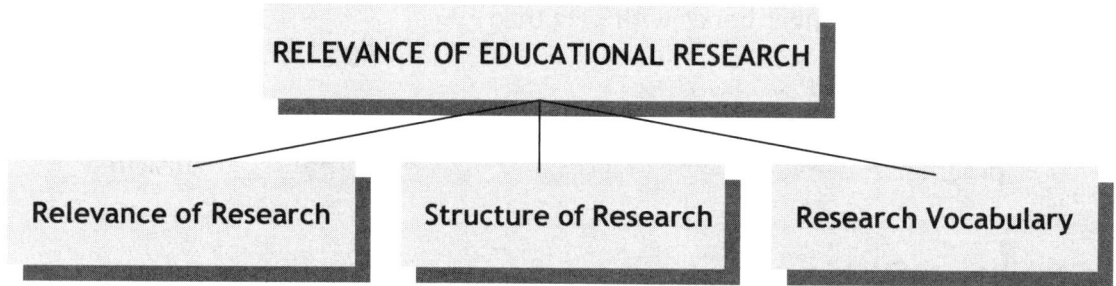

Why Research Is Relevant

In 1955 a medical researcher named Jonas Salk introduced the first vaccine for poliomyelitis (polio), also called infantile paralysis because of its devastating effect on children. Until Salk's discovery, polio was one of the most feared diseases in the world. Tens of thousands of children were stricken each year with fever, pain, and paralysis that condemned them to live with braces or in iron lungs, huge metal chambers that literally took the place of the muscles necessary for breathing. So great was the fear of polio – particularly during the summer – that parents routinely isolated their children, and communities shut down swimming pools in an attempt to prevent the disease from spreading. The Salk vaccine was the product of years of systematic experimentation, and today polio has been virtually eliminated as a health threat in the United States. Every year the USDA approves thousands of new drugs that fight diseases or add to our collective wellness. Each new drug is thoroughly researched and tested before it is released to the public.

Medical research may be the most dramatic research domain, but research in the physical sciences and engineering have led to astonishing technological advances which have touched all of us in deep and permanent ways. Every large corporation has the equivalent of an R&D (research and development) division. During the last 70 years agricultural researchers have made vast improvements in farm productivity by means of research. In fact, many of the statistical methods used in the behavioral sciences and education are derived directly from agricultural research that systematically manipulated chemicals, soil types, amounts of water and sunlight, temperature and other variables to find out what combinations produce the best crops.

In education and the behavioral sciences, the research of the last 100 years has given us a knowledge base in teaching, learning, and counseling that guides professionals in those areas. For example, in spite of the debate that has raged for decades over the relative merits of phonics instruction, the research literature – which is composed of hundreds of individual studies – clearly shows that systematic instruction in decoding and related activities is highly beneficial to children learning to read (Stahl, Duffy-Hester, & Stahl, 1998). Whether your area of study is Elementary Education, School Counseling, Special Education, or Teaching English as a Second Language, there is a huge body of research made up of thousands of studies that together inform you about best practices and programs.

Definition of Research

Research is any discovery procedure that requires the systematic collection of information. The first thing to note in the definition is that, to be research, it must involve discovery. If you are not trying to find something out, it isn't research. For example, the telephone company systematically collects information about individuals and businesses so that they can be listed in the telephone book, but this is not research because the purpose of the activity is not discovery. The second thing to note in the definition of research is that it must be systematic. Guessing or estimating based upon casual observations is not research.

Suppose you want to find out how many miles per gallon your car gets. You fill the tank and set the trip odometer to zero. The next time you stop for gas you note the number of gallons it takes to fill the tank. Then you divide the number of miles on the trip odometer by the number of gallons it took to fill the tank. Assuming that the trip odometer read 390 miles and number of gallons used was 16.7, the number of miles per gallon was 23.35 (390 miles / 16.7 gallons = 23.35 miles per gallon). We would classify this as research because it fits our definition. It is also an example of what is usually referred to as *quantitative research* because the research is dependent upon numerical computation.

The information collected in research does not have to be numerical. It may also involve observations that are not easily reduced to numbers. For example, if you wanted to investigate the interactions of children on a particular school playground, you could observe the children at every recess for a week. You could enter your observations in a journal and then review them after you finished your observations. Some questions you might be able to answer are: Do boys and girls participate in the same activities? In what ways are the games of older children different from those of younger children? Do the children seem happier in the morning or the afternoon? It would, of course, be possible to collect numerical information (for example, by counting aggressive behaviors in the morning and afternoon), but it is not a requirement to qualify as research. You could simply provide a written account of your systematic observations. This type of research is often referred to as *qualitative research*.

Both quantitative and qualitative research can be subclassified as pure research, applied research, and action research. These terms refer to the purposes of research rather than to the methods that are used. *Pure research* – sometimes referred to as "hard" or "fundamental" research – is designed to advance knowledge for the sake of knowledge without regard for practical applications. Pure research aims to create new knowledge and theories that contribute to the overall understanding of the natural or social sciences.

Applied research – often referred to as research and development (R&D) in business and industry - utilizes the knowledge and theories of natural and social sciences to solve real world problems or to create new products. It is often the case that pure research ultimately leads to applied research. Newton's laws of motion (Newton, 1687) (pure) were fundamental in the development of transportation systems (applied); Einstein's theory of relativity (Einstein, 1905) (pure) was essential in the development of nuclear energy (applied); and the linguistic research of the 1950s on the acoustic properties of speech (pure) was critical in the design of modern telecommunications (applied).

Action research is a form of applied research, and it may be qualitative or quantitative. Action research is designed to resolve practical problems and immediate concerns at a local level. The focus of the research is on the investigator's clients, students, or school. It is possible that the results of action research will be relevant to others, but the focus of the research is on acquiring information or resolving problems of importance to the researcher.

Activity 1

Paragraph 1

Each of the paragraphs below describes research. Classify each study as Qualitative or Quantitative and Pure, Applied, or Action research. Check the appropriate boxes and justify your answers in the space provided.

"A significant component of the interior noise of aircraft and automobiles is a result of turbulent boundary layer excitation of the vehicular structure. In this work, active robust feedback control of the noise due to this non-predictable excitation is investigated. Both an analytical model and experimental investigations are used to determine the characteristics of the flow induced structural sound radiation problem. The problem is shown to be broadband in nature with large system uncertainties associated with the various operating conditions" (Heatwole, 1998).

Qualitative ___   Quantitative ___   Pure ___   Applied ___   Action ___

Rationale: _____

_____

_____

Paragraph 2

Thor Heyerdahl believed that people from South America during pre-Columbian times were the original settlers of Polynesia. In 1947 Heyerdahl and five companions built the raft Kon-Tiki using only balsa wood and other materials and technologies that would have been available to Peruvian people 1,500 years ago. Heyerdahl sailed the Kon-Tiki from South America for 101 days across 4,300 miles of the Pacific Ocean and reached the Tuamotu Islands of Polynesia on August 7, 1947. The only modern equipment aboard the Kon-Tiki was a radio and a watch. The book *Kon-Tiki* details this extraordinary experiment (Heyerdahl, 1950)

Qualitative ___ Quantitative ___ Pure ___ Applied ___ Action ___

Rationale: _____

_____

_____

Paragraph 3

"The purpose of this study was to increase time on task by observing student behaviors in four Grade 2 classrooms throughout The School District of the City of Erie using the *Student Engagement Rate Instrument* (SERI). The *Student Engagement Rate Instrument* allowed the evaluators to identify those students who were deemed to be off task. Therefore, the *Student Engagement Rate Instrument* helped the observers to identify the off-task behaviors and supplied the research team with a percentage of students who were on task. Using this information, the research team provided appropriate feedback and training to the participating classroom teachers to assist them in engaging students in learning for a higher percentage of time." (Barker, Bernard, Cappabianca, Dahlstrand, Maguire, Meredith, and Rewers, 2004)

Qualitative ___ Quantitative ___ Pure ___ Applied ___ Action ___

Rationale: _____

_____

_____

Discussion of Activity 1

The three paragraphs in this activity are not comprehensive; so there is room for debate, and our solutions are not necessarily the only options.

Paragraph 1 is classified as Quantitative and Applied. It seems designed to deal specifically with vehicle noise; and the descriptive language (e.g., "experimental investigations") suggests a quantitative approach. Could it be qualitative?

Paragraph 2 is classified as Qualitative and Pure. Heyerdahl was testing a theory that had no practical applications, which makes it pure research. The paragraph doesn't come right out and say so, but our inference is that the adventure would have lent itself to qualitative approaches involving careful observation and detailed journal writing. Could it have been both qualitative and quantitative?

Paragraph 3 is classified as Quantitative and Action. It is clearly action research because it is designed to address a local school problem. And while the research may have had qualitative elements, it did involve the collection of numerical information, which makes it quantitative.

Activity 2

Read the article "Pet Bonding and Pet Bereavement among Adolescents." As you encounter each of the research terms listed below, indicate your level of comprehension by circling the appropriate number on the scale. This will give you a baseline sense of how well you understand research terminology and procedures at the beginning of the course. By the time you complete this course you should be able to read an article like this with confidence. This activity will also give your instructor information that will be useful in designing class presentations and discussions.

5 = complete understanding of the term
3 = fuzzy idea of what the term means
1 = zero understanding of the term

Hypothesis	5	4	3	2	1
Sample	5	4	3	2	1
Descriptive data	5	4	3	2	1
Method	5	4	3	2	1
Participants	5	4	3	2	1
Reliability	5	4	3	2	1
Internal consistency	5	4	3	2	1
$r = .54$	5	4	3	2	1
Range	5	4	3	2	1
$p < .001$	5	4	3	2	1
Mean	5	4	3	2	1
Standard Deviation	5	4	3	2	1
Rank order	5	4	3	2	1
Statistics	5	4	3	2	1
Validity	5	4	3	2	1
Correlation	5	4	3	2	1
Positively correlated	5	4	3	2	1

Negatively correlated	5	4	3	2	1
Results	5	4	3	2	1
Table 1	5	4	3	2	1
F-ratio	5	4	3	2	1
t-ratio	5	4	3	2	1
$F(2, 52) = 12.75$	5	4	3	2	1
Mean differences	5	4	3	2	1
$n = 19$	5	4	3	2	1
Analysis	5	4	3	2	1
Dependent variables	5	4	3	2	1
Significant results	5	4	3	2	1
M	5	4	3	2	1
SD	5	4	3	2	1
Statistically significant	5	4	3	2	1
Distributions	5	4	3	2	1
Discussion	5	4	3	2	1
References	5	4	3	2	1

Total Score _____

Discussion of Activity 2

The loss of a family pet is an almost universal experience, so we would expect everyone to begin reading the article with high prior knowledge and some interest in the subject. Our guess is that your comprehension was excellent until you hit page two and some of the unfamiliar terms and obscure numbers. By the time you got to the third page you began to feel frustrated and at least considered saying "the heck with it" and jumping to the conclusion on the last page of the article. And if you rolled your eyeballs, gritted your teeth, or said a naughty word when you looked at Table 1, you wouldn't be the first student to do so. The entire Results section was probably on a frustration reading level for you. This is a natural feeling that comes from not knowing the specialized vocabulary of research. However, your discomfort will fade into confidence as you master the concepts and vocabulary in the rest of this book.

Template for Writing a Research Paper

Master's students in an introductory research course are typically required to prepare a research paper or project. Your instructor will provide you with specific information, but the structure of the project will probably take one of the following forms:

A. Three Chapter Format: Planning a Study

   Chapter 1: Introduction
   Chapter 2: Review of the Literature
   Chapter 3: Research Methods

B. Five Chapter Format: Planning and Conducting a Study

   Chapter 1: Introduction
   Chapter 2: Review of the Literature
   Chapter 3: Research Methods
   Chapter 4: Data Presentation and Results
   Chapter 5: Discussion

C. Journal-Style Manuscript

   This format contains the same information as the five chapter format. However, the paper is typically much shorter in length. The manuscript is written according to the *Publication Manual of the American Psychological Association (2001)*, and – in the ideal case – is suitable for publication in a professional journal.

Depending upon the format your instructor selects, some combination of the topics listed below will be part of your research paper. The outline below indicates where information about those topics is found in this text. For example, the abstract for a research paper is usually the last in the writing chronology, so suggestions for writing an abstract are found in Chapter 13. In contrast, selecting topics and asking research questions is in the beginning stage of the research process and is presented in Chapter 2.

Abstract: Chapter 13

Introduction
    Topic and Questions: Chapter 2
    Review of Literature: Chapter 3

Methods: Chapter 8

Results: Chapter 9

Discussion: Chapter 10

References: Chapter 3

Reaction Guide

1. ___ Figuring your gas mileage is research.   Confirmed _____ Disconfirmed _____

2. ___ Research without numbers is not research.   Confirmed _____ Disconfirmed _____

3. ___ Statistical methods used in education and the behavioral sciences are derived from agricultural research methods.   Confirmed _____ Disconfirmed _____

4. ___ Girls have stronger bonds with pets than do boys.   Confirmed _____ Disconfirmed _____

5. ___ Reading research supports strong phonics programs.   Confirmed _____ Disconfirmed _____

Why my choice is confirmed.   Why my choice is not confirmed.

1. _____   _____

2. _____   _____

3. _____   _____

4. _____   _____

5. _____   _____

Chapter 1 Self-Test *

True or False

1. ____ Calculating your average monthly electric bill could be an example of qualitative research.

2. ____ The primary purpose of this text is to make you a smart consumer of research.

3. ____ Educational research rarely leads to improved instructional methods.

4. ____ Some of the research methods used to improve crop yields are also used to study teaching and learning.

5. ____ It is possible to read and comprehend research without understanding the specialized vocabulary of educational research.

Matching

6. ____ quantitative research

7. ____ anticipation guide

8. ____ qualitative research

9. ____ reaction guide

10. ____ stall

A. research in which numerical computations are critical
B. an instructional technique for introducing new material
C. a member of a mob of pick-pockets
D. research in which descriptive observations are more important than numerical computations
E. an instructional device for bringing closure to a lesson.

* Answers are in Appendix A.

Companion Website

Additional resources and chapter activities are located at www.edinboro.edu/press.

2 Research Topics, Questions & Statements

Anticipation Guide

1. All unsolved questions are research questions. Agree _____ Disagree _____

2. A research question is the same as a research statement. Agree _____ Disagree _____

3. "I wonder if extraterrestrials exist?" is a good research question. Agree _____ Disagree _____

4. You must have a research question to do research. Agree _____ Disagree _____

5. Lack of clarity is the most serious shortcoming of research questions. Agree _____ Disagree _____

6. Minimal harm to subjects is permitted in the interest of research. Agree _____ Disagree _____

Chapter Rationale

One February a few years ago I was attending an educational conference in Chicago. It was late at night and snowing like crazy. As I was walking back to my hotel I saw a young man under a bright streetlight frantically searching the snow-covered ground. I stopped and asked what was wrong and he breathlessly informed me that he'd lost his wedding ring. I got down on my knees and started raking the snow with my bare hands hunting for the ring. After a few minutes of this I asked the guy if he was sure he'd lost the ring in this particular spot. He pointed and said, "No, I lost it in that alley over there." My immediate question was, "Then why in the world are we looking for the ring over here?" To which he replied, "The light's better!" (Scott)

The purpose of this chapter is to show you how to identify good and bad research questions and how to develop appropriate research questions of your own. If you select an inappropriate topic or frame your research questions haphazardly, you will end up out in the cold and looking under the wrong streetlight.

Objectives

In this chapter you will learn how to select a research topic and then develop it into a research question and finally into an appropriate research statement.

Graphic Organizer

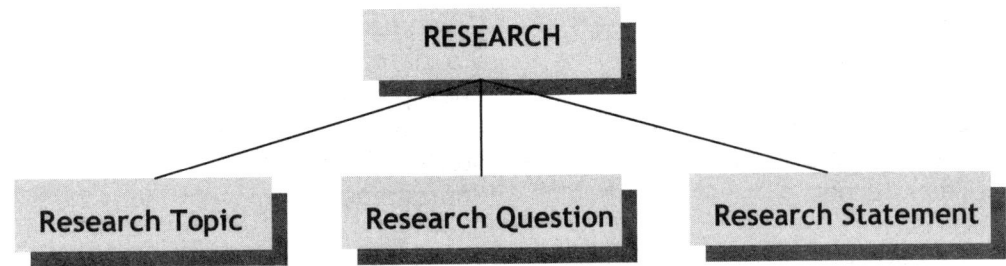

Research Topics

A *research topic* is a broad area of possible scientific inquiry. Identifying a good research topic is a critical first step in selecting a specific research project. This is not always as easy as it sounds because there is a universe of possible topics lurking out there, and they will be more or less suitable depending upon your interests, knowledge, and purposes. Here are four rules for selecting a good topic:

Rule #1: Select a topic that is consistent with your instructor's course objectives and/or your current program of study.

Rule #2: Select a topic that is of personal interest to you.

Rule #3: Select a topic about which you already have some knowledge.

Rule #4: Select a topic that is sufficiently well documented that it will lend itself to fruitful library research.

Activity 1

The following is a tiny sample of possible research topics. Following the four rules for selecting a topic, pick three and be prepared to justify your choices in class discussion.

Possible Topics

Study Skills
Movement Therapy
Educational Uses of Multimedia
Year Round Schools
Language Acquisition
Gay Marriage
Whole Language
Career Counseling
Marriage Counseling
The Internet
Division
Technology
Post Traumatic Shock
Sports Psychology
English Only
Addictions
Adolescent Sex
Divorce
Teacher Pay
Tort Law
Management Styles
No Child Left Behind
Counseling AIDS Patients
Education Reform
Term Papers in Education
Multicultural Education
Smoking Cessation
IQ Tests
Evaluation of Educational Software

Phonics
Math Phobia
Science Education in the Primary Grades
Sleep Therapy
Grouping for Reading Instruction
Standardized Tests
Therapy for Depression
Classroom Management
Student Teaching
Photography
Bulimia
Performance-based Education
Hypnosis
Sleep Disorders
Learning Disabilities
Drug Use
Adult Sex
Learning Disorders
Counselor Pay
Inclusion
Employee Motivation
Wellness
Dyslexia
Managed Care in Counseling
Cognitive Dissonance
Student Achievement
Weight Loss
Critical Pedagogy
School Accreditation

Research Questions

Research topics are broad; research questions are narrow and usually associated with quantitative research. A *research question* is a query that guides scientific investigation and data gathering. Developing a good research question – or set of research questions – is critical in the planning phases of research. To get from a research topic to an appropriate research question usually requires a good bit of thinking as well as some research in the library. Your research question will probably evolve while you are doing your library research of the topic (Chapter 3, Review of Literature). However, for purposes of explanation we will discuss research questions without reference to a literature review.

What makes a research question good?

A good research question is one that will assist you in designing a study that is valid and adds accurate information to your personal knowledge base or to the profession. Here are the four *SMEC* principles (**S**cope, **M**easurement, **E**mbedded Questions, and **C**larity) for developing a good research question from a research topic.

Principle #1: The research question must have a reasonable scope.

If the scope of your study is too big, you may never be able to accomplish it. Consider the question:

> What is the best way to improve student achievement?

This research question is massive and includes just about everything that might influence student achievement. Any research design that derived from such a question would be essentially undoable. To determine if the scope of your research question is reasonable, you have to ask yourself some practical questions:

1. Do I have the resources to conduct the study?
2. Can I get permission to do the study?
3. Can the research question be answered using ethical methods?
4. Can I gather the data in a timely manner?
5. Do I have to create my own assessments?
6. Do I have the necessary expertise to complete the tasks involved?

Principle #2: The research question must have a measurable solution.

The answer to a quantitative research question must involve measuring something: achievement, emotions, beliefs, or physical attributes. This means that you have to have some sort of practical instrumentation. It is pointless to pose a research question if you can't measure whatever it is you want to study. For example:
What is the intellectual potential of children born into low income families?

The question is provocative, but there is at this time no known way to measure the contributions of inherited ability independent of interaction with the environment.

Principle #3: The research question must not contain embedded questions.

Some research studies pose numerous questions, but the questions are usually written separately to avoid ambiguity. Your research question should be one and only one question. For instance:

In a virtual learning environment, will girls outperform boys in writing and arithmetic?

There are two research questions embedded in the question above: (1) In a virtual learning environment, will girls outperform boys in **writing**? and (2) In a virtual learning environment, will girls outperform boys in **arithmetic**?

Principle #4: The research question must be clear and unambiguous.

If your research question lacks precision or is confusing, there is a strong possibility that your research design and the results of your study will be invalid or subject to dispute. Think about the following question:

Will students in the Far Out program outperform students in the Sting program?

The research question is vague and uninformative. In what ways will the Far Out students outperform the Sting students? What subjects? What age groups? A better question would be: Will sixth-grade students in the Far Out program outperform students in the Sting program in reading achievement as measured by an informal reading inventory?

Converting Research Topics into Research Questions

Example 1: Ms. Frost, a 10th grade social studies teacher, is interested in the role homework plays in academic achievement.

Her research topic is: How Homework Affects Student Achievement. Ms. Frost's first attempt to convert the topic into a research question results in the following:

Does homework improve achievement in social studies?

Applying the SMEC principles, it should be obvious that the research question is inadequate because its scope is way too broad and it lacks clarity. The improved question reduces the scope of the question and increases clarity:

Do moderate amounts of homework (versus no homework) in American history improve the classroom test performances of 11th grade students in an urban school?

Example 2: Mr. Romero is a high school counselor who wonders if he is making good use of his time. His research topic is: Most Efficient Use of a Counselor's Time. His hunch is that he is spending extraordinary amounts of time with a few students. Mr. Romero's review of the literature suggests that he might make more of a difference in his school if he could spend time in the classroom instead of counseling individual students all day long. He wonders if this would have an effect on those students: personally, socially, behaviorally and academically? Mr. Holmes is an English teacher who is willing to experiment, and they decide to team-teach a class in world literature once a week. In addition to the traditional readings and related class discussions, Mr. Romero will add some social skills, coping skills and life skills to the curriculum. Mr. Romero's research question is framed as follows:

What are the effects on the academic performance and social behavior of tenth grade students of a school counselor serving as a team teacher?

Using the SMEC principles, you could argue successfully that the scope of the question is too large, that measurement of social behavior is problematical, and that the question is vague. However, the main error is embedded questions. Mr. Romero has asked two questions:

What are the effects of a school counselor serving as a team teacher on the academic performance of tenth grade students? And,

What are the effects of a school counselor serving as a team teacher on the social behavior of tenth grade students?

Having two questions certainly increases the complexity of any study; so Mr. Romero decides to eliminate the focus on behavior, and rewrites his research question as follows:

How will the inclusion of social skills in a tenth grade world literature course affect student achievement as measured by ability to comprehend daily reading assignments?

Mr. Romero now has a clear direction for designing an appropriate experiment. Furthermore, anyone reading his research question will have a pretty good idea of what Mr. Romero wants to study.

Example 3: Ms. McCartney is a therapist in a mental health center. She has been treating adult clients with symptoms of depression by placing them in individual therapy and in groups. Some of her clients are receiving medication, but overall she believes that while some are improving, few have improved enough to cease therapy. Ms. McCartney is also a wellness enthusiast and is curious about the relationship between depression and exercise. Her research topic is: The Relationship between Depression and Exercise. Ms. McCartney reasons that if depressed clients gained something new in their lives as intrusive as their own depression, the depression would not be so overwhelming. A review of the literature suggested that exercise might be just the right kind of intrusion. Her research question is:

Will non-medicated depressed adult clients who participate in individual therapy and strenuous exercise show more signs of recovery than clients receiving therapy alone?

Following the SMEC principles, this appears to be a good research question. You should note that it you want to get picky, you can almost always reduce the scope, question the difficulty of measurement, and add additional clarification. How much is a matter of professional judgment.

These examples should provide you with a feel for taking your topic and narrowing it down to a researchable question. Good questions help to keep you focused and clarify for everyone the purpose of your research.

Bad Questions

Bad questions are research questions that violate the SMEC principles. Bad questions are too broad; they are not researchable; they cover too many questions; or they are vague and confusing. Read and think about the following examples:

Example 1

Topic: The Cost of Education

Bad Question: What are the costs of education?

Why the question is bad: This question fails the SMEC principle of scope. It is too broad and needs to be narrowed into a manageable subject for study. For instance, are you going to include the cost of teacher salaries, instructional supplies, construction, transportation, maintenance, sports, and so on? The revised and more constrained question provides the researcher and reader with a clear picture of what is being proposed.

Revised Question: What is the per-pupil transportation cost of an inner city public school in comparison to a suburban public school?

Example 2

Topic: Empathic Counseling

Bad Question: Are empathic counseling techniques important to client progress?

Why the question is bad: This question fails the SMEC principle of clarity. It is not clear whether the word "important" refers to the client or the therapist. The revised question adds clarity.

Revised Question: Do empathic counseling techniques increase clients' recovery when compared to traditional counseling techniques?

Example 3

Topic: Phonics

Bad Question: What are the effects of teaching phonics in reading?

Why the question is bad: This question does not tell what effects are under investigation. You could argue that it violates all four of SMEC principles. The revised question is very clear on what the issues are and the nature of the proposed investigation.

Revised Question: Does teaching phonics increase third graders' word recognition scores as measured by the *Stanford Achievement Test*?

Activity 2

Using the SMEC principles, explain why each of the following research questions is bad. Then revise the question to make it better.

Topic: Eating Disorders

Bad Question: What causes bulimia and anorexia?

Why the question is bad: _____

_____

Revised Question: _____

_____

Topic: Technology in Education

Bad Question: Does technology improve education?

Why the question is bad: _____

_____

Revised Question: _____

_____

Topic: Literacy

Bad Question: Will reading cease to be an essential skill in the future?

Why the question is bad: _____

_____

Revised Question: _____

Research Statements

A research statement is a research question that has been transformed into a declarative statement that predicts the outcome of the research or proposes to test a specific hypothesis. Some professors prefer to guide research with a statement rather than a question. A question implies objectivity and the researcher's belief that a number of outcomes are plausible. For example, the following research question by itself suggests that costs could be higher for inner city or for suburban schools.

What is the per-pupil transportation cost of an inner city public school in comparison to a suburban public school?

However, suppose the researcher has a hunch or hypothesis about the relative costs of transportation; it may make sense to reframe the research question as a statement that reflects the researcher's beliefs. For instance: The per-pupil cost of transportation will be higher for an inner city school than for a suburban school.

The choice of using a research statement rather than a research question to guide the design of a study is really a matter of personal preference.

Activity 3

Convert the following research questions into research statements:

Does homework improve achievement in social studies? _____

_____

What are the effects of a school counselor serving as a team teacher on the academic performance and social behavior of tenth grade students?

_____

_____

Will non-medicated depressed adult clients who participate in individual therapy and strenuous exercise show more signs of recovery than clients receiving therapy alone?

___

___

___

Activity 4

Reread the introduction to the article, "Pet Bonding and Pet Bereavement among Adolescents," and be prepared to answer the following questions:

1. Did the researchers use research questions or research statements?

2. Why do you think the researchers made the decision to use questions (or statements)?

3. Do the research questions/statements adhere to the SMEC principles? If not, which principles are violated?

Ethical Considerations

Research in education, counseling and other social sciences frequently involves human subjects. Designing research that deals with people must consider their safety as study participants. Beyond physical safety, researchers must carefully evaluate risks for mental, emotional, and even social safety when studying human behavior. Just as the be- kind-to-others rule crosses a myriad of religions, there is one prevailing rule for conducting ethical research: Do no harm.

Obvious as this one rule may seem, researchers can easily step across the invisible threshold that defines harm to others. Sometimes the step taken is easy to see as in the reported "Monster Study" conducted by researchers at a large university in the 1930s. Researchers trying to determine the causes of stuttering, subjected very young children in a state-run orphanage to continuous verbal harassment and other negative responses to see if they could cause the children to stutter. As they grew, these children suffered from a variety of psychological disorders. It is not difficult to see the lack of ethical behavior in the design and implementation of this research plan. The emotional stress of interruptions and other harassment while speaking; the resulting lack of confidence in ability to speak well socially; the physiological reactions to frequent negative feedback are all readily evident in this technically well designed but thoroughly unethical research study.

Not all research studies break the do-no-harm rule in such an obvious manner. Perhaps, a physical education teacher wants to address the growing concern of obesity in her students. After providing instruction on healthy eating habits to all of her classes, she randomly assigns the students in the classes to two groups. One group is given a nutritionally balanced eating plan that limits caloric intake to 1,200 calories daily for six weeks. The other group continues eating as they usually do. Following six weeks of implementation, the children are weighed and results from both groups are compared.

On the surface this may seem like a viable study that has the best interest of students at the front. But, has this teacher considered the physical safety of overweight students who suddenly drop daily caloric intake by thousands of calories. Have the emotional implications of being told what and how much you can eat been considered? Will there be social implications for students who may lose weight and others who do not have the opportunity to participate in the experimental eating plan?

The American Educational Research Association (2007) and the American Psychological Association (2007) provide detailed explanations of ethical guidelines that should govern all research involving human and other animal subjects. These guidelines are available in AERA and APA publications and on their websites. We encourage you to become familiar with these guidelines as you develop your skills as an educational researcher.

Writing Your Research Report: Topics & Questions

The topic is usually reflected in the title of the research report. In a journal-style research report the topic is inserted at the beginning of the introduction as a lead-in to the review of literature. Research statements and questions usually come at the end of the review of literature, the results of which are typically used as evidence of the need for the study and the importance of answering the research questions posed by the researcher. If your instructor requires a chapter format, follow her directions for placement of the topic discussion, review of literature, and research questions or statements.

Reaction Guide

1. All unsolved questions are research questions.   Confirmed _____ Disconfirmed _____
2. A research question is the same as a research statement.   Confirmed _____ Disconfirmed _____
3. "I wonder if extraterrestrials exist?" is a good research question.   Confirmed _____ Disconfirmed _____
4. You must have a research question to do research.   Confirmed _____ Disconfirmed _____
5. Lack of clarity is the most serious shortcoming of research questions.   Confirmed _____ Disconfirmed _____
6. Minimal harm to subjects is permitted in the interest of research.   Confirmed _____ Disconfirmed _____

Why my choice is confirmed.   Why my choice is not confirmed.

1. _____   _____
2. _____   _____
3. _____   _____
4. _____   _____
5. _____   _____

Chapter 2 Self-Test*

True or False

1. _____ Research topics are more narrow than research questions.
2. _____ You must have a research question to do research.
3. _____ Topic selection precedes the development of a research question.
4. _____ Available resources affect the desirable scope of a study.
5. _____ There is no such thing as a bad question.

Matching

6. _____ Guides scientific investigation and data gathering.
7. _____ SMEC principle that keeps you from getting in over your head.
8. _____ Is it more healthy for humans to eat poultry and fish than red meat?
9. _____ Phonics Method A is superior to Phonics Method B.
10 _____ Is education as good today as it was 100 years ago?

A. research question
B. bad question
C. contains an embedded question
D. research statement
E. scope

* Answers are in Appendix A.

Companion Website

Additional resources and chapter activities are located at www.edinboro.edu/press.

3 Review of the Literature

Anticipation Guide

1. A review of the literature is optional in conducting research. Agree _____ Disagree _____

2. The review of literature provides you with a knowledge base for your research idea. Agree _____ Disagree _____

3. An adequate review of the literature can be conducted just by searching the Internet. Agree _____ Disagree _____

4. Writing a review of the literature is basically a matter of quoting other sources. Agree _____ Disagree _____

Chapter Rationale

In 1926 Arthur C. Gates published *A Study of the Role of Visual Perception, Intelligence, and Certain Associative Processes in Reading and Spelling*, which demonstrated that visual perception is not a unified skill in humans. In other words, it would be inaccurate to say that people are good or poor visual perceivers. We can be fast and accurate in visually perceiving some events and slow and inaccurate in perceiving others. In the 1960s and 1970s the new field of learning disabilities widely supported the notion that one of the causes of delayed development of decoding skills in reading was inferior visual perception. Tests such as the *Marianne Frostig Developmental Test of Visual Perception* (Frostig, 1963) and related instructional materials were based on the concept of unity in visual perception and promoted a curriculum in which primary grade students engaged in visual training exercises with shapes and pictures rather than letters and words as a means of improving reading skills. These methods have long since been discarded. We now know that if you want children to be good recognizers of letters and words, they need practice with letters and words and not with triangles and pictures of trees. The point is that this huge waste of time, money, and instructional progress could have been avoided by a systematic review of the literature on visual perception and reading.

The literature found in journals, books, monographs and other sources provides the knowledge base for a research topic. Without a review of literature relevant to the topic, the researchers would be starting over with each topic they explored. Reinventing the wheel is an inefficient use of time and a poor way to conduct research. Learning what has been tried and what has succeeded or failed can help you begin your own research from a base of knowledge. Investigating the origins of your topic and discovering what other researchers have already explored is invaluable. Most of us who research a topic are surprised to find that someone else has already thought of the topic and in many instances has experimented with the topic. By searching the relevant literature, researchers quickly find a background of knowledge on their topics. In addition to refining your topic and giving you background information, a good review of the literature will help you to avoid selecting a research question that is irrelevant or has already been fully answered.

As a side note, Gates' methods included the new statistical tool of correlation, which will be introduced in Chapter 6. Gates and his colleagues computed over 1,000 correlations with hundreds of subjects using pencil and paper in an era in which radio was in its infancy; television was a dream, and hand calculators were unimagined and 50 years in the future.

Objective

In this chapter you will learn how to conduct and organize a review of literature. Having selected your topic and an initial research question, you will learn how to focus a literature search, refine your search, validate your topic and question, and organize the results of your findings into a systematic review of what others have discovered about your topic.

Graphic Organizer

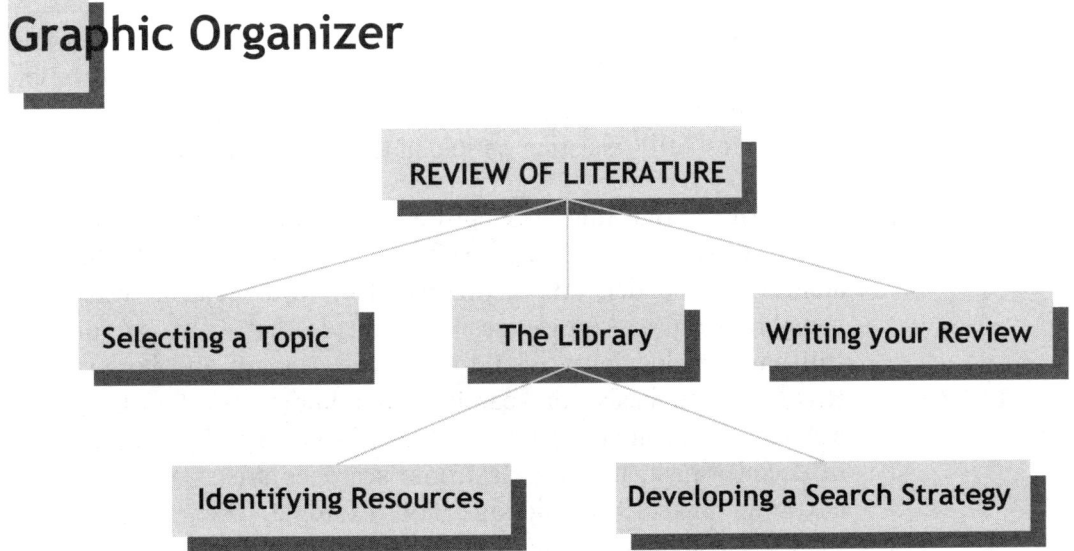

Procedures for Conducting a Literature Review

The Wrong Way to Conduct a Search

The easiest way to do a review of the literature – and one that should earn you a hot spot in Dante's *Inferno* – is to jump on the Internet, do a quick search, and grab whatever you find that seems to make sense. On October 7, 2007, the authors did a Google search for the term "classroom management" and got 40,800,000 hits. If we evaluated one reference each second 24 hours a day, it would take 1.31 years to complete the task. Obviously, this kind of evaluation isn't feasible, which means that a simple Internet review will be incomplete. A second problem is that the Internet search has no systematic mechanism for establishing the credibility of its sources. The Internet is also loaded with commercial hype and misinformation. This type of search is haphazard and should not be the basis for any review of the literature that purports to be scholarly.

Visit the library

Your review of the literature will require the services of a college or public library. While modern libraries have many common features, their systems are not identical. If you are not already familiar with the organization, search engines, and other electronic resources of your chosen library, ask for a tour and demonstration of online search procedures. Nothing makes a librarian happier than successfully assisting people in their search for information.

In one of the old Star Trek episodes, *Spock's Brain*, an alien race had a device called "the teacher." It looked a little like an aluminum colander, and if you put it on your head it would zap your brain full of knowledge. We can't do that – yet, so you will still have to do plenty of old fashioned reading and note-taking. However, the basis for searching the library is almost entirely electronic; and in comparison with the laborious physical searches of decades past, today's electronic searches are as marvelous as anything in science fiction. For example, *PsycINFO* is an EBSCOHost database supported by the American Psychological Association. It contains more than 2.3 million citations and scholarly summaries from books, dissertations, and over 2,000 peer reviewed journals that go back as far as 1887. Authors, titles, key words, and phrases can be used to find resources in psychology, counseling, and related disciplines in seconds. Other common resources in education and counseling are listed below. Resources with free information are provided on the companion website with direct links.

Authoritative Resources for Educational Research

Encyclopedia of Educational Research
Encyclopedia of Special Education
International Encyclopedia of Education
Encyclopedia of American Education
Handbook of Research on Multicultural Education
Encyclopedia of Education
Philosophy of Education: An Encyclopedia
Handbook of Research on Teaching
Educator's Desk Reference
Handbook of Educational Ideas and Practices
Handbook of Educational Psychology
Handbook of Research in Reading
Educational Index

On-line Resources

Online Computer Library Center (OCLC)
ProQuest
Resource Page for K-12 Instructors
Cisco Educational Archive
School Library Hotspots
Children's Literature Web Guide
National Institute for Literature
U.S. Department of Education
Links to Educational Sites
ACLIN
U.S. Federal Government Agencies

Educational Professional Organizations

American Library Association
Council for Exceptional Children
International Montessori Society
International Reading Association
National Association for the Education of Young Children
National Association of School Psychologists
National Association Elementary and Secondary School Principal
National Council for Accreditation of Teacher Education
National Council of Teachers of English
National Council of Teachers of Mathematics

National Education Association
National Reading Conference
National Rural Education Association
National Home School Association
Teachers of English to Speakers of Other Languages

Psychology and Counseling Resources

Psychware Sourcebook
Encyclopedia of Adult Development
Handbook of Educational Psychology
Encyclopedia of Drugs and Alcohol
Alternative Health Medical Encyclopedia
Encyclopedia of Phobias, Fears, and Anxieties
Handbook of Social and Clinical Psychology
Psychological Abstracts
Statistical Abstract of the United States
Social Science Index
Encyclopedia of Human Intelligence
Encyclopedia of Human Psychology
Test Critiques
Human Sexuality: An Encyclopedia
Diagnostic and Statistical Manual (DSM IV)
Encyclopedia of Human Behavior
Encyclopedia of Mental Health
Burros Mental Measurements Yearbook

On-line Resources

Psychcrawler
Clinical Psychology Resources
Cyber Psych Link
PsychRef
ACLIN
U.S. Federal Government Agencies Page
Psychology Journal Article Database

Psychology and Counseling Professional Associations

American Counseling Association
American Psychological Association
American Psychiatric Association
American Psychoanalytic Association
American Psychological Society
American Association of Pastoral Counselors

Select a Research Topic

There is no one correct way to acquire an appropriate research topic. Most of us have areas of special interest in education or counseling and most of us have theories about how to solve educational or interpersonal problems, particularly those that are a part of our daily work environment. So, one of the first steps in selecting a research topic is to explore your own interests. Another approach is to read research articles in journals looking for ideas that intrigue you. You can also find a topic by talking with your colleagues. There are no shortages of issues and problems in work and school settings, and some of these may be research opportunities. For purposes of this chapter, we have selected classroom management as the broad topic because it is an area of interest for us as educators.

Develop a Search Strategy

Reduce the Scope of the Topic to Manageable Size

If you have a topic that is too broad, the first objective of the literature search strategy is to narrow the topic so that you can develop an answerable research question. We used the *Thesaurus of ERIC Descriptors* to identify key words and topics related to classroom management and found several hundred of them. We selected "conflict management in the elementary school" and then did another Google search. This time the Google search indicated 1,830,000 hits, less than 5% of the number of hits when we used "classroom management." Another search using the *Thesaurus of ERIC Descriptors* yielded another set of descriptors, one of which was "peer mediated conflict management in the elementary school." One more Google search using "peer mediated conflict management elementary school" resulted in only 23,000 hits, only one half of 1% of the number found in our original Google search. Similar reductions in the numbers of citations occurred in authoritative databases such as Education Full-Text EBSCOHost. This helped us to narrow our initial topic of "classroom management" to "peer mediated conflict management in the elementary school" as our manageable final topic.

Identify Key Words, Phrases, and Names of Authors

These will be your inputs in the electronic searches. Sources include your professors, handbooks, research encyclopedia, textbooks, and *Thesaurus of ERIC Descriptors.* Some of the descriptors we found that relate to "peer mediated conflict management in the elementary school" were: restorive justice, restorive discipline, classroom bullying, Internet bullying, peace psychology, creative conflict, peer mediation training, managing conflict, and classroom peace.

Locate primary sources and avoid secondary sources whenever possible. Remember that the authors of secondary sources are providing their summaries and interpretations of what primary sources or other secondary sources said, and these interpretations may be biased or inaccurate. The only way to know what the original researcher found is to read the primary report of the research.

The articles and books you find will contain more references and the names of authors and researchers well known in the area of study. In addition, the articles will have citations that go back farther and farther in time. Eventually you will reach a point where there are no additional references on the topic. As you search the databases recommended by your reference librarian, including *Dissertation Abstracts* and pertinent conference proceedings, you will reach a point were the references become redundant. This redundancy signals the end of your search.

By reading the abstracts that are usually available as search output, you will be able to identify journal articles and other documents that are highly relevant to your topic. There may be dozens or hundreds of these articles depending upon the topic and the scope of your search. You can read these and take notes, but you will need photocopies of the ones that provide critical information.

Read each article carefully, highlighting information pertinent to your research question. Look for information that specifically references your identified variables and your anticipated subjects. Always take notes verbatim from your resources. When you extract material directly from a text, copy the author's words exactly so that you will not have to decide later which notes are already paraphrased and which are not. Do not rely on your memory. Trusting your memory will almost certainly lead to a failed literature review. It will not only cause you distress, anxiety and time retracing your steps, but likely will lead to some other more serious mental disorders as you try to remember where you found a quote or other piece of information for which you no longer have a source to reference. Depending upon the circumstances, failure to cite your sources of information may be plagiarism, a serious infraction of scholarly etiquette.

Critique the literature

Some of the references you acquire in your search will be discarded after a cursory inspection; some you will skim and retain the reference with a very brief statement in your journal or note card; others you will photocopy and read in their entirety; and for some you will take extensive notes. Your decision will depend upon your perception of the significance of each article. It is important that you critique the literature and not just read articles for general information. You cannot afford to be an information vacuum cleaner. You will need to determine which articles are seminal, which research studies are done well, and which ones are seriously flawed. In the chapters to come you will learn how to evaluate the quality of research reports.

Keep a Careful Record of Your Search

This record could be a running journal that documents the history of your search, or a collection of note cards. Your search record should include all of the databases and references you have used as well as a list of books, journal articles, and other materials you need to read. As you find each reference, write down all pertinent information on a 3x5 card or enter it into your laptop, i.e. author, title, publisher, dates, page number, whatever you will need later to find the article or to create an American Psychological Association (APA) style reference.

In the fields of education and counseling, the *Publication Manual of the American Psychological Association* (2001) is the standard authority on grammar, mechanics of writing, references, citations, and copyright issues. It also shows how to organize research reports, present statistical information, and create tables and figures in reports.

When to Abandon your Search

It will be the rare student who finds a topic with merit that hasn't been researched already. You might even find that the specific study you had in mind has already been done. But, was it completed perfectly and with no questions left unanswered? Do you have a new twist on the idea, or were there were some fundamental errors in how the topic was previously explored?

Your topic need not be a completely new idea to be worthy of pursuit. As you go through this class, you will find that there are many reasons to revisit topics as any number of problems exist in previous research that, if corrected, could make your idea very worthy of examination. Most studies include in the discussion section suggestions for future research and limitations of the study. One of these suggestions for additional research or a replication without some of the limitations of the original may provide a great opportunity. Don't give up on your topic just because you think the research has already been done.

Generating the Research Question

The research question, or statement, was discussed in the previous chapter. What is provided here is a review of the research question.

Once you completely review the topic, you must do a difficult thing, and that is to reduce your topic into a research question. This involves stating your topic in a one-sentence question. Most of us can talk ad nauseam about our ideas, but putting them into concise questions is more difficult. The trick in this process is making the topic understandable for others while accurately stating the purpose of the research. The research question needs to be clear, concise, understandable, and doable. A reader of your research should be able to read the research question and understand your specific intent immediately. The question we generated on the subject of peer mediated conflict resolution in the elementary school was: Will the implementation of a peer mediated conflict resolution program reduce classroom bullying in an urban elementary school?

Writing Your Research Report: Literature Review

In Chapter 1 we indicated that there were two approaches to writing a review of literature. The first is suitable for chapter one in a three-chapter proposal format or in the traditional five-chapter format of theses and dissertations. The alternative approach is suitable as the introduction to a journal length article written in APA style. The primary difference between the two is that the chapter approach is exhaustive and requires some discussion of most of the articles that are referenced. In journal articles space is a significant consideration, so the review of the literature is compressed.

No matter which approach you employ, begin by preparing an outline for your review of literature chapter. The major topics of your outline should directly address the variables in your research question. For example, our research question is: Will the implementation of a peer mediated conflict resolution program reduce school bullying in an urban elementary school? Therefore, the major topics of our outline should definitely be peer mediation and bullying. Other possible topics might be related to the use of peer mediation in conflict resolution, peer mediation, and in-school bullying.

Once you have an outline for your review of literature, organize your notes from your resources within the outline. You will begin to see where you have sufficient resources and where you still need to gather resources.

In "Pet Bonding and Pet Bereavement among Adolescents," the review of literature and introduction to the article is approximately 800 words, about three double-spaced typed pages. In the first paragraph the authors introduce the broad topic and references to support it: "Most children and adolescents at one time or another express a strong desire to own a pet" (Kidd & Kidd, 1985; Salmon, 1982). The second paragraph narrows the topic to focus on pet bonding. The third paragraph further narrows the topic to pet bereavement, attempts to make an argument for the relevance of the study, and presents hypotheses, which are research statements. Note that in a chapter format review of the literature, the studies by Kid and Kid (1985) and Salmon (1982) would have been summarized rather than reduced to a reference.

Another common approach is to introduce the literature historically or chronologically. For example, a study of visual perception in reading might begin with one or more paragraphs discussing psychological processes in reading, leading to the topic of the role of visual perception in reading. An appropriate sentence at this point might be: The first comprehensive study of the role of visual perception in reading was conducted by Gates (1926). The discussion and references that might follow would describe the research in this area from 1926 to the present. Usually, that author indicates what knowledge is missing and how the proposed research will add to the existing knowledge base on the topic.

The writing style for the review of literature is formal and serious. The purpose is to communicate information clearly, accurately, and concisely. Creativity and variety are not appropriate. This is not the place to be clever or amusing. Your readers will expect to learn the content of your study, not to be entertained. Write the chapter to educate the reader about the major topics of your outline. Present your information by combining facts and references to support these topics. Write the review of literature using your own words, paraphrasing others carefully and sparingly. Use quotations infrequently, but use citations often.

This is a standard format for a literature review and introduction to a research study:

- Introduce the broad topic: pets, classroom management, or reading skills.

- Refine the topic: pet bereavement, peer mediated conflict resolution, or visual perception in reading.

- Discuss the relevant literature on the refined topic chronologically or by subtopic.

- Make the case for the relevance and importance of your proposed study.

- Present your research question(s) or statement(s).

Writing Your Research Report: References

Unless there are appendices, the references section will be the conclusion of your report following the discussion. In Education and Counseling, references almost always follow the guidelines in the *Publication Manual of the American Psychological Association* (2001), which includes detailed descriptions as well as examples. While there are hundreds of reference variations, the most common are articles in periodicals, books, book chapters, and electronic sources. The References section in *Educational Research: Insights and Applications* can serve as a model for the development of a reference list. However, APA is the final authority.

Reaction Guide

1. A review of the literature is optional in conducting research. Confirmed _____   Disconfirmed _____

2. The review of literature provides you with a knowledge base for your research idea. Confirmed _____   Disconfirmed _____

3. A review of the literature can be conducted without going to a library. Confirmed _____   Disconfirmed _____

4. Writing a review of the literature basically a matter of quoting other sources. Confirmed _____   Disconfirmed _____

Why my choice is confirmed.   Why my choice is not confirmed.

1. _____   _____

2. _____   _____

3. _____   _____

4. _____   _____

Chapter 3 Self-Test

True or False

1. _____ It is a waste of time to take notes during your literature review.

2. _____ You should compile your findings before you identify your topic.

3. _____ An idea should be a new one to make it worthy of research.

4. _____ Research questions tend to be broader than topics.

5. _____ Plagiarism is acceptable in a review of literature because you are quoting.

Matching

6. _____ A searchable database

7. _____ A search strategy

8. _____ An online resource in psychology

9. _____ A search engine

10. ____ Provides the knowledge base for a research topic

A. EBSCOHost
B. Google
C. Psychcrawler
D. identify key words, phrases, and names
E. the existing literature on the subject

Companion Website

Additional resources and chapter activities are located at www.edinboro.edu/press.

4 Overview of Quantitative Research

Anticipation Guide

1. Quantitative research is deductive in nature.   Agree _____ Disagree _____
2. Unsound arguments suffer from insufficient data.   Agree _____ Disagree _____
3. The ultimate goal of science is prediction.   Agree _____ Disagree _____
4. A formal argument can be valid but unsound.   Agree _____ Disagree _____
5. Qualitative and quantitative research methods
   are essentially the same.   Agree _____ Disagree _____

Chapter Rationale

"I guess I've been a researcher all my life. When I was five-years-old, my little sister and I were playing at a neighbor's house with a bunch of other children. Some big kids came down the street and told us we could get to China by digging a hole in the ground and coming out on the other side of the world. I wanted to see if this was true, so after the big kids left, we went into the neighbor's garage, got some shovels, and started digging for China - in a different neighbor's perfectly manicured front yard! We had a ragged hole about 10 inches deep and two feet in diameter when the owner pulled into the driveway and beheld his torn up yard. He started yelling at us. We all dropped our shovels and ran like the hounds of hell were after us. I never did make it to China, but I haven't lost my sense of curiosity." (Scott)

We give the kids credit for their interest in testing a hypothesis. Unfortunately, they had the wrong tools and little to no knowledge of geography, geology, physics, and mathematics, all of which would be required to test the validity of the hypothetical hole to China. The unit on statistics and quantitative research methods is designed to give you a set of tools for interpreting and conducting psychological and educational research.

Objectives

When you have completed this chapter, you will be able to define *quantitative research* and its purposes.

Graphic Organizer

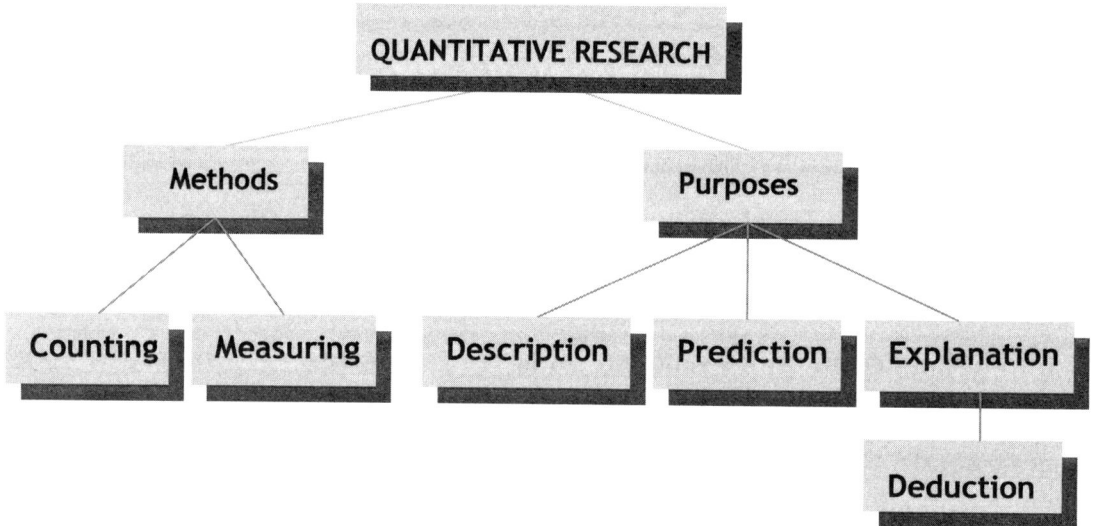

The Purposes of Research

Phenomena are all the events in the universe: the pathways of comets, the propagation of dandelions, the dancing of bees, the movements of tectonic plates, and the collective thoughts of all humanity. We can observe these phenomena directly or indirectly with our senses. Often the phenomena of interest are too small, too distant, or simply outside the range of human sensation, so we build instruments such as microscopes, telescopes, Geiger counters, or personality inventories to enhance our perceptual capabilities. *Quantitative research methods* examine phenomena by counting and measuring, usually with the assistance of instrumentation. Quantitative methods also employ precise experimental procedures in which conditions and behaviors are manipulated or controlled in order to test very specific hypotheses. By contrast, qualitative methods examine phenomena in social contexts without using experimental manipulations or statistical procedures. The purposes of quantitative research are description, prediction, and explanation.

A *description* is an inventory, chronology, or representation of a phenomenon. It can be a story. For instance, when your doctor asks you to describe what happened after you accidentally stepped on your son's skateboard. Or, you might be asked to describe your physical and emotional sensations the first time you looked down into the Grand Canyon. Or you might have to describe a missing pet: *mixed breed shorthaired dog, 55 pounds, blind in left eye, three legs, crooked tail, answers to the name "Lucky."* These are all common, everyday types of descriptions. However, in social science research and in the performance of professional responsibilities, it is frequently the case that adequate descriptions require mathematical applications. For instance, suppose you are the principal of an elementary school, and the school board asks you to describe the math skills of the 320 students in your school. You have recent math achievement scores for all of them, but the school board probably doesn't want you to send them a long list of scores. Somehow you must convert that raw information into statistics that will bring meaning to the chaos of hundreds or thousands of numbers. In Chapter 5 you will be introduced to the following descriptive statistics: mean, median, mode, range, percentile, variance, standard deviation, z-score, and T-score. You will become good friends.

Prediction is the ability to forecast the future. This probably brings to mind a crystal ball or Nostradamus. However, in social and behavioral science research, *prediction* is the ability to forecast phenomena based on systematic observation and measurement. As the principal in the elementary school with 320 children, imagine what a powerful tool you would have if you could predict which curricula, teachers, schedules or reward systems would have the greatest positive impact on individual students or students of different ages, genders, or levels of home support. The most common type of predictive statistic used in educational and psychological research is correlation, and you will learn about it in Chapter 6.

The ultimate goal of science is *explanation*, which incorporates the description and prediction of phenomena but also states why the phenomena occur. In addition, the explanation should make sense within the context of social and behavioral science theories. As the instructional leader in the elementary school, you should have the tools to explain phenomena in your school. In Chapter 9 you will learn about analysis of variance (ANOVA). In the social and behavioral sciences, ANOVA is the most frequently used procedure for explaining phenomena and establishing cause and effect.

The Role of Deduction in Research

There are two basic types of formal arguments: deductive and inductive (non-deductive). As you will learn in Chapter 11, inductive reasoning leads to a general conclusion based on the observation of individual events (i.e., reasoning from the specific to the general). In contrast, d*eductive arguments* involve reasoning from a set of premises (statements or generalizations) to a conclusion that must logically follow (i.e., reasoning from the general to the specific).

There are two criteria for assessing deductive arguments; validity and soundness. Validity refers to the form of the argument and soundness refers to the truth of the premises. A *valid argument* is one in which the conclusion follows logically from the premises even if the premises are false. A *sound argument* is one that is valid and in addition contains only true premises. The argument in (1) is valid because the conclusion follows from the premises. However, the argument is unsound because one of the premises is false. It is untrue that all women have wings. The argument in (2) is both valid and sound because the conclusion follows from the premises and all of the premises are true.

(1) All women have wings. (Premise)
Sacajawea is a woman. (Premise)
Therefore, Sacajawea has wings. (Conclusion)

(2) All men are mortal. (Premise)
Socrates is a man. (Premise)
Therefore, Socrates is mortal. (Conclusion)

If it is true that all men are mortal and if it is true that Socrates is a man, then Socrates must be mortal.

The cornerstone of quantitative research is deductive reasoning; and, in an ideal world, educational and psychological research would be so wonderful that we would only need to read the conclusions at the end of a researcher's published paper. Unfortunately, the authors estimate that 40-50% of all published social science research would be classified as invalid or unsound if held to close scrutiny. In Chapters 8, 9, and 10 you will learn about quantitative methods and how to evaluate research by examining the premises and conclusions of the researchers.

Activity 1

This activity requires you to search for the components of an argument embedded in a real world vignette. The reason for the activity is that you must learn to think deductively when you are evaluating reports of research. First, classify the purpose of the research vignette as description, prediction, or explanation. Second, identify the premises and conclusion in the deductive argument. Third, indicate whether the argument is valid or invalid and sound or unsound.

The hardest part of this exercise is identifying the premises and conclusion. Begin with the conclusion. What is it that Dr. Wadsworth wants to conclude from his experiment? Then, identify the facts, beliefs, and assumptions (the premises) that are essential to the argument. This is not an easy activity, and there may be more than one solution; so give yourself time to think. (See Appendix A for our solution.)

Vignette

The superintendent of the Mesquite School District, Dr. Wadsworth, believes that segregation leads to racial hostility because it creates an "us against them" mentality. The African-American and white students in Mesquite elementary schools tend to self-segregate during lunch and at recess. Dr. Wadsworth reasons that desegregating lunch and recess activities should reduce the number of cross-racial incidents of physical and verbal aggression. There are six elementary schools in the Mesquite School District, and Dr. Wadsworth randomly assigns three of them to be experimental schools and three to be control schools.

All of the teachers and principals participate in a week-long program in multicultural education and desegregation training. The principals in the experimental groups create a plan in which the teachers control seating arrangements during lunch and organize teams and recess activities so that they are desegregated. The teachers at the control schools continue to allow students to sit where they want during lunch and to choose their own groups during recess.

Over the course of the school year, the principals at all six schools count the number and measure the intensity of cross-racial incidents of physical and verbal aggression. At the end of the school year Dr. Wadsworth finds that the number of incidents and the intensity of incidents declined significantly in the experimental schools but not in the control schools. He concludes that desegregation of lunch and recess activities reduces racial hostility in elementary schools and that the program implemented by the Mesquite School District is a success.

1. Purpose of the research: Description ___ Prediction ___ Explanation ___

2. List Dr. Wadsworth's Premises and Conclusion

Premise 1: _____

Premise 2: _____

Premise 3: _____

Premise 4: _____

Premise 5: _____

Premise 6: _____

Conclusion: _____

3. Validity of the argument: Valid ___   Invalid ___

4. Soundness of the argument (check one):   Sound ___ Unsound ___

5. List the premises, if any, that you believe are untrue:_____

_____

_____

Reaction Guide

1. Quantitative research in deductive in nature. Confirmed _____ Disconfirmed _____

2. Weak arguments suffer from insufficient data. Confirmed _____ Disconfirmed _____

3. The ultimate goal of science is prediction. Confirmed _____ Disconfirmed _____

4. A formal argument can be valid but unsound. Confirmed _____ Disconfirmed _____

5. Qualitative and quantitative research methods are essentially the same. Confirmed _____ Disconfirmed _____

Why my choice is confirmed.   Why my choice is not confirmed.

1. _____   _____
2. _____   _____
3. _____   _____
4. _____   _____
5. _____   _____

Chapter 4 Self-Test

True or False

1. _____ A sound argument is always a valid argument.

2. _____ The ultimate goal of science is accurate prediction.

3. _____ The ultimate goal of science is to explain phenomena.

4. _____ Qualitative researchers rely on experimental manipulations.

5. _____ Qualitative and quantitative methods both use descriptive techniques.

Multiple-choice

6. An experiment that attempts to predict the academic performances of high school juniors based on expressed career interests is probably:

A. valid   B. inductive   C. unsound   D. quantitative

7. If a deductive argument is sound, the probability that the conclusion is false is:

A. 0%   B. 9%   C. 50%   D. 100%

8. What makes a deductive argument sound?

A. true premises   B. a good research question   C. a true conclusion
D. reliable data

9. ANOVA is used by quantitative researchers to establish:

A. theories   B. strong arguments   C. truth   D. cause and effect

10. Which is not a purpose of quantitative research?
A. explanation   B. triangulation   C. description   D. prediction

Companion Website

Additional resources and chapter activities are located at www.edinboro.edu/press.

5 Descriptive Statistics

Anticipation Guide

1. Ninety percent correct on a test is a good score. Agree _____ Disagree _____

2. If your score on a test is in the 70th percentile, it means you answered 70% of the items correctly. Agree _____ Disagree _____

3. Statistics are really a lot like adjectives. Agree _____ Disagree _____

4. It is possible for variance on a test to be zero. Agree _____ Disagree _____

5. A z-score of 3 would be a very high test score. Agree _____ Disagree _____

Chapter Rationale

Fahrenheit 451, the famous Ray Bradbury novel about censorship in the future, contains a number with a special meaning; 451 degrees Fahrenheit is the temperature at which paper burns. In *Fahrenheit 451*, firemen do not put out fires; they burn books. No other numbers or comparisons are needed to understand the significance of the number. However, this is frequently not the case in the universe of measurement and educational research. For example, suppose you take a multiple-choice examination in astronomy and get 85% of the questions correct. How well have you done? Is your performance worth a B? Should you be embarrassed or elated with your performance? Suppose there were 20 people in your class and 85% was the lowest grade. Oops! What if the next highest grade in the class was 55%? Yippee! Test scores and other numbers often have meaning only when they are compared with other numbers. In this chapter we will show you how to interpret *descriptive statistics*, a special kind of numbers that will assist you in making such comparisons. Knowledge of basic descriptive statistics will vastly improve your ability to understand educational research.

Objectives

When you have completed this chapter, you will understand the basic purposes for summarizing numerical data, and you will be able to calculate the most commonly used descriptive statistics.

Graphic Organizer

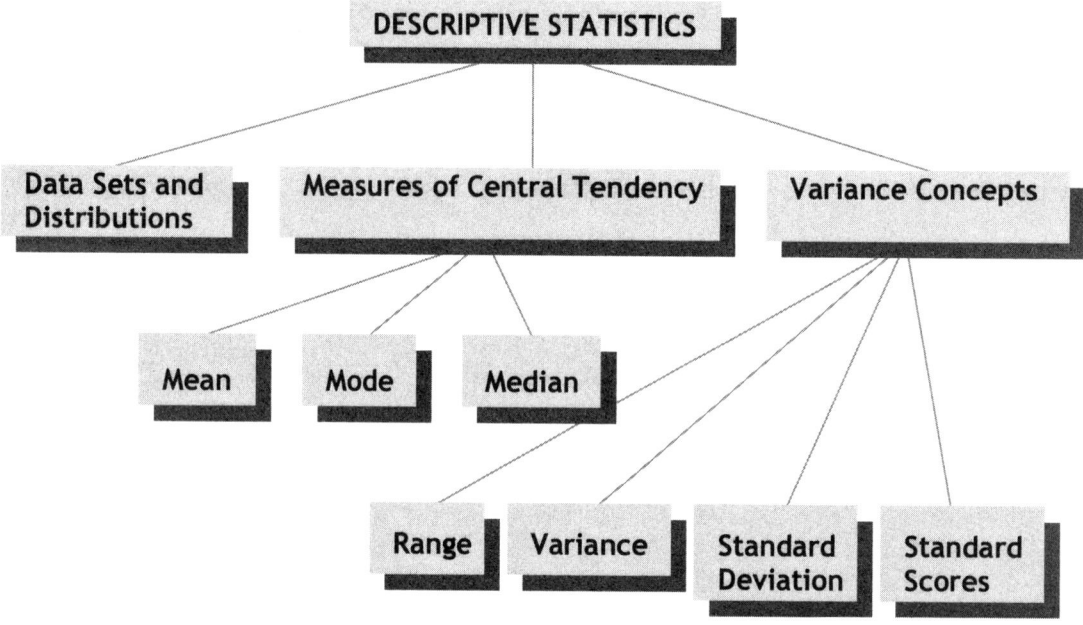

Definition of Descriptive Statistics

The word *statistics* is word derived from the Greek *statistik*, the study of political facts and figures. The English word *statistics* was first used in the 18th century and refers to the branch of mathematics that deals with the collection and interpretation of large quantities of numerical information. A *statistic* is a number that is created from a group – or set – of numbers. A *descriptive statistic* is a number that helps to describe a set of numbers. You might want to think of a statistic as a kind of adjective. If someone asked you to describe the sky, you might use adjectives such as blue or cloudless or starry for clarification. Statistics are the adjectives of educational research.

Data Sets

Data refers to factual information that is used as a basis for reasoning or calculation. Data may be – but don't have to be – numerical. For example, if you were writing a history of technology in the United States and one of your facts was that the Apple computer was first marketed in 1977, you would be well within your rights to refer to this piece of information as data. However, in this chapter we will be concerned only with numerical data. Some people still insist that data is the plural form and datum is the singular, but this is archaic and we will use *data* as both singular and plural (i.e., "the data was collected" is acceptable parlance). *Set* is simply another term for a group. And a *data set* is a group of numbers that have not yet been converted into a statistic. The numbers in a data set are sometimes referred to as *raw* (unprocessed) *scores* or *raw data*.

There are four data sets listed below: A, B, C, and D. These data sets will be used to illustrate and explain a variety of descriptive statistics.

Data Set A: Raw Scores on a 20 Item English Quiz

11 20 17 17 15 12 13 13 12 19 18 15 18 15

15 16 15 16 10 18 16 17 14 14 14 13 15 14

16

Data Set B: Family Income in a Remote Columbian Village in US $ x 1,000

2 2 2 1 200 2 1 1 2 3 2 3 3 1 2

3 2 1

Data Set C: Salaries of First-Year Teachers in a Colorado School District

35,000   35,000   35,000   35,000   35,000   35,000

35,000   35,000   35,000

Data Set D: Raw Scores on a 20 Item High School Algebra Test

14 11 7 19 10 11 20 6 3 18 11 10 0

Data Set E: Midterm Exam Grades in a Graduate Course in Educational Research

10 5 5 1 8 10 8 6 3 5 2 10 9

10 5 9 10 7 5 10 5

Data Distributions

Data distribution refers to how the numbers in a data set are spread out. To get a visual representation of the data distribution, you can stack the raw scores as we have from Data Set A. Then draw a continuous line linking the top of each stack.

```
                        15
                        15
                 14     15     16
          13     14     15     16     17
      12  13     14     15     16     17     18
10 11 12  13     14     15     16     17     18     19     20
```

This type of distribution is typically referred to as a *normal* or *bell curve* distribution because of its shape, which is thick in the middle and balanced on both sides. When thousands of raw scores from a personality or educational test are plotted or stacked in this fashion, they tend to have a bell curve distribution. However, data distributions frequently do not have a bell shape, especially when the number of individual scores in the data distribution is small (Micceri, 1989).

Activity 1

Create a visual distribution of the numbers from Data Set B. How is the distribution different from the distribution of Data Set A?

Discussion of Activity 1

Your visual of the data from Set B should **not** look like a normal distribution. In fact, it should be very lopsided. The technical term for this is a *skewed distribution*. Because of interpretive problems caused by skewed distributions, researchers rely on statistics to describe a distribution of numbers. In this case the distribution is skewed because one family in the village makes more money than all the other families combined.

Measures of Central Tendency

Measures of central tendency are statistics that provide information about the center of a distribution of numbers. There are three descriptive statistics that are defined as measures of central tendency. They are the mean, median, and mode. The range is not really a measure of central tendency, but it is a useful statistic that is frequently employed to describe score distributions.

The *mean* (abbreviated as M or   ) is the arithmetic average of all the raw scores in a data set. This is simply the total of all the numbers in the data set divided by the number of individual scores. In research reports the number of scores in a data set is usually referred to as *n*.

The *median* is the middle score in a data set. If the number of scores in the data set is an even number, the median is the average of the two middle scores.

The *mode* is the score that occurs most frequently in a data set.

The *range* is the difference between the highest and lowest scores in a data set.

To calculate the measures of central tendency, order the numbers in the set from lowest to highest or from highest to lowest. You can try to just "eyeball it," but this will cause you to make errors. Here are the ordered numbers from Data Set A.

10 11 12 12 13 13 13 14 14 14 14 15

15 15 15 15 15 16 16 16 16 17 17 17

18 18 19 20

There are 28 scores in the data set (n = 28). To find the mean, add all the scores together and divide by 28. The mean is 15 (420/28 = 15).

The median in this data set will be the average of the 14th and 15th numbers. If there were an odd number of scores, the median would just be the score in the middle. The 14th and 15th scores are both 15, so the average of the two is 15, and the median is 15.

The mode in this distribution is 15 because it is the score that occurs most frequently.

The range is 10 (20 – 10 = 10).

Note that the mean, median, and mode are all 15 for Data Set A. In a perfectly normal distribution of scores the measures of central tendency will be identical.

Activity 2

Order the numbers for Data Set B:

Calculate the mean, median, mode, and range for Data Set B.

Mean   _____

Median _____

Mode   _____

Range _____

Is the distribution normal? _____

Which measure(s) of central tendency do you believe give the most accurate picture of income in the village and why?

_____

_____.

Discussion of Activity 2

The distribution of Data Set B is clearly not normal, bell shaped, or balanced because the mean ($12,944) is quite different from the mode ($2,000) and the median ($2,000). From our point of view the median and the mode are better indicators of what constitutes "being income average" in the village. It would be very misleading to say that on the average families in the village earn about $13,000. Note also that the range ($199,000) is about 100 times the median income.

Variance

Diversity is a fact of human existence. We are not all the same height and weight. Some of us get better school grades than others. We don't all have the same level of interest and ability in sports. Some of us manage stress better than others. In thousands of ways, some critical and some trivial, human beings are different from each other. These differences can also be described as variations. We can say that people vary in physical appearance and mental attributes. And, when we look at a data set, we can talk about the variation in the data. If the differences among raw scores in a data set are big, we can say that there is a lot of variation. When differences among scores are small, we can say that there is little variation. Distributions of scores that have little variation tend to look like this.

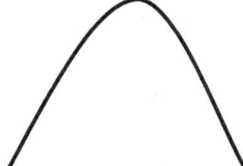

Look at the salaries in Data Set C. Every teacher is being paid the same thing, so there is no variation at all. Now observe the test scores in Data Set E. On a 20-item test the scores range from 0 to 20 correct. Distributions with a lot of variation tend to look like this.

The *variance* is a statistic that is used to measure the amount of variation (fluctuation) from the mean of a data set. The variance in a data set is calculated by: (1) subtracting each score from the mean, (2) squaring the result, (3) adding all the squares together, and (4) dividing the total squares by n-1. Here is the calculation of the variance for Data Set A. Note that the more deviant the individual scores are from the mean, the greater the number of squares, resulting in a bigger variance.

Mean	Raw Score	Difference	Square
15	10	5	25
15	11	4	16

15	12	3	9
15	12	3	9
15	13	2	4
15	13	2	4
15	13	2	4
15	14	1	1
15	14	1	1
15	14	1	1
15	14	1	1
15	15	0	0
15	15	0	0
15	15	0	0
15	15	0	0
15	15	0	0
15	15	0	0
15	16	-1	1
15	16	-1	1
15	16	-1	1
15	16	-1	1
15	17	-2	4
15	17	-2	4
15	17	-2	4
15	18	-3	9
15	18	-3	9
15	19	-4	16
15	20	-5	<u>25</u>

Total Squares 150
n = 28
n – 1 = 27

Variance is 5.56 (150 / 27)

Statistical Notation

Over the years we have noticed that many students have a great fear of symbols that represent mathematical procedures or individual statistics such as n, $\bar{x}$, γ, and $\sum$.

n represents the number of items in a set of numbers

$\bar{x}$ represents the arithmetic mean

γ represents the variance

Σ is the summation sign and simply indicates the addition of a set of numbers.

This book could have been written without the use of mathematical notation. However, such symbols are common in research literature, and we would be doing you a disservice not to introduce those which are most common. Symbols have been inserted into Activity 3 so that you can see how easy they are to work with.

Activity 3 A

You can determine the variance using a hand calculator or a statistical software package such as MINITAB®; and that certainly makes sense in professional practice and especially when working with large data sets. However, you will have a superior feel for the statistic if you thoroughly understand where the number comes from. For this reason you should be able to compute the variance of a set of numbers without having to look up the procedure. Calculate the variance of the following numbers (No peeking!):

16 7 10 6 5 13 9 8 12 10 15 19

$\gamma = $ _____

Discussion of Activity 3

$\bar{x}$	Raw Score	Difference	Square
10	16	-6	36
10	7	3	9
10	10	0	0
10	6	-4	16
10	5	-5	25
10	13	3	9
10	9	-1	1
10	8	-2	4
10	12	2	4
10	10	0	0
10	15	5	25
10	19	9	<u>81</u>

Σ Squares   210
n = 13
n − 1 = 12
γ = 17.5 (210/12)

Activity 3 B

If you need more practice in computing the variance of a set of numbers, try again using the numbers below. The answer is in Appendix A:

13   29   15   33   40   24   18   22   37   18   29   17   34   28   31

Standard Deviation

A statistic that is more often used by researchers as a measure of variation is called the *standard deviation* (abbreviated as SD or σ). It is calculated by taking the square root of the variance. The standard deviation of the scores in Data Set A is 2.36.

$$\sigma = \sqrt{\gamma}$$

We realize that the *standard deviation* (SD) is still a fuzzy concept and that you may be asking yourself questions like: "2.36 what?" and "Why is this standard deviation thing important?" Don't worry; you're normal. To make the concept and its purpose clearer we need to refer again to the bell curve.

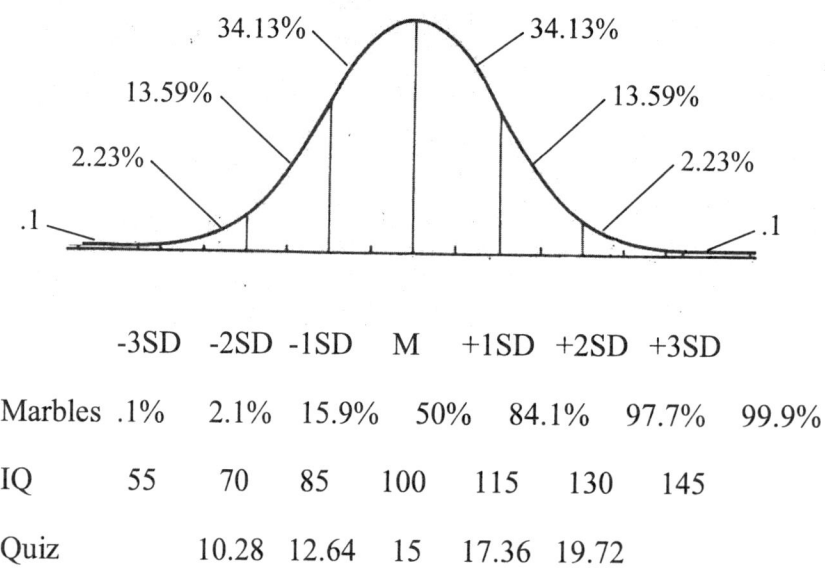

	-3SD	-2SD	-1SD	M	+1SD	+2SD	+3SD
Marbles	.1%	2.1%	15.9%	50%	84.1%	97.7%	99.9%
IQ		55	70	85	100	115	130 145
Quiz			10.28	12.64	15	17.36	19.72

Think of the bell shaped curve as a narrow, three dimensional glass container into which you could throw marbles. If you filled the container with marbles, most of them would be stacked up in the middle and only a few would be in the tails (sides). The numbers inside the curve above show the percentages of marbles that could fit into the area defined by the lines on either side of the number. The numbers on the line "Marbles" show the cumulative percentages of marbles that would fit into the curve beginning on the left. Only about 1 tenth of one percent would fit in the area below –3 SD. About 2% of the marbles would fit in all the area below –2 SD. A bit more than 68% of the marbles would be stacked up in the area between –1 and +1 SD. Only about 2% of the marbles would be in the area above +2 SD. Another way of saying it is that 97.7% of all the marbles would be in the area below +2 SD. Instead of marbles we can talk about human performances and attributes using the same curve and standard deviation markers.

Look at the IQ scores on the second line below the curve. IQ tests generally have a mean of 100 and a standard deviation of 15. An IQ of 130 or higher is typically considered gifted and an IQ below 70 is frequently used as the cutoff score for mental retardation. Being one SD above the mean on an IQ test should now be a meaningful statement to you even if no score is cited. The same is true with the English quiz. The meaning of a score is at least in part determined by comparison with other scores. For instance, if you get 60 correct on a 100 item objective test, it is hard to know the meaning of the score without reference to the performances of other test-takers. Sixty doesn't sound great, but if you discover that the data set for the class had a mean of 40 and a standard deviation of 10, you scored two SDs above the mean and should probably go out and celebrate because it means that you outscored about 97% of those who took the test.

Transformed Scores

A *transformed score* is one in which the numerical value of the raw score is changed into a number that shows the relationship of raw scores to each other. Test developers and researchers frequently transform raw test scores to make them easier to interpret. There are many different kinds of transformations, and a complete discussion of them is beyond the scope of this book; however, we can give you an illustration. Transformed scores are often related to the standard deviation of a distribution of scores. The most common transformation is called the *z-score*. A z-score shows in standard deviation units how far above or below the mean a given raw score is. The z-score is calculated by subtracting the mean from a raw score and dividing it by the standard deviation:

$$z = \frac{(\text{raw score} - \text{the mean})}{\text{standard deviation}}$$

Z-scores can be negative or positive numbers. If the mean is greater than the raw score, the resulting z-score will be a negative number. If the mean is less than the raw score, the z-score will be a positive number. For example, remember that most IQ tests have a mean of 100 points and a standard deviation of 15 points. If a student is tested and found to have an IQ of 115, the score is 1 SD above the mean. Let's plug those numbers into the z-score formula above.

$$z = \frac{(115 - 100)}{15}$$

$$z = +1$$

A z-score of +1 shows that the raw score is 1 SD above the mean. If a student is tested and the resulting IQ score is 65, the z-score reveals a score that is 2.33 SDs below the mean.

$$z = \frac{(65 - 100)}{15}$$

$$z = -2.33$$

The *T-score* is another commonly used transformation. A set of test scores – or other numerical data – can be transformed into z-scores, which in turn can be converted to T-scores. T-scores have a mean of 50 and a standard deviation of 10 and are created from z-scores using the following formula: $10z + 50 = T$. In other words, if you multiply a z-score by 10 and then add 50, you have the T-score. For example, a z-score of –2 is equal to a T-score of 30, $(10 \times -2) + 50 = 30$. A z-score of –2 has the same meaning as a T-score of 30. A z-score of .50 has the same meaning as a T-score of 55.

Activity 4

The mean and standard deviation for Data Set A are 15 and 2.36, respectively. Calculate the z-scores and T-scores for the raw scores below. After you have finished your computations, go back and look at the raw scores in Data Set A. What makes the numbers 10 and 20 special in this set of scores? Based on your z-score calculations, would you say that the scores in Data Set A show moderate or large amounts of variation?

	z-score	T-score
10		
20		
15		

Discussion of Activity 4

The scores 10 and 20 are special because they are the lowest and highest scores in the data set. The z-scores for 10, 20, and 15 are –.90, .90, and 0, respectively. The T-scores for 10, 20, and 15 are 41, 59, and 50, respectively. Because the lowest and highest scores in the distribution are within one standard deviation of the mean, the distribution has only moderate variance. Usually, if a set of scores has a lot of variance, there will be scores that fall 2 or 3 SDs above or below the mean.

Percentiles

The percentile is one of the most commonly reported statistics and also one of most commonly misinterpreted – especially by teachers and parents when it comes to interpreting the results of achievement tests. A *percentile* is a point on a distribution of scores below which a certain percentage of scores fall. There are 99 percentile points in a distribution. If a student scores in the 44th percentile, it means that his or her performance was superior to 44% of those who took the test. A percentile score of 78 on the Graduate Record Examination (GRE) indicates that the test-taker had a higher raw score than 78% of the people who took the test. If you take a test and your score is in the 1st percentile, it means that 99% of the test-takes did better than you. If your score was in the 99th percentile, your performance was better than 99% of those who took the test. Remember that the median was defined as the middle score in a distribution. In a perfectly normal distribution of scores the median and the 50th percentile are the same. Percentiles do not indicate the percentage of items correctly answered on a test.

Activity 5

You should now be able to interpret a table of means and standard deviations in a research article. Go to Table 3 on page 508 of "Pet Bonding and Pet Bereavement among Adolescents." Ignore the t-ratios and the footnote.

How many boys were in the study? _____

(T or F) Boys had higher bonding and grief scores than girls. _____

What is the mean difference between boys and girls on the PAS? _____

What is the standard deviation for boys on the combined grief scale? _____

(T or F) Girls demonstrated more variance than boys on the grief scales. _____

What can you infer from comparing the SDs for boys and girls on the various assessments?

Answers and Discussion of Activity 5

How many boys were in the study? 27 ($n = 27$)

(T or F) Boys had higher bonding and grief scores than girls. False

What is the mean difference between boys and girls on the PAS? 7.61 points

What is the standard deviation for boys on the combined grief scale? 17.53 points

(T or F) Girls demonstrated more variance than boys on the grief scales. False

On all of the bonding and grief scales the boys have larger SDs than the girls, indicating more variation in their responses. Another way of stating this is that the girls in the study tended to have similar responses while the boys did not. It may have been that some boys had very low bonding and grief scores in comparison to the girls. Or, one might even speculate that boys tended to have more extreme scores than girls in both directions. We can't tell for sure because the authors did not give us the range of scores for girls and boys on the various tests.

Reaction Guide

1. Ninety percent correct on a test is a good score. Confirmed _____ Disconfirmed _____

2. If your score on a test is in the 70th percentile, it means you answered 70% of the items correctly. Confirmed _____ Disconfirmed _____

3. Statistics are really a lot like adjectives. Confirmed _____ Disconfirmed _____

4. It is possible for variance on a test to be zero. Confirmed _____ Disconfirmed _____

5. A z-score of 3 would be a very high score. Confirmed _____ Disconfirmed _____

Why my choice is confirmed.   Why my choice is not confirmed.

1. _____   _____

2. _____   _____

3. _____   _____

4. _____   _____

5. _____   _____

Chapter 5 Self-Test

True or False

1. _____ The range is a measure of central tendency.

2. _____ If the mean of a data set is 12 and the SD is 3, a raw score of 18 is 2 standard deviations above the mean.

3. _____ If the variance of a data set is 16, then the standard deviation is 5

4. _____ The percentage of people with IQs over 130 is about 13%.

5. _____ If everyone gets the same score on a test, there is zero variance.

Matching

6. _____ percentile

7. _____ a skewed distribution

8. _____ (raw score – Mean) / SD

9. _____ mode

10. _____ 6 4 9 9 1 3 8 9 7 5 5 3 4 8

A. 5 5 3 5 7 2 506 3 5 8 2
B. z-score
C. the most frequently occurring score in a data set
D. a point on a distribution of scores
E. median = 5.5
F. mean = 6.1

Computation

Given the set of numbers below, find the answers to items 11 – 20.

3 9 10 4 4 7 8 5 9 12 5 0 13 5 11

11. _____ n

12. _____ M

13. _____ Range

14. _____ Median

15. _____ Mode

16. _____ Σ squares

17. _____ γ

18. _____ σ

19. _____ z-score of the number 12 in this set

20. _____ Number in the set with a z-score of −.81

Companion Website

Additional resources and chapter activities are located at www.edinboro.edu/press.

6 Correlation

Anticipation Guide

1. Negative correlations are usually bad. Agree _____ Disagree _____

2. A correlation of −.65 is bigger than a correlation of .25. Agree _____ Disagree _____

3. Correlation implies causality. Agree _____ Disagree _____

4. The plot of a perfect correlation looks like a circle. Agree _____ Disagree _____

5. It is impossible to have a correlation greater than 1. Agree _____ Disagree _____

Chapter Rationale

According to the old Frank Sinatra song, "Love and marriage go together like a horse and carriage." The sentiment is clear enough, and most of us would agree that there is at least a tendency for people who are in love to get married. We also understand that married people don't necessarily love each other and that there are many reasons why romantic love doesn't automatically lead to the alter. However, there is a cultural relationship between love and the institution of marriage, and we can describe this relationship as a *correlation* (co *together* + relation). Literally, phenomena are correlated if they tend to go together. The question is: to what extent do phenomena go together? How predicable is the relationship? In this chapter we will explain how researchers in education and counseling quantify relationships. It is essential that you understand correlation because it is one of the most frequently used of research techniques as well as one of the most misinterpreted.

Objectives

In this chapter you will learn how to interpret statistics related to correlation.

Graphic Organizer

```
                    CORRELATION
        ┌──────────────┼──────────┬──────────────┐
Bivariate Correlation  Multiple Correlation  Size  Correlation Fallacy
    ┌───────┐
Positive  Negative
```

Definition of Statistical Correlation

A *correlation* is a statistic that is computed from two sets of data or *variables*. Because there are two sets of data or variables, such correlations are sometimes referred to as *bivariate* or *simple correlations*. The correlation statistic suggests the strength of a relationship and is sometimes referred to as a *coefficient of correlation*. All correlation coefficients are expressed as numbers that range from minus 1 to plus 1. The size of the correlation is defined without reference to its sign (e.g., correlations of + .76 and −.76 are exactly the same size. If a correlation is zero, there is no relationship between the two sets of data or variables, so the smallest possible correlation is 0.00. The most commonly used correlation is the Pearson correlation.

Plotting and Interpreting Correlations

Pretend that the two sets of numbers in Table 1 represent test scores of a group of students in grade 11. The first set of scores is from an aptitude test of mathematical ability with standardized scores that range from 200 to 800 (M = 500, SD = 100). The second set of scores is from a 40-item test created by Mr. Wilson, the head of the high school math department. The scores on Mr. Wilson's test are the number of items correct. The scores are plotted in Figure 1. The plotted scores together are referred to as a scatter plot.

Table 1
Aptitude and Math Test Scores for Mr. Wilson's Class

	Aptitude Test	Mr. Wilson's Math Test (number of correct items)
Fred	400	15
Esther	350	12
Tom	600	27
Bill	250	6
Susan	500	21
Jason	800	39
Milka	750	36
Jim	200	3
Sam	450	18
Phoebe	300	9
Ralph	550	24
Sally	650	30
Rollo	700	33

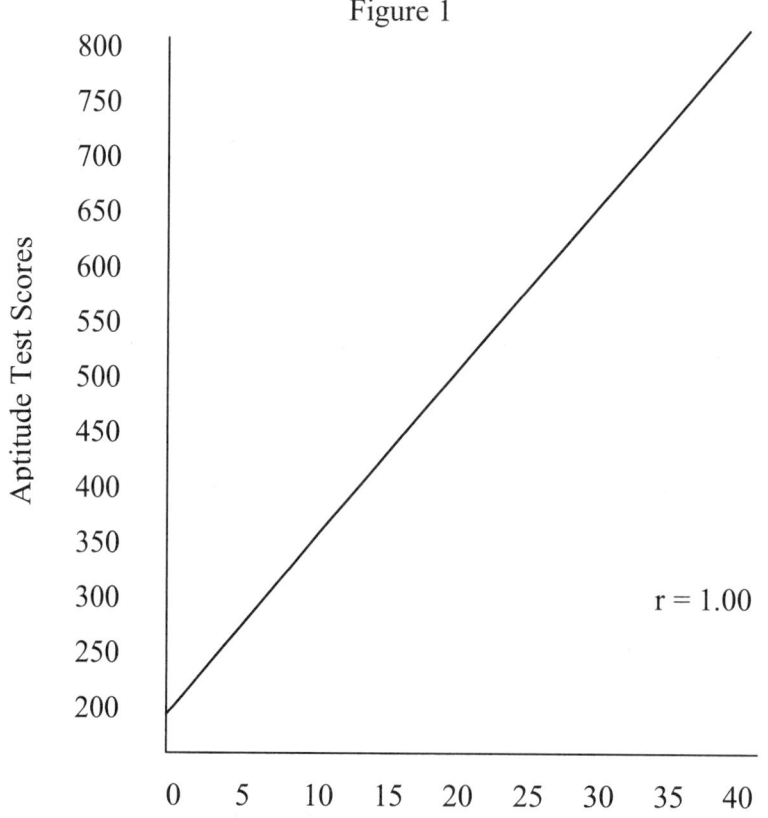

Figure 1

Mr. Wilson's Math Test Scores

Notice that all of the scores fall on a straight line. This is because the order of scores from highest to lowest is the same on both assessments. For example, Jim had the lowest score on the aptitude test and also the lowest score on Mr. Wilson's test. Jason had the highest score on the aptitude test and also the highest score on Mr. Wilson's test. In fact, all of the student performances were in identical order on both tests. This is a *perfect correlation* of 1.00 because each student's score on one test precisely predicts the score on the other test. If you know the aptitude score you can accurately predict the Wilson test result. If you know the student's score on Mr. Wilson's math test, you can absolutely predict the score on the aptitude test. The correlation coefficient of 1.00 is a *positive correlation* because high scores on one test predict high scores on the other, and low scores on one test predict low scores on the other. The correlation coefficient is usually represented by the letter *r*. Please note that neat, perfect correlations like this are almost nonexistent in the real worlds of educational and psychological research.

Activity 1

The aptitude and math test data from Mr. Wilson's class are presented again, except that the scores from Mr. Wilson's 40-item test are the number wrong instead of the number correct. For example, in the first data set Fred had a score of 15 correct. In the data set below Fred's score is the number of wrong items (40 items – 15 correct = 25 incorrect). Plot the students' scores in Figure 2. What is the major difference between this plot and the one in Figure 1? What do you think the coefficient of correlation is for the second set of scores?

	Aptitude Test Scores	Mr. Wilson's Math Test (number of incorrect items)
Fred	400	25
Esther	350	28
Tom	600	13
Bill	250	34
Susan	500	19
Jason	800	1
Milka	750	4
Jim	200	37
Sam	450	22
Phoebe	300	31
Ralph	550	16

| Sally | 650 | 10 |
| Rollo | 700 | 7 |

Figure 2

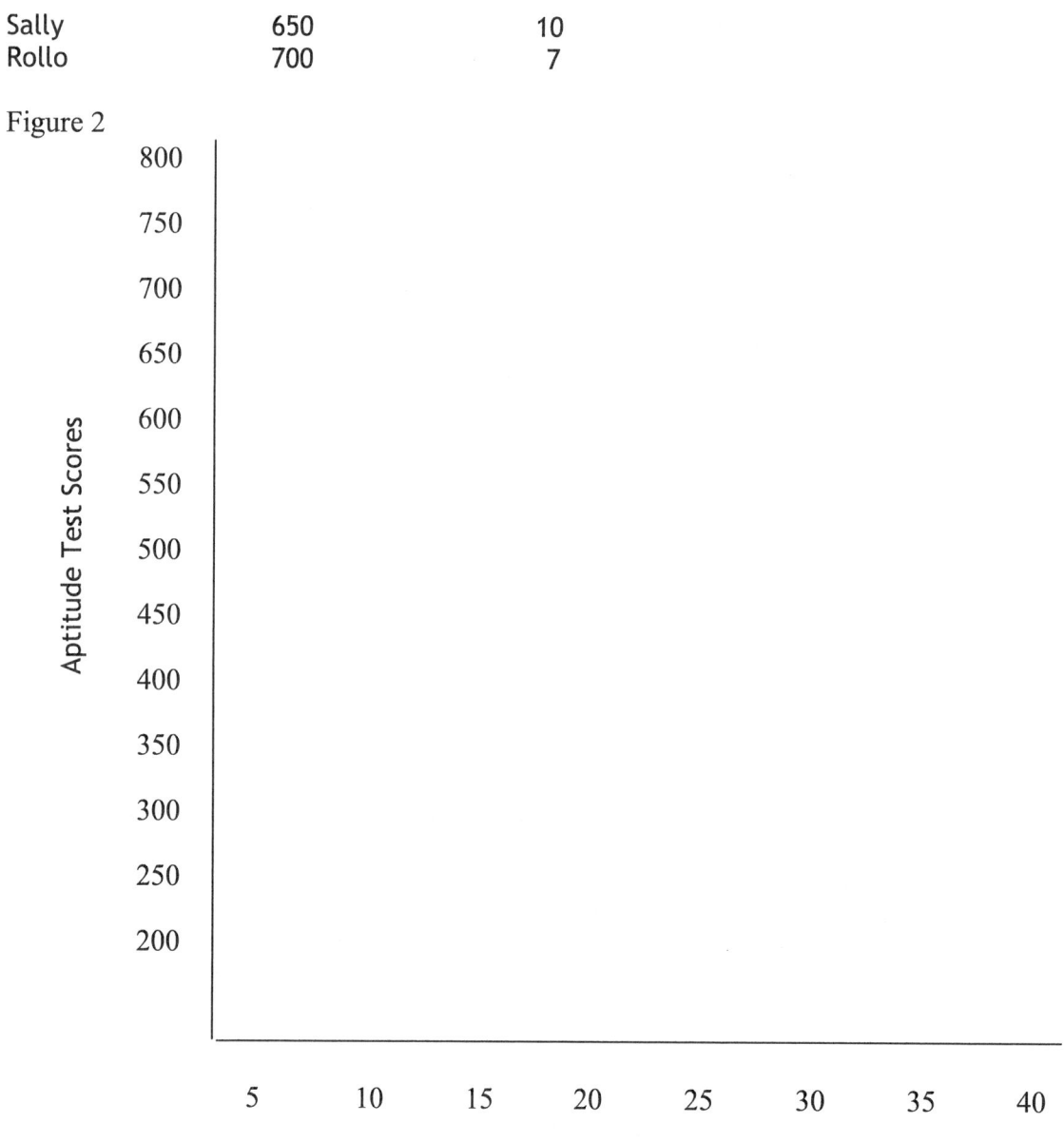

Mr. Wilson's Math Test Scores

Discussion of Activity 1

If you plotted the scores correctly, they should all be on a straight line that runs from the upper left to the lower right of the graph. The only difference between the two graphs is the direction of the line of plotted scores. In this case r = −1.00. It is a *negative correlation* because as one set of scores goes higher, the other set of scores goes lower. The higher the aptitude test score the fewer the number of incorrect answers on Mr. Wilson's math test. The correlation is a perfect correlation because a student's score on any one test perfectly predicts the score on the other test.

Positive and Negative Correlations

Positive correlations are not necessarily good and negative correlations aren't necessarily bad. There is a positive correlation between amount of cigarette smoking and the chances of getting lung cancer, and that's bad. **The more** you smoke **the more** likely you are to get lung cancer. On the other hand there is a negative correlation between the amount of green vegetables people eat and the probability of them getting colon cancer, and that's good. **The more** leafy green vegetables you eat **the less** likely you are to develop colon cancer. A positive correlation simply means that the two sets of numbers that are being correlated tend to go up and down with each other. A negative correlation means that high numbers in one data set tend to go with low numbers in the other data set. There is also no difference in the predictive power of positive and negative correlations. A correlation of - .45 ($r = - 45$) is just as large or small, strong or weak as a correlation of .45 ($r = .45$). You should interpret the power of a correlation without reference to its sign. The *absolute value* of a correlation is the size of the correlation coefficient without any reference to it being positive or negative.

Size of Correlations

In general, correlations with an absolute value less than .40 are considered small; correlations with an absolute value between .40 and .70 are considered moderate; and correlations greater than .70 are considered large. The size of a correlation is also referred to as its *magnitude*. Look at the scatter plots of the following correlations:

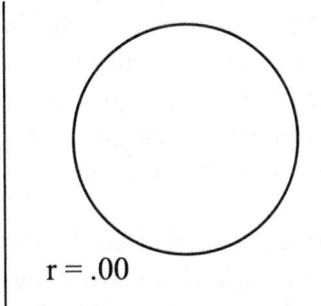
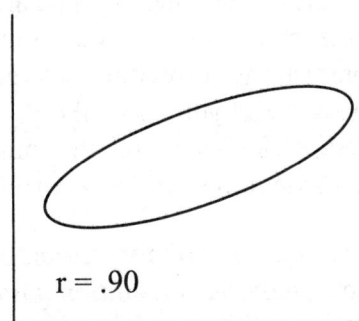

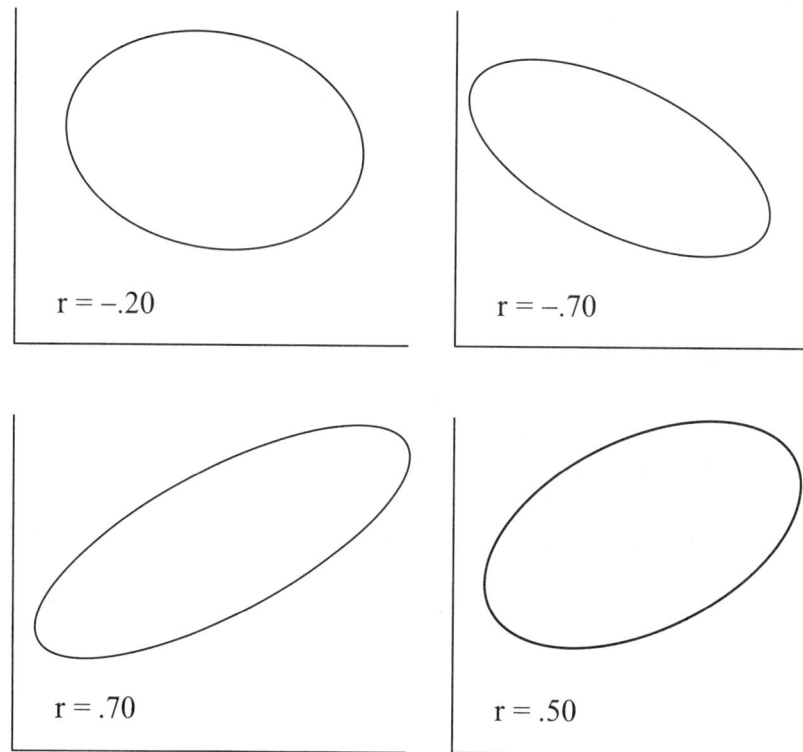

The more tightly packed and closer the dots are to being on a straight line, the higher the correlation and the greater the power of one set of numbers or scores to predict the other. A correlation of 1 or –1 gives perfect predictive power. A correlation of .00 means that there is no predictive power at all. If two tests have a correlation of .00, knowing a person's score on one test will not help you at all to predict what their score might be on the other test. The correlation between height and IQ in adult Americans is .00. Height and intelligence are unrelated, and knowing how smart someone is will give you no information about his or her height. In contrast, the correlation between the IQ scores of identical twins is about .90. If you know the IQ score of one twin you can just about predict the score of the other twin. In most educational and psychological research a correlation of .90 is considered huge.

It is not unusual for researchers to do many correlations in the same study. A *correlation matrix* is a chart or grid that shows how each variable is correlated with every other data set or variable. For instance, suppose we administered three tests to a group of third grade children: an arithmetic test, a test of reading comprehension, and a spelling test. The correlation matrix would show the correlation of each test with every other test. In the matrix below you will notice that some of the correlations are perfect correlations of 1.00. These are the correlations of each test with itself and are often not included in the matrix because they provide no information. You will also notice the bold letters in place of numbers in the matrix. There is no number in the space occupied by **a**, for instance, because the correlation between reading and arithmetic is already there in row one column two of the matrix. Usually a correlation matrix will just have blank spaces instead of including the redundant correlations. In this hypothetical matrix the correlation between reading and arithmetic is .56, the correlation between reading and spelling is .66, and the correlation between arithmetic and spelling is .43.

	Reading	Arithmetic	Spelling	
Reading	1.00	56	.66	
Arithmetic	**a**	1.00	.43	Correlation Matrix
Spelling	**b**	**c**	1.00	

Accounting for Variance

In Chapter 5 you learned that variance refers to the fluctuation of scores in a data set. If a correlation is –1 or 1, all of the variance in one set of scores can be predicted by knowing the scores in the other data set. *Accounting for variance* is a research term that refers to the ability to predict the fluctuations of scores in a set of data. In a perfect correlation, all variance can be accounted for, as in the case of the aptitude test and Mr. Wilson's math test. With a correlation of zero, no variation can be accounted for at all. To find out what percentage of variation can be accounted for by a correlation, one must square the correlation (multiply the correlation by itself). The resulting statistic is referred to as *r squared* and is written as r^2. If a correlation is .30, squaring it gives you .09, which means that 9% of the fluctuations in one set of scores can be predicted by knowing the scores in the second set. If a correlation is –.80, the r^2 is .64, meaning that 64% of the fluctuations in one set of scores can be predicted by knowing the scores in the second set. To find the correlation from r^2 you calculate the square root of r^2. For example, if $r^2 = .36$, the correlation is .60.

Activity 2

1. Calculate r^2 for a correlation of .63.
2. Place the following correlations in order from largest to smallest:
   −.71   .55   .88   −.16
3. How much variance is accounted for by a correlation of .27?
4. If r^2 is .44, what is the correlation?
5. How impressed would you be with a correlation of .20 in a research study?

Discussion of Activity 2

The answers for activity items 1–4 are in Appendix A. What is most important at this point is that you begin to get a feel for the relevance of a correlation based on its size. Note that a correlation of .20 accounts for only 4% of the variation in test scores. That leaves a whopping 96% of the variation unexplained! Of course, it's not quite as simple as this, and the meaning of a correlation is influenced by the data being correlated. For instance, humans are so complicated that it is difficult to predict behavioral outcomes from tests, and psychologists sometimes have to be satisfied with small correlations between personality tests and the future behaviors of clients.

Multiple Correlation or Multiple Regression

Multiple correlation (sometimes called *multiple regression*) is a statistical procedure in which more than one variable is used to make a prediction. For example, suppose you were a medical researcher and wanted to predict the probability of heart attacks in adult males. Age would probably be correlated with heart attacks, but so would family history, eating and smoking habits, stress levels at work, and a variety of other variables. Multiple correlation would permit you to use data about all of these variables to make a more powerful predictor of heart attacks than any one of the variables alone. R is the symbol for the coefficient of multiple correlation. Variance accounted for in a multiple regression is also calculated by multiplying the multiple regression coefficient by itself, and the symbol is R^2.

Calculating the Pearson Correlation

The *Pearson correlation* is one of the most commonly employed and useful statistics in social science research. However, computing the value of a correlation is far more complicated than computing the variance of a single set of numbers, and you may need to calculate one or more correlations as part of your research project. Using MINITAB®, the authors obtained the correlation in Activity 3 in less than two minutes; that's the easy way. However, if you do not have ready access to a statistical package, you can calculate a correlation with only a hand calculator using the procedure below. Activity 3 will lead you through the process with a concrete example.

Activity 3

Mr. Wilson administers a second 40-item math test later in the semester and is curious to know the correlation between the two sets of scores. You are a student in Mr. Wilson's advanced statistics class and volunteer to do the correlation for him. You could compute r and r^2 using a software package, but you decide to do it by hand because calculating statistics is so much fun.

Before you calculate r for Mr. Wilson's two sets of test scores, plot the scores on the graph below. Is the correlation positive or negative? Estimate the magnitude of the correlation based on the shape and dispersion of the plots (see pages 69-70).

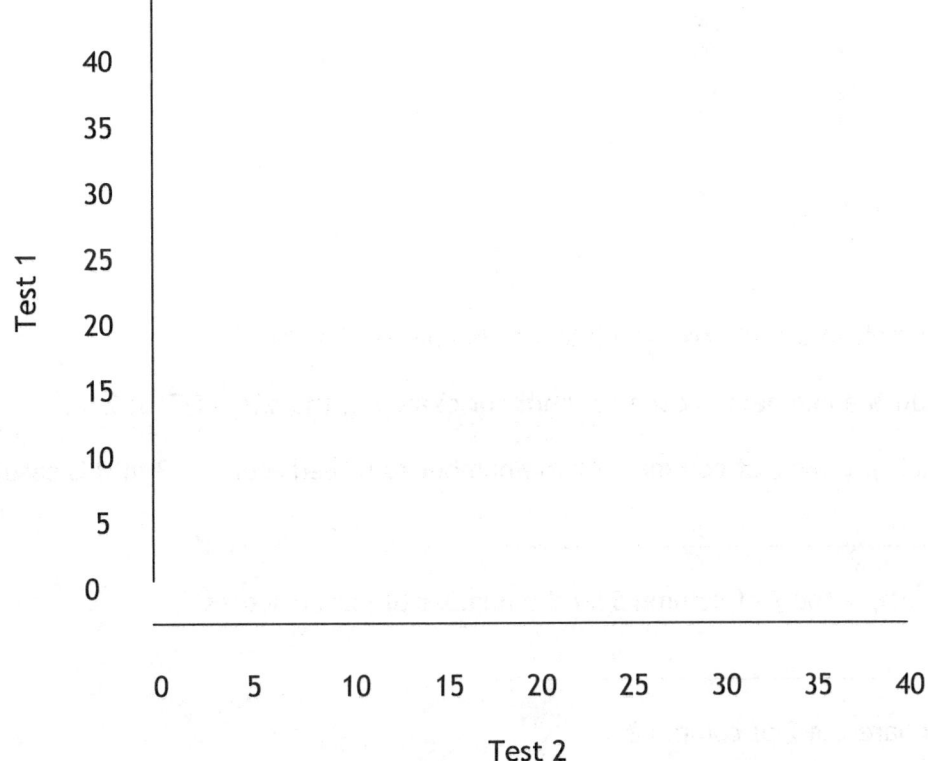

Estimated Magnitude: _____

Calculate *r* using the steps below.

STEP 1: Arrange the data in a matrix in which T1 is the first test score for each student, T2 is the second test score for each student, T1 x T2 is the product of the two scores, $T1^2$ is the square of the first test score, and $T2^2$ is the square of the second test score. This exercise looks daunting, but if you follow each step carefully you will get the answer in about 15 minutes; and you will feel satisfaction in the accomplishment.

Mr. Wilson's Matrix

Col 1	Col 2	Col 3	Col 4	Col 5	Col 6
Student	T1	T2	T1 x T2	$T1^2$	$T2^2$
Kyle	25	29	725	625	841
Esther	28	35			
Tom	13	27			
Donna	34	15			
Susan	19	22			
Jason	1	7			
Courtney	4	13			
Jim	37	32			
Sam	22	31			
Jamie	31	24			
Ralph	16	19			
Jo	10	12			
Ann	7	5			
Σ	247				

STEP 2: Complete the matrix. The first row is finished for you.

STEP 3: Add the numbers in each column. For example, the sum of T1 is 247.

STEP 4: Multiply the Σ of column 4 by the number of paired scores, 13 in this case.

_____

STEP 5: Multiply the Σ of column 5 by the number of paired scores.

_____

STEP 6: Square the Σ of column 2.

_____

STEP 7: Multiply the Σ of column 6 by the number of paired scores.

_____

STEP 8: Square the Σ of column 3.

_____

STEP 9: Multiply the Σ of column 1 by the Σ of column 2.

_____

STEP 10: Subtract the result of STEP 9 from the result of STEP 4.

_____

STEP 11: Subtract the result of STEP 6 from the result of STEP 5.

_____

STEP 12: Subtract the result of STEP 8 from the result of STEP 7.

_____

STEP 13: Multiply the result of STEP 11 by the result of STEP 12.

_____

STEP 14: Take the square root of STEP 13.

_____

STEP 15: Divide the result of STEP 10 by the result of STEP 14.

r = _____

Discussion of Activity 3

The plots of the students' scores form a pattern that extends from the lower left portion of the graph to the upper right, so the correlation is positive. Students who performed well on test 1 tended to perform well on test 2 and vice versa. If your estimate of the magnitude of the correlation based on the scatter plot was anything from .60 to point .80, give yourself a pat on the back.

The Pearson correlation between tests 1 and 2 is .70, and r^2 is .49. To get a better understanding of what this means, go back to the scatter plot you created in the graph above. Take a straight edge and draw a line through the scatter plot so that the individual data points are as close as possible to the line (guess). This is called a *regression line*, and it has a precise mathematical formula – which we will skip. If you were to measure the distance from each dot to the closest point on the regression line and then add the distances together, the total would be less than with any other line you could draw. (Draw several lines through the scatter plot to test this concept.) The total of the distances represents score variations that the correlation cannot predict. If the score variations were 100% predictable, all the data points would fall on the line, and the correlation would be a perfect 1.

Mr. Wilson's correlation is not perfect; it is .70 and accounts for only 49% of the variance. Another way to state this is that each test predicts 49% of the variation in the other test. Since this is a moderate to large correlation, we might expect that many of the scores will come close to the line while others will not. For example, Susan's scores of 19 and 22 should be plotted very close to your regression line. On the other hand, the plot for Donna's scores of 34 and 15 should be far from the line. Perhaps Donna was lucky at guessing on the first test, or perhaps she was ill when she took the second test. Is it possible that the students' performances on test 1 caused most of them to perform in a similar manner on test 2? Is it possible that the performances on test 1 caused the performances on test 2 to be similar?

The Correlation Fallacy

The *correlation fallacy* – also called the fallacy of false cause - is the belief that if two variables are correlated, then one must be causing the other. **Correlation does not prove cause**. The fact that reading comprehension and spelling are correlated does not mean that one causes the other or that improvement in one will automatically lead to improvement in the other. The correlation between shoe size and reading achievement in elementary school children is about .50. Does having bigger feet make children read better? Maybe we should stretch the kids' feet or make them wear oversized shoes to improve their reading skills! Age is a hidden variable in the correlation between reading and shoe size. Because the age of elementary school children is correlated with both shoe size and reading achievement, shoe size and reading achievement are also correlated. What hidden variable might be the cause of the correlation between test 1 and test 2 performances in the preceding example?

In addition to the correlation fallacy, correlational statistics are subject to misinterpretation because there are many different types of correlations. If the wrong correlation is used it can erroneously inflate or deflate the size of the correlation. Other correlations include: Spearman Rank-Order, Kendall Rank-Order, and Point-Biserial correlation (Bruning & Kintz, 1987; Gay & Airasian, 2008). The Pearson *r* is the most widely used of all correlational measures. However, you should check with your instructor before using it in your project.

Reaction Guide

1. Negative correlations are usually bad. Agree _____ Disagree _____

2. A correlation of −.65 is bigger than a correlation of .25. Agree _____ Disagree _____

3. Correlation implies causality. Agree _____ Disagree _____

4. The plot of a perfect correlation looks like a circle. Agree _____ Disagree _____

5. It is impossible to have a correlation greater than 1. Agree _____ Disagree _____

Why my choice is confirmed.   Why my choice is not confirmed.

1. _____   _____
2. _____   _____
3. _____   _____
4. _____   _____
5. _____   _____

Chapter 6 Self-Test

True or False

1. _____ Correlations of .55 and −.55 are exactly the same size.

2. _____ The absolute value of a correlation is its magnitude.

3. _____ The higher the correlation the higher the probability of a causal relationship.

4. _____ A correlation of zero has the shape of a straight line.

5. _____ A negative correlation is a bad correlation.

Matching

6. _____ $R^2 = .25$

7. _____ Accounts for 41% of the variance

8. _____ A medium sized Pearson correlation

9. _____ The square root of the variance

10. _____ The coefficient of multiple correlation

A. $r = .64$
B. r
C. $R = .50$
D. SD
E. R
F. $r = .52$

Computation

Using Set X and Set Y raw data below, find the answers to items 11 - 20.

Set X   3   8   -2   9   -5   7   5   5   -1   10   -7   4   5   -3 (M=2.71)

Set Y   -3 -8   2   -9   5   -7 -5 -5   1 -10   7   -4 -5   3

11. _____ Median of Set Y

12. _____ Range of Set X

13. _____ M X + M Y

14. _____ Σ Y

15. _____ SD of Set Y

16. _____ z-score for 8 in Set X

17. _____ T-score for −7 in Set Y

18. _____ Describe the scatter plot of X and Y.

19. _____ Pearson *r* for X and Y

20. _____ Variance accounted for by the correlation.

Companion Website

Additional resources and chapter activities are located at www.edinboro.edu/press.

7 Measurement

Anticipation Guide

1. Line B below is longer than line A.   Agree _____ Disagree _____

2. Measurement is subjective.   Agree _____ Disagree _____

3. All standardized tests are norm-referenced.   Agree _____ Disagree _____

4. A reliability coefficient of .90 is good.   Agree _____ Disagree _____

5. A reliable test is a valid test.   Agree _____ Disagree _____

A _____   B _____

Chapter Rationale

If you haven't done it already, take a ruler and measure the length of lines A and B above. You will find that B actually is longer than A. We attempted to trick you by making you think that this was simply another instance of a commonly demonstrated optical illusion. The point we wish to make is that "eyeballing" frequently isn't enough to draw accurate conclusions. We all filter what we see and hear through our memories, beliefs, and knowledge base; and our personal experiences alter our perceptions. Educational and psychological research requires objectivity, which in turn requires accurate measurements. The purpose of this chapter is to introduce you to measurement concepts that are directly related to research in the social and behavioral sciences.

Objectives

Measurement and assessment are complex disciplines, and the scope of this text permits only a limited overview of the concepts most essential for understanding social and behavioral science research. Consequently, this chapter will not include test construction, the role of objectives in educational and psychological evaluation, development and interpretation of standardized tests, discussions of achievement versus aptitude tests, and examinations of individual assessments. However, when you finish this chapter you will understand why measurement is critical to social and behavioral science research and you will be able to comprehend the concepts of reliability and validity as they are used in real research.

Graphic Organizer

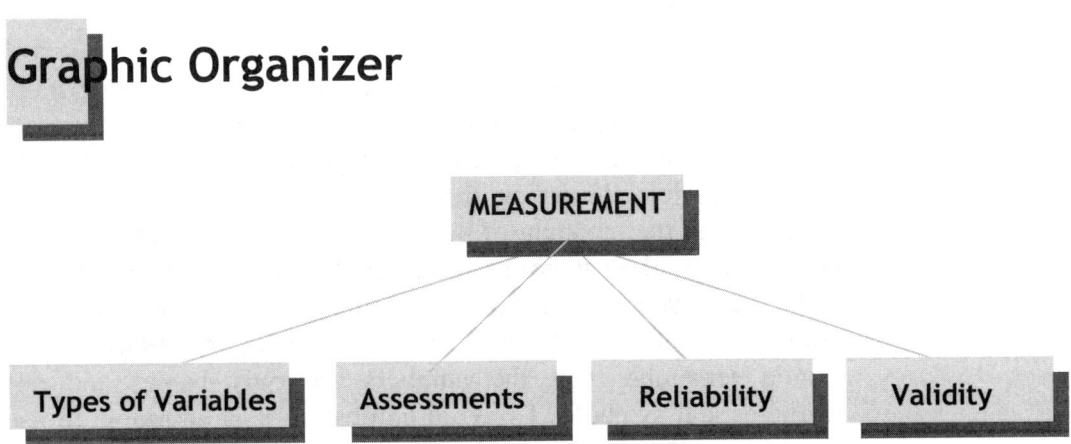

Definition of Measurement

Measurement refers to any activity or device that allows us to quantify experience. A measurement could be derived from a physical device such as a measuring spoon or from an achievement, personality, or aptitude test such as the *Scholastic Aptitude Test*. Checklists and other observational methods used in qualitative research may also be considered measurements. In all cases, the purpose of measuring is to provide objective observations and to establish dependable standards that make individual measurements or assessments meaningful.

Types of Variables

A variable is an idea that can be measured or counted. In actual research, a variable is usually a set of numbers that represents the variable as a concept or idea. For example, reading ability is an idea that is measured on a regular basis in American schools. The scores students receive on a particular assessment constitute a variable, a measure of the idea of reading ability or achievement. There are four types of variables and data in social science research: nominal, ordinal, interval, and ratio.

Nominal Variables

Nominal variables classify objects or events into one or more categories. These categories have no order or mathematical values; they are just names. For example, the gender variable is typically {male, female}. Reversing the order {female, male} makes no difference in the meaning of the variable. Sometimes numbers are used to name the categories in nominal variables, for example, 1 and 2 for male and female on a survey form. When you see nominal variables with categories represented by numbers, you should remember that the numbers are only names and not mathematical symbols. To avoid confusion, it is advisable to use letters or other non-numeric symbols rather than numbers to represent nominal data.

Ordinal Variables

An *ordinal variable* in one in which the order of the numbers in the variable is meaningful, but the intervals between the numbers are not. For example, survey instruments commonly ask subjects to respond to statements using ordinal scales such as the following: Strongly Agree, Agree, Disagree, and Strongly Disagree. The variable is ordinal because the order is meaningful. As a measure of agreement, Strongly Agree is more than Agree, which is more than Disagree, which is more than Strongly Disagree. However, it is impossible to determine whether the difference between Strongly Agree and Agree is the same as, for example, the difference between Agree and Disagree. This nonequivalence of intervals – size of steps – makes ordinal data inappropriate for many statistical analyses. Generally speaking, in quantitative research an ordinal scale is inferior to interval and ratio scales.

Interval Variables

An *interval variable* is one in which the order of the numbers is meaningful; but, in addition, the sizes of the – intervals - are identical. Interval scales are the most frequently used in social science research (e.g., norm-referenced achievement tests, aptitude tests, and personality assessments). If we count the number of items answered correctly on a 30-item multiple-choice test, we will have a variable with 29 equal intervals of one. This equivalence of intervals makes interval variables superior to nominal and ordinal variables for purposes of measurement and statistical analysis.

Ratio Variables

A *ratio variable* has all the properties of an interval variable; and, in addition, the scale has a true zero. Mass and velocity have absolute points at which there is no weight within a gravitational field and no speed. If Jim weighs 180 pounds and Jen weighs 120, it is accurate to say that Jen is 2/3 the weight of Jim (ratio). Note that if Jim has an IQ of 100 and Jen has an IQ of 150, it is not accurate to say that Jim is 2/3 as intelligent as Jen. This is because IQ assessments use interval scales. Instruments with ratio scales are fully appropriate for measurement and statistical applications, but they are relatively rare in social science research.

Activity 1

Identify the type of variable that best describes each of the sets below. The answers are in Appendix A.

1. _____ Microscopic   Small   Medium-sized   Large   Enormous

2. _____ 5   10   15   20   25   30   35

3. _____ Dog   Fish   Tree   Worm   Fungus

4. _____ 0 MPH   20 MPH   1,000 MPH   1,000,000 MPH   C

Types of Tests

There are thousands of tests for sale in the fields of counseling and education. There are tens of thousands more created for instructional and scholarly purposes every day by teachers and researchers. And, there are hundreds of ways of classifying tests. However, for our purposes we will limit the scope of the discussion to standardized tests, non-standardized tests, norm-referenced tests, and criterion-referenced tests.

Standardized and Non-standardized Tests

Standardized tests are assessments that have a uniform set of procedures. This means that there is a fixed number of test items, that the test is administered under a fixed set of conditions and time constraints, and that the test is always scored the same way. Most commercial tests in education and counseling are standardized and have been scrutinized by researchers and evaluation experts so that the properties of the tests are well understood (for example, how well an aptitude test predicts future achievement). In contrast, *non-standardized tests* may not have uniform procedures, and their properties may not be known at all. This uncertainty about what non-standardized tests measure and how well they do it is a critical issue in the evaluation of research. Examples of non-standardized tests include teacher-made classroom assessments and tests invented by researchers when there are no appropriate standardized tests available.

Norm-referenced Tests

A *norm-referenced test* is one in which an individual's performance is compared with a group. The quality of one's performance is relative to the performances of other test-takers. Commercially prepared norm-referenced tests use something called a *norming group*, a group of individuals – sometimes several thousand - who took the test at some point in the past as part of the development of the assessment. On a norm-referenced test, test-takers are not compared with others who took the test at the same time they did but rather with the original norming group. For instance, if you took the *Graduate Record Examination* and your percentile rank on the verbal portion of the test was 60, it would mean that your performance was better than the performance of 60% of the people in the norming group. It is possible for norm-referenced tests to be non-standardized. For example, a teacher could design a chemistry test for a particular class and then assign letter grades based on z-scores (e.g., everyone with a z-score of + 1 or higher gets an A).

Criterion-referenced Tests

Criterion-referenced tests are assessments in which performances are compared against a fixed standard, or criterion, and not against the performances of other individuals who have taken the same test. For example, if a history teacher gives an exam on the Civil War and determines that students who correctly answer 95% of the items will get an A, the test is criterion-referenced and not norm-referenced. In theory, everyone in the class could get an A by meeting the teacher's pre-established criterion or standard. Note that criterion-referenced tests may also be standardized. For instance, many state exams for teachers and school counselors have a uniform set of procedures but are not norm-referenced. A certain score is required for passing, and the score is independent of the performances of others.

Reliability

Fred has a habit of arriving late for work and calling in sick on Fridays. He tends to be moody at the office– sometimes happy and sometimes depressed. On good days his work is excellent, but on bad days the rest of the staff has to carry him. Fred's co-workers can't count on him; he's unpredictable. In common parlance, Fred is unreliable. Part of what makes a test good is our ability to count on it the way you would a reliable employee. Test *Reliability* is the consistency of a measurement. Hypothetically, if you could give a test to the same individual over and over again – assuming the person gained nothing from the experience of taking the test – the ideal case would be for the test-taker's score to be the same every time. This would make the test 100% reliable. On the other hand, if our fictional testing scenario resulted in wildly different scores at each retesting we would consider the test to be unreliable. If you administered a reading achievement test to a third grade girl on four occasions and her percentile scores were, 15, 76, 44, and 94, you would correctly wonder whether any of those scores had any real meaning at all. By contrast, if the same student had successive percentile scores of 33, 29, 38, and 34 on the reading achievement test you would have much more faith in the meanings of the scores as well as a sense of how well the student was performing relative to other children in her age group. If a research study uses tests with low reliabilities or if no reliabilities are reported, the results and interpretation of the research should be questioned.

Test-retest Reliability

Measures of reliability are correlational, which means that the highest possible reliability is + 1.00. These correlations are often referred to as *reliability coefficients*. One way to assess the reliability of a test is to administer the test to one group on two separate occasions and then correlate the results. This is referred to as *test-retest reliability*. If the correlation (reliability coefficient) is high (> .80), the test is said to be reliable. If the correlation is low (< .60), the test is said to be unreliable. In order to achieve a perfect reliability coefficient of + 1.00, each test-taker would have to get exactly the same score on both administrations of the test or at least perform identically relative to all others on each test administration. Of course, the correlations of .80 and .60 are ballpark figures only. A reliability of .80 would be unacceptably low for commercial, norm-referenced achievement tests. On the other hand, for a non-standardized personality test a reliability of .60 might be perfectly acceptable as a research tool.

There are some practical problems with test-retest measures. People change between test administrations and they may learn from taking the tests. Establishing test-retest reliability is a bit like weighing a group of people, waiting a while, and then weighing them again. One alternative to test-retest reliability is the use of equivalent forms. Two forms (e.g., A and B) of the same test are created and then administered to one group. The correlation between the students' performances on the two forms is referred to as the *equivalent forms method of reliability*. Doing equivalent forms reliability is a little like weighing people on two different scales and then correlating the results. The obvious difficulty with the equivalent forms method is the effort and difficulty in creating forms that are truly equivalent.

Activity 2

Donna is working on her master's thesis in School Counseling and wants to establish the reliability of an instrument she has created to measure the comfort level of students in their high school environments. After obtaining the necessary permissions, Donna randomly selects 20 students from Rasputin High School and administers the test to them on two different occasions. Using the scores listed below, establish the test-retest reliability of Donna's instrument. The solution is in Appendix A.

Subject	Test Administration 1	Test Administration 2
S1	15	20
S2	14	18
S3	17	18
S4	20	20
S5	15	18
S6	9	10
S7	17	19
S8	11	9
S9	13	14
S10	12	9
S11	15	14
S12	12	14
S13	16	15
S14	18	18
S15	8	11
S16	18	17
S17	14	13
S18	20	20
S19	17	13
S20	16	17

Internal Consistency

In the real world of budgets and timelines, it is often impractical to obtain test-retest or equivalent forms reliability. Measures of *internal consistency* provide good estimates of reliability based on the extent to which the parts of a test correlate with the total test score. Researchers who design their own tests prefer these estimates of reliability because they are less expensive and less time consuming than the test-retest alternative.

The *split-half reliability* method is a measure of internal consistency and a common alternative to the equivalent forms method. As the name split-half suggests, the items on a test are randomly sorted into two sets (A and B) after the administration of a test, in effect creating two smaller tests. The students' scores on A and B are then correlated to create the reliability coefficient.

Steps in establishing a split-half reliability:

1. Administer the full instrument to subjects and score the tests.
2. Randomly assign the items on the test to one of two groups: A or B
3. Create two scores for each subject, one for each half (A and B).
4. Correlate the two sets of scores.

Activity 3

Donna is in a panic. She has just discovered that the results from the initial administration of her test are worthless because the students were given incorrect directions; and she doesn't have time to arrange for another testing. Donna's thesis advisor suggests the split-half procedure. From the second test administration, Donna creates two scores for each subject by randomly assigning the items to split-half A and split-half B. There were a total of 20 items on the original assessment. For example, S6 got 9 answers correct of the 10 items assigned to A and all 10 correct on B.

What is Donna's split-half reliability coefficient? _____ See Appendix A)

Subject	Split-Half A Score	Split-Half B Score
S1	10	10
S2	7	8
S3	8	9
S4	10	10
S5	7	4
S6	9	10
S7	7	9
S8	10	9
S9	6	4
S10	5	6
S11	7	8
S12	6	7
S13	8	8
S14	9	9
S15	4	6
S16	9	8
S17	7	6
S18	10	10
S19	8	7
S20	8	9

The split-half method is a time consuming procedure. A commonly used and acceptable estimate of internal consistency is the Kuder-Richardson 21 formula (KR-21). The advantage of using the KR-21 is that it is fast and easy to calculate. Don't let the formula frighten you. Once you have the mean and standard deviation, the solution takes only about 60 seconds with a calculator

$$r = \frac{(K)(SD^2) - M(K-M)}{(SD^2)(K-1)}$$

Where:

r = reliability
K = the number of items on the test
M = the mean
SD = the standard deviation

Activity 4

Donna's thesis advisor suggests that she use the KR-21 as a second estimate of reliability. She uses the scores from Test Administration 2 (see Activity 2).

What was Donna's KR-21 reliability estimate? _____

Factors that Influence Test Reliability

Test reliability tends to increase with the number of items on the test. All other things being equal, an astronomy test with 40 items will be more reliable than an astronomy test with only 20 items. The narrower the scope of knowledge being assessed the higher the reliability is likely to be. For example, an astronomy test that is limited to types of stars will probably be more reliable than a test that attempts to cover the entire cosmos. Tests in which the difficulty of individual items varies will tend to be more reliable than tests that are very easy or very difficult. Finally, speed tests – sometimes referred to as *power tests* - tend to be less reliable than tests where test-takers have adequate time to respond to each item. To remember the four factors influencing reliability, think TIDS (Time, Items, Difficulty, and Scope).

Validity

In general, *validity* refers to whether or not a test measures what it claims to measure. If a research study uses a test that in fact does not measure the intended trait or behavior, the value of the study is in serious doubt. Moreover, the validity of the test may have as much to do with testing conditions and the test-takers as it does with the properties of the test. A classic example from literacy research involves the concept of passage dependency. In reading comprehension tests, *passage dependent questions* are questions that can only be answered from reading the passage and not from prior knowledge. *Passage independent questions* can be answered without reading the passage if the test-taker is sufficiently knowledgeable about the subject. A common error in assessment occurs when older students who read poorly for their age group are assessed with text materials that are difficult for them to read and comprehend but simple in an informational sense. The students may not be able to read the material, but their prior knowledge allows them to answer questions, which gives the illusion that they have been reading adequately. Under such conditions the reading test is invalid because it is measuring what the students know rather than how well the students can comprehend written text.

Face Validity

Face validity is the common sense determination that a test is valid. If you claim a test has face validity it means you have no evidence that it measures what it's supposed to measure, but your experience and expertise in your field suggest the test's validity – at least on the surface. About 30 years ago a researcher attempted to predict reading skills based on children's identification with specific animals. Even though the research revealed some correlations between animal identifications and reading skills, no one took the research seriously because it had a complete lack of face validity. Face validity is usually addressed through appeals to common sense, professional knowledge, and logic.

Concurrent Validity

A test has *concurrent validity* if its results are highly correlated with another test that already has established validity. For example, if you were to design a personality test that was positively correlated with a well-established personality test of the same type, you would have evidence of concurrent validity. Concurrent validity is usually established through correlation.

Construct Validity

Construct validity refers to the extent to which the test adequately measures the domain of knowledge implied by the researchers or test developers. A domain of knowledge could be narrow or broad; for example, a test of knowledge of educational technology would be a very large domain and would require many test items to cover the domain properly. On the other hand, a test on how to create a

PowerPoint presentation would be much more finite. If you were to create a test called the *Cherry Creek Test of Educational Technology* and the test included only items on designing PowerPoint presentations, the test would certainly suffer from a lack of construct validity. Generally, the greater the domain of knowledge claimed for the test, the more items are required to establish adequate construct validity. Construct validity is usually demonstrated by describing the process through which the test domain was established and how items were selected to represent that domain.

Predictive Validity

Tests are said to have *predictive validity* if they can predict events or behaviors in the future. A high school aptitude test that is highly correlated with grade point averages in college could be said to have strong or good predictive validity. Predictive validity is usually established through correlation.

External Validity

In educational and psychological research *external validity* usually refers to how well the results of research will apply to other schools, clients, and to real world conditions. For example, suppose a research study demonstrates that a constructivist, whole language reading and writing program in well-to-do schools in suburban Chicago was superior to other reading programs. Even if the study is well done in other respects, it may have limited validity for urban and rural schools. External validity is usually established by examining the research sample and the experimental environment and then asking whether or not other populations and environments are sufficiently alike to make the research generalizable.

The Relationship between Reliability and Validity

There are many assessments that are both reliable and valid. However, there is no automatic correlation between reliability and validity. It is possible for a test to be highly reliable but invalid (e.g., a reading comprehension assessment with a large number of passage independent questions). It is also possible for a test to be valid (e.g., to have face and construct validity) but to be unreliable because it violates TIDS principles. The assessment may have too few items; subjects may have too little time to complete the assessment; there may be a lack of diversity in item difficulty; or the test may be too broad in its scope.

It is usual for published research to include reliability coefficients for their assessments. Unfortunately, researchers are often satisfied to report reliabilities and assume that their assessments are also valid. In any quantitative study, the validity of its instrumentation should be addressed.

Activity 5

Go to the companion Web site and read "The Effect of Inclusion vs. Resource Room Instruction on Reading Achievement." Note: Focus on the research concepts you have been exposed to so far. Do not expect to be familiar with everything in the article.

Do the researchers provide adequate information on the reliability and validity of their assessments? What familiar measurement terms did you find?

1. _____

In the first table on page 10, the authors report a correlation of .68 between WRAT READING and K-TEA COMPREHENSION.

Why is .68 referred to as a validity coefficient?

2. _____

Do you think this coefficient is strong or weak? Why?

3. _____

The researchers found that it didn't make any difference whether or not students were in an inclusive environment or a resource. What might have caused this outcome?

4. _____

Are the results of the study consistent with the recommendation in the last line of the article?

5. _____

Reaction Guide

1. Line B is longer than line A.   Agree _____ Disagree _____

2. Measurement is subjective.   Agree _____ Disagree _____

3. All standardized tests are norm-referenced. Agree _____ Disagree _____

4. A reliability coefficient of .90 is good. Agree _____ Disagree _____

5. A reliable test is a valid test.   Agree _____ Disagree _____

_____   _____

    A _____   B _____

Why my choice is confirmed.   Why my choice is not confirmed.

1. _____   _____

2. _____   _____

3. _____   _____

4. _____   _____

5. _____   _____

Chapter 7 Self-Test

True or False

1. _____ Concurrent validity is established using correlation.

2. _____ Criterion-referenced tests cannot be standardized.

3. _____ If a test covers a large and complex knowledge domain, decreasing the number of items on the test will tend to increase the reliability of the test.

4. _____ The passing score on a criterion-referenced test is 60%.

5. _____ A reliability coefficient of .75 should be interpreted in the same manner regardless of the nature of the assessment.

6. _____ A test with a reliability of .90 is also a valid test.

7. _____ {Single, Married, Divorced, Remarried} is an ordinal scale.

8. _____ A reliability coefficient of .80 is better than a coefficient of .20.

9. _____ Most criterion-referenced tests use a ratio scale.

10. _____ Internal consistency is usually on an ordinal scale.

Matching

11. _____ KR-21   A. the quantification of experience

12. _____ Measurement   B. grading based on T-scores

13. _____ Norm-referencing   C. a measure of internal consistency

14. _____ 1.25   D. .96

15. _____ Test-retest Reliability   E. impossible reliability coefficient

16. _____ TIDS   F. requires two test administrations

17. _____ High Reliability   G. factors affecting reliability

18. _____ Ordinal Scale   H. a type of validity

19. _____ Passage Dependence   I. ordered but uneven intervals

20. _____ Predictive   J. answers found only in the tex

Multiple-Choice

21. Which of the following does not belong?

    A. Nominal   B. Radial   C. Ordinal   D. Interval

22. Weight as measured in kilograms is what kind of scale?

    A. Ordinal   B. Interval   C. nominal   D. Ratio

23. Which of the following is not a type of validity?

    A. Interval   B. External   C. Construct   D. Predictive

24. In the KR-21 formula, SD^2 is the:

    A. Mean   B. Correlation   C. Reliability   D. Variance

25. "All test-takers who earn a score of 15 or better will receive an A" suggests:

    A. Interval Scaling   B. Criterion-referencing   C. High Reliability   D. TIDD

Companion Website

Additional resources and chapter activities are located at www.edinboro.edu/press.

8 Quantitative Methods

Anticipation Guide

1. Control and experimental groups are typically utilized in quantitative research designs.

   Agree _____ Disagree _____

2. Manipulation and control of variables are the essence of experimental research.

   Agree _____ Disagree _____

3. It is impossible to have a true experimental design without a dependent variable.

   Agree _____ Disagree _____

4. Randomization is a key distinction between true experimental and quasi-experimental research.

   Agree _____ Disagree _____

5. Snowball sampling is a technique developed in Alaska.

   Agree _____ Disagree _____

Chapter Rationale

Methodology refers to the participants, instrumentation, procedures for collecting data, and the design for analyzing the data in a study. The *methods section* in most research articles follows the review of literature and describes the researcher's methodology. When you read a research article in a professional journal (e.g., *Reading Research Quarterly* or *Journal of Counseling & Development*), how do you know if the researcher really did a good job? What kinds of things do you need to be aware of when you are reading the methodology section of the article? Our experience has been that most teachers and counselors tend to skip the methods sections of research articles because this part of the manuscript appears boring or hopelessly complicated. In this chapter and in Chapters 9 and 10, we will attempt to demonstrate why it is essential to read and critically evaluate the methods sections of research articles. If you don't do this, you are reduced to simply accepting the researchers' conclusions based on faith or superficial appeal. As you read the methodology section in a research article, it is important to think about how much trust you can place in the researchers' results. Many studies reported in the literature are seriously flawed and the results and conclusions are not trustworthy. The focus of this chapter is on research consumerism. We want you to be able to read, comprehend, and critique quantitative research.

Objectives

After completing this chapter you will be able to define quantitative research and recognize the important characteristics of several types of quantitative designs. You will also be able to apply specific criteria in the evaluation of quantitative research.

Graphic Organizer

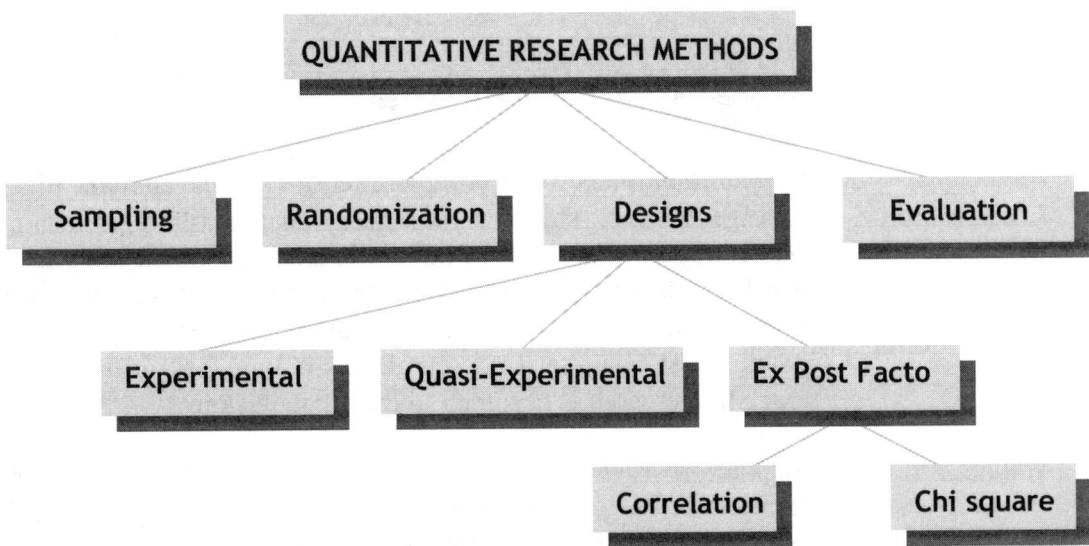

Definition of Quantitative Research

In Chapter 1 we described research as any discovery procedure that requires the systematic collection of information. Krathwohl (2004, p.740) defines *qualitative research* as "research that describes phenomena in words instead of numbers or measures" and *quantitative research* as "research that describes phenomena in numbers and measures instead of words." However, there are other important distinctions. Quantitative research is associated with *positivism*, the belief that reality exists and that it is the researcher's task to define and describe that reality. Qualitative research tends to be more constructivist in nature. Qualitative research tends to be inductive, drawing conclusions from huge numbers of observations that researchers use to establish patterns of behavior and cultural generalizations. Quantitative research follows the scientific method and is deductive and theory-driven. Quantitative research involves a lot of if-then thinking. If quantitative researchers believe there is a connection between peer tutoring and academic improvement, then they will design an experiment to find out how and if these two concepts are correlated or if one causes the other. The quantitative researcher is a tester of hypotheses.

Population Sampling

A *population* refers to the complete set of humans, animals, plants, or objects that share a common characteristic or set of characteristics. Examples of populations would be all seals in the world, dandelions in Scott's front yard, women in Japan over 80 years of age, or all practicing first grade teachers in the United States. Most quantitative research has a target population about which the research is designed to draw conclusions.

Suppose we wanted to assess the performances of all first grade teachers in the United States in the teaching of mathematical concepts. This would be quite a job considering there are about 500,000 first grade teachers spread out over four million square miles of U.S. geography. Obviously, assessing all of the subjects in this huge population is impractical. The alternative is to draw a sample that represents the population of first grade teachers; but even this would be a logistical nightmare considering we would have to select teachers from many different states. In order to make the project practical, we need to redefine the population to, for example, first grade teachers in Philadelphia. Even with this great reduction in the size of the population, the project would probably still be too expensive, too time consuming, and – as it turns out – unnecessary. The solution is to draw from the population a sample that will represent the population of interest. The most common types of sampling are: simple random sampling, stratified random sampling, snowball sampling, and convenience sampling; but before we can describe these procedures we need to define the concept of randomness.

Randomness

The common meaning of *random* is haphazard or lacking in a definite plan or purpose, as in: The boy committed a random act of violence. In social science research the words *random* and *randomization* refer to techniques that are designed to ensure that the selection of subjects in a sample is free from bias that might lead to false conclusions. For example, let's assume we ask 20 elementary school principals in Philadelphia to each recommend one first grade teacher for our study; this would constitute our sample. Do you think the principals might be biased in their choices? Would they select their weakest teachers or their strongest? What is the likelihood that the performances of those 20 first grade teachers would be representative of all first grade teachers in Philadelphia? Randomization is designed to eliminate such biases. One randomization technique would be to throw the names of all the first grade teachers into a hat, mix them up, and then blindly select the required number of names from the hat. Another method would be to assign a number to each member of the population and then have a computer select the required number of subjects using a random number generator.

In social science research, randomization is an ideal that is almost impossible to achieve in practice. Some of the teachers or schools might refuse to participate; some teachers might quit their jobs in the middle of the project; or – heaven forbid – the researcher might make a mistake and forget to invite a school to participate. Imperfections notwithstanding, a study will be better to the extent that randomization is used in the selection of its sample.

Simple Random Sampling

Simple random sampling means that all individuals in the population have an equal and independent chance of being selected. From the example above, every practicing first grade teacher in Philadelphia would have an equal opportunity to participate. This type of sampling technique would be like putting tens of thousands of names in a hat and then selecting 5, 50, or 500 names out of that hat. The sample would be a random one. Random sampling, in this case, means that every teacher in the United States would have an equal chance of being in our study, and the researchers would have no idea who was going to be selected.

Stratified Random Sampling

Another sampling technique is *stratified random sampling*. This procedure creates subsamples from the original sample and then employs simple random sampling for each subsample. Stratified random sampling ensures that individuals in the population who share a certain characteristic will be represented in the study. For example, if we want to make sure that we have an equal number of male and female teachers in our Philadelphia study, we sort the population into males and females and then select an equal number from each using a simple random sampling technique. This would be like having two hats with names from our population; one hat would have all the male teachers and the other would have all the female teachers.

Convenience and Snowball Sampling

Both simple random sampling and stratified random sampling give every person in the population an equal chance of being selected. Unfortunately, it is frequently the case that finances, politics, and other logistical barriers make random sampling impractical. For instance, what do you think the likelihood is of 200 schools in a large city all agreeing to allow a researcher to select individual teachers for an experiment that carries with it the possibility of negative reflections on the school?

The alternative to random sampling is *convenience sampling*, where the sample is created from those who are available and willing to participate. For example, suppose a school district with 45 first grade teachers gives us permission to conduct our assessments using all of their first grade teachers, then we are simply using the subjects that are most convenient. Another sampling procedure similar to convenience sampling is *snowball sampling*, in which the researcher selects several individuals with the right characteristics and then uses those individuals to identify additional participants ("Find a buddy to be in our control group."). For reasons that should be apparent, sampling in psychology and education is almost never completely randomized, and it is frequently based on convenience. Convenience sampling makes it impossible to clearly identify a target population. The result is that researchers often overstate and over generalize the implications of their research.

Activity 1

Identify the type of sampling procedure described in each of the scenarios below. The answers are in Appendix A.

1. Ethel and 24 other high school students have been selected to participate in a program designed to improve attendance. The counselors have asked each of the participants to identify a friend who is willing to be in the control group.

_____

2. Mrs. Hershey and Mr. Kirk teach fifth grade and their classes are in adjoining rooms. A doctoral student from the local university has asked them to try a set of techniques for improving textbook comprehension. There are a total of 56 students in the two classes. To assign the students to two groups, the teachers put 56 slips of paper in a hat and mix them up. There are 28 slips that say "Group 1" and 28 that say "Group 2." Each student picks a slip without looking.

_____

3. The assistant principal, Mr. Frantic, has been assigned the task of testing a new classroom management technique that involves having the students hold hands with imaginary characters from history. With the exception of Ms. Dinger, all the teachers in the school think it's a stupid idea, so Mr. Frantic asks Ms. Dinger to have her sixth graders to participate.

_____

4. The reading specialist in Landisville Elementary School, Mrs. Saccade, wants to assess the reading attitudes of the children to see if there is a correlation between grade level and attitude. Because there are 550 children in the school and she can't afford to test all of them, Mrs. Saccade randomly selects 20 students from each grade level.

_____

Quantitative Designs

There are hundreds of different research designs, some relatively simple and some extraordinarily complex. However, they all fall into one of the following categories: experimental, quasi-experimental, or ex post facto.

Characteristics of True Experimental Research Designs

In a true experimental design there is always at least one independent and one dependent variable. The *dependent variable* is the assessment. The *independent variable* is the method, intervention, or treatment. If Method A is compared with Method B and the basis of the comparison is a test, then the test is the dependent variable and the method is the independent variable. For example, a counselor wants to know if changes in diet can cause changes in depression. Based on a review of the literature, the counselor selects two diets. A group of people suffering from depression are assigned to two groups: Diet Method A and Diet Method B. The diets of the people will be controlled by the counselor, and they will be different for each group. After the participants have followed the diets for a predetermined period of time, the counselor will give the subjects a depression test and then compare the mean scores of the two groups to see if one group is less depressed than the other. In this case, the dependent variable is the depression test, and the independent variable is the diet.

In a true experimental design all sources of variation must be controlled so that the independent variable is the only possible cause of changes in the dependent variable. In our example, if the people in Diet Method A discover that the counselor thinks their diet will help them, and the people in Diet Method B do not know what the counselor believes, then an improvement in depression (dependent variable) by Diet Method A could be caused by the expectations of the people in group A and not by their diet. If the people in Method B cheat on their diets and become more depressed by guilt, then differences in depression between the two groups could be partially or entirely the result of cheating as opposed to dieting. Ruling out these alternative explanations, also referred to as *threats to validity* (see Chapter 10), is challenging; and the fact that research studies are published is no guarantee that the proper controls have been exercised.

In a true experimental design the participants in the sample (representing the target population) must be randomly assigned to treatments. If they are not randomly assigned, the study cannot be a true experiment. In the diet study the participants must not be allowed to choose their own diet; they cannot be assigned to one group or the other based on weight, age, or any other characteristic; they must not be assigned haphazardly. It must be a random assignment that uses a table of random numbers, a computer with a random number generator, or some similar device.

The reason for insisting on random assignment of participants to treatments is to ensure that people with various characteristics have an equal – and predictable – chance of being selected for each group (e.g., sugar freaks, meat eaters, and people with no willpower whatsoever).

Notice that a true experiment is deductive in nature, which means it can be reduced to a series of premises and a conclusion that should logically follow from the premises:

Premise 1: The conditions of the experiment have been controlled so that the independent variable is the only possible cause of changes measured by the dependent variable.

Premise 2: Randomization has been used in selecting the sample and assigning subjects in the sample to intervention groups.

Premise 3: The dependent variable is a reliable and valid measure.

Conclusion: Changes in the dependent variable are caused by the independent variable.

Incomplete True Experimental Designs

Educational and psychological research studies frequently have the appearance of true experimental designs when in reality they are based on false premises that lead to unsound and inappropriate conclusions. One common design of this sort involves administering an assessment (dependent variable) to a group of subjects, providing an intervention or treatment (independent variable), administering the assessment again, comparing the results of the two assessments, and then drawing a causal conclusion. This is called the *Pretest-Posttest Single Group Design*. These are the steps in the design:

Step 1: Select a sample, which becomes the experimental group
Step 2: Test the experimental group (dependent variable)
Step 3: Conduct the treatment, program, or intervention (independent variable)
Step 4: Test the experimental group again (dependent variable)
Step 5: Compare the group means of the two assessments
Step 6: If the means are different, conclude that the treatment is the cause

The main flaw in the Pretest-Posttest Single Group Design is that it always violates Premise #1 of true experimental designs because there are always alternative explanations for changes in the group's performances. For example, the group might have improved because they matured and would have done better anyway; the teacher rather than the treatment could have caused the difference; the subjects may have tried harder on the second testing because they thought they were supposed to improve.

Activity 2

Read "Selected Differentiated Instructional Strategies & Reading Comprehension Levels" in Snodgrass and Adams (2004) (Educational Research Website). Hint: The chart on page 15 shows that the study is really three separate Pretest-Posttest Single Group Designs.

1. What sampling technique did the authors use?

   _____

2. What is the dependent variable in the study?   _____

3. Did the authors address reliability and validity?   _____

4. What is the independent variable in the study?   _____

5. Is Premise #1 met   _____

6. Is Premise #2 met?   _____

7. Is Premise #3 met?   _____

8. Did the authors draw causal conclusions?   _____

9. Explain why the conclusions were or were not appropriate.

   _____

   _____

Completely Randomized Control Group Design

The *Completely Randomized Control Group Design* is an improvement over the Pretest-Posttest Single Group Design because it attempts to fulfill Premise #1.

Premise 1: The conditions of the experiment have been controlled so that the independent variable is the only possible cause of changes measured by the dependent variable.

In the Completely Randomized Control Group Design, the researchers might do only one assessment at the end of the treatment period, a *posttest only design*. Or, the researchers may want to obtain a *baseline* or an initial assessment of the dependent variable as a check on the equivalency of the two groups at the beginning of the experiment – even with random assignment. A second assessment is completed immediately following the administration of the treatment to determine if there is a change in the performances of the groups. The pretest score for each individual is subtracted from the posttest score to create a *gain score*, which then serves as the dependent variable. This is referred to as a *Pre-post design*. It is also possible to have two or more experimental groups instead of one experimental and one control group.

There are many variations of the true experimental design, but the following steps are basic:

Step 1: Randomly select a sample from the population of interest
Step 2: Randomly assign members of the sample to treatment and control groups
Step 3: Establish the reliability and validity of the Dependent variable
Step 4: Conduct the treatment, program, or intervention (independent variable)
Step 5: Assess all groups using the dependent variable
Step 6: Compare group means
Step 7: Draw appropriate causal conclusions

"Everything that can go wrong will go wrong" (Murphy's Law) applies nicely to educational and psychological research. Cost prohibits you from sampling the complete population; people refuse to be in your sample; you are working in a setting with intact groups and can't get permission to randomly assign individuals to treatment and control conditions; you have a flat tire on your way the teachers' training session; there are problems implementing the experimental program; subjects drop out of your experiment; a teacher gives the control group extra time to complete the posttest. You start thinking about jumping out a window. Real world social science research is exacting in theory, but in reality it is fraught with limitations and compromise.

Quasi-Experimental Research Designs

Quasi-experimental research designs are used when random assignment of the sample is impossible. Typically, quasi-experimental designs are utilized when pre-existing groups are assigned to treatments. This is very common in clinical and educational settings where naturally occurring, intact groups are present. It is important to note that the researcher can and should randomly assign the intact groups to treatment and control conditions. In other respects, quasi-experimental designs are the same as true experimental designs in form. The primary limitation of quasi-experimental designs is that without random assignment of individual participants to treatments, it is difficult to establish the equivalence of the groups being compared; and that makes it more difficult for the researcher to make the case that differences between groups have been caused by the treatment (independent) variable and not by some pre-existing difference between the groups.

Ex Post Facto Designs

In Latin the literal meaning of ex post facto is "from a thing done afterward" (i.e., after the fact). In ex post facto designs there is no systematic manipulation of an independent variable in an attempt to establish cause and effect. The designs are either descriptive or correlational. The results tell something about what currently exists or about what has happened already.

Sometimes a study will have the appearance of a true experimental design when in reality it is only ex post facto. For example, Mr. Firem, a human resources officer in a large company wants to investigate the relationship between smoking and attendance at work. The researcher obtains a sample of smokers and a sample of non-smokers in the company and the number of days absent for each individual over the course of a year. Mr. Firem compares the means of the two groups and finds that the smokers missed more days than nonsmokers. His conclusion is that smoking causes absenteeism. It may well be that smoking causes absenteeism, but this experiment doesn't prove it. There is no randomization and no experimental treatment of any kind. The proper analysis for this data is correlation.

Correlational Research

In Chapter 6 we defined a correlation as a statistic that is computed from two sets of data. A statistic is just a number, and a correlation by itself proves nothing. Unless a correlation is supported by other data, logic, and theory, it means only that one variable can predict another variable to an extent defined by the magnitude of the correlation. Shoe size and reading achievement may be correlated when all the children in an elementary school are tested, but what other data, what logic, or what theory would support the notion that such a correlation has any practical value or theoretical significance? By contrast, cigarette manufacturers for decades rigorously denied that the high positive correlation between cigarette smoking and lung cancer was causal based on the fact that correlation does not prove cause. However, in the case of smoking and cancer there are huge amounts of data (e.g., from experiments with animals), logic (e.g., lung cancer certainly does not cause smoking), and medical theory (e.g., understanding of carcinogens) to support a causal relationship.

Sometimes correlations and other ex post facto methods are the only alternatives available to researchers. For example, it is not possible to randomly assign human beings to experimental and control groups for smoking behavior, poor diet, child abuse, and thousands of other conditions. However, this does not free researchers from the obligation to establish causality by methods other than correlation. It is not uncommon for research reports to talk about using correlation to explore the relationship between two variables. *The relationship* is a fuzzy term that some researchers use to refer to prediction, but too often this is a disguised reference to causality. Beware. Any report of research that uses correlational procedures and then addresses causality should be viewed with skepticism unless the authors supply additional data, logic, and theory.

2x2 Chi-Square

The *Chi square* statistic is used to determine if there is a systematic relationship between the two nominal variables. There are other variations of the Chi Square, but the 2x2 Chi-square is particularly useful. The symbol for Chi square is χ^2.

Suppose you wanted to find out if male and female teachers were different in their preferences for taking online and face-to-face graduate courses. If you were able to ask all of the 120 teachers in

a rural school district which they preferred, your data might look like Table 1 below:

Table 1

	Female	Male
Online	20	60
F2F	30	10

Male/Female and Online/F2F are nominal variables and the number in each box is the *observed frequency* of response. These variables are also dichotomous, which means they are split into two categories. For instance, out of 50 female teachers, 30 indicated that they would prefer face-to-face classes. Table 2 shows the *expected frequencies* if there are no preferences at all among men and women for type of course delivery. Table 1 shows that the frequencies are different for men and women, but these differences might be due to chance.

Table 2

	Female	Male
Online	25	35
F2F	25	35

Activity 3

Calculate x^2 using the data in Table 1 and the steps below. Answers are in Appendix A.

STEP 1:   Arrange the data in a matrix by column and row, and add the numbers in each row and column.

	R1	R2	Σ Rows
C1	20	60	80
C2	30	10	40
Σ Columns	50	70	

STEP 2:   Σ all the numbers in the table. _____

STEP 3:   Multiply the row and columns sums: 80 x 40 x 50 x 70. _____

STEP 4: Multiply R1C1 and R2C2: 20 x 10. _____

STEP 5: Multiply R2C1 and R1C2: 60 x 30. _____

STEP 6: Subtract the smaller of Steps 4 and 5 from the larger number. _____

STEP 7: Square the result of STEP 6. _____

STEP 8: Multiple the result of STEP 7 by N (120 in this case). _____

STEP 9: Divide STEP 8 by STEP 3. x^2 = _____

If the value of x^2 is greater than 3.8, the chances are less than 5% that the frequencies in Table 1 are the result of chance. If there is a relationship between the two variables, its strength can be computed from the x^2. The resulting statistic is called the *Phi coefficient* and is interpreted like a correlation. Two additional steps are required to calculate Phi:

STEP 10: Divide x^2 by N. _____

STEP 11: Take the square root of STEP 10: Phi = _____

At least within the sample surveyed, there appears to be a relationship between gender and format of graduate classes. Inspection of the cells in Table 1 indicates that – in this sample – men have a higher preference for online courses than do women; and women prefer the face to face classes. Chi squares are ex post facto analyses because there are no experimental manipulations, and they do not demonstrate cause and effect.

Writing Your Research Report: Methods Section

When you read a research article written in APA format (American Psychological Association) or in the chapter format used in most thesis writing, there is almost always a *Methods Section*. This is the part of the article that describes the population and sample, dependent and independent variables, experimental procedures, the research design, and statistical procedures for analyzing the data. If researchers provide sufficient detail and clarity in the methods section, other scholars should be able to replicate the experiment.

Evaluating the Sample

The researcher needs to provide a detailed description of the population of interest and the sample. This means describing the population and sample along with any factors that might influence the outcome of the study. The researcher needs to describe the sample in rich detail. For example, the number of participants, gender, ethnicity, age, and any other factors that may impact the results such as geographic location, social economic status, and vocational status.

Situational variables are those things that happen to the sample or participants during the study. They need to be reported as well because they can influence the results. Sampling techniques and randomization procedures should be clearly stated.

Instruments/Apparatus/Measures

Research reports should list, describe, and provide a rationale for the tests, assessments, observation instruments, technology, and apparatus used in the study. In particular, the dependent variable should be presented in detail along with evidence of reliability and validity.

Procedures

Once the sample and instruments have been described, the report should give a detailed account of all procedures in the study. In an experimental design this would include a description of the experimental and control groups, how subjects were assigned to groups, and a complete chronology of events and activities, including assessments. In an ex post facto or correlational study, the procedures section of the report would describe how the data were collected.

Analytical Techniques/Statistical Analyses

In this part of the methods section, the researcher indicates what statistical techniques will be used to analyze the data, such as correlation or Chi-square. In addition, the researcher should explain how the statistical procedure will support or refute the research hypothesis or answer the research question.

Activity 4

Using a scale from 5 to 1 with 5 being Excellent and 1 being Inadequate, evaluate the components in the method section of "Pet Bonding and Pet Bereavement among Adolescents" (see Appendix B).

Scale: Excellent   5   4   3   2   1   Inadequate

_____ Sample

_____ Instruments/Apparatus/Measures

_____ Procedures

_____ Analytical Techniques/Statistical Analyses

_____ Methods section overall

Would you classify the Pet Bonding study as True Experimental, Quasi-Experimental, or Ex post facto? Give a justification. (See Appendix A for the solution.)

_____

Reaction Guide

1. Control and experimental groups are typically utilized in quantitative research designs. Agree _____ Disagree _____

2. Manipulation and control of variables is the essence of experimental research. Agree _____ Disagree _____

3. It is impossible to have a true experimental design without a dependent variable. Agree _____ Disagree _____

4. Randomization is a key distinction between true experimental and quasi-experimental research. Agree _____ Disagree _____

5. Snowball sampling is a technique developed in Alaska. Agree _____ Disagree _____

Why my choice is confirmed.   Why my choice is not confirmed.

1. _____   _____

2. _____   _____

3. _____   _____

4. _____   _____

5. _____   _____

Chapter 8 Self-Test

True or False

1. _____ All other things being equal, a true experimental design is better than a quasi-experimental design.

2. _____ A high correlation means there is a causal relationship between the variables.

3. _____ A random sample is part of a population.

4. _____ χ^2 measures dependent variable changes caused by the independent variable.

5. _____ A stratified sampling procedure is also a random procedure.

Matching

6. _____ placebo

7. _____ independent variable

8. _____ positivism

9. _____ ex post facto

10. _____ true experimental design

A. belief in an objective reality
B. must have random assignment of participants to treatments
C. the intervention
D. a phony treatment
E. design that focuses on what has already occurred
F. correlational procedure

Companion Website

Additional resources and chapter activities are located at www.edinboro.edu/press.

9 Analysis of Variance

Anticipation Guide

1. Significant differences are important differences. Agree _____ Disagree _____

2. ANOVA is an exploding star. Agree _____ Disagree _____

3. It is just as bad to have too many as too few participants in a quantitative study. Agree _____ Disagree _____

4. Statistical significance tests are overrated. Agree _____ Disagree _____

5. When a correlation is statistically significant, it is unnecessary to report the correlation itself. Agree _____ Disagree _____

Chapter Rationale

The results sections of almost all research reports discuss the importance of the research, its implications for teachers and counselors and/or its contributions to psychological or educational theory. It is not unusual for the authors of these reports to overstate the case for the value of their research or even to misinterpret their own statistics. To be a critical, informed reader of social science research, it is essential that you are able to make your own professional judgments regarding the value of published research. One of the corollaries of Murphy's Law is "Half of everything is crud." Unfortunately, this is probably as true of educational research as anything else. The purpose of this chapter is to help you figure out which half is which.

Objectives

When you have completed this chapter, you will have acquired three important new competencies. First, you will be familiar with the basic terminology that quantitative researchers use to present the results of their research. Second, you will be able to make informed judgments about the credibility of quantitative research reports and their importance to you as a consumer of educational research. Finally, you will be able to write the results section of a research report in APA style.

Graphic Organizer

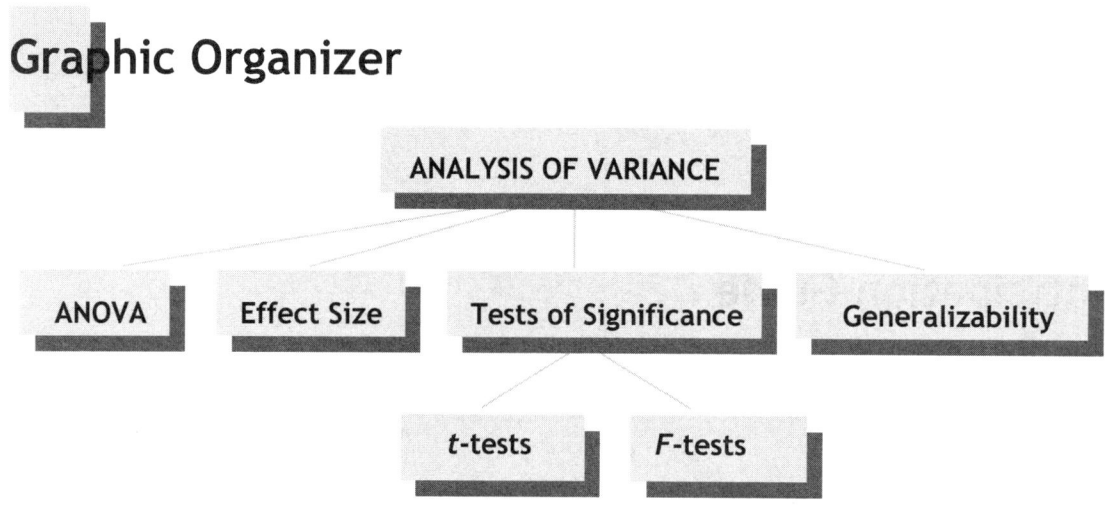

The Hampton Experiment

Sample, Research Design, and Procedures

Sample: Hampton Elementary is a fictitious urban school on the east coast. Most of the children are from blue collar homes and live in neighborhoods that are well maintained and relatively safe. Hampton provides an upbeat, multicultural environment with an enthusiastic principal and a competent and caring faculty who are always looking for new ways to improve their curricula. Hampton Elementary has two first-grade classrooms with a total of 48 students and two teachers, Mr. Gibbons and Ms. Pickles. The first grade teachers are eager to improve the children's reading comprehension and have received permission from the principal and the students' parents or guardians to conduct an experiment in their own classrooms.

Topic: Reading

Research Statement: Reading achievement will increase if teachers read exciting and grade-appropriate literature to first grade children for 10 minutes immediately before daily reading instruction.

Research Rationale: The teacher's reading will heighten the children's attention and interest in learning to read, which, in turn, will focus attention on learning new words and comprehending text.

Research Design: Mr. Gibbons and Ms. Pickles have selected a true experimental design (Posttest-Only-Control-Group) whose purpose is to compare group performances. In this design, participants are randomly assigned to the experimental or control group by drawing names from a hat. The experimental group gets a treatment and the control group receives nothing. At the end of the treatment period both groups are tested and the means of the two groups are compared.

Group 1: randomly assigned, received treatment, post-tested

Group 2: randomly assigned, received no treatment, post-tested

Procedure: The students are randomly assigned to one of two groups, experimental (Group 1) and control (Group 2). At 9:40 each morning the students in the experimental group all go to Mr. Gibbons classroom to listen to him read for 10 minutes (the treatment). The remaining students go to Ms. Pickles classroom and participate in activities unrelated to reading. Mr. Gibbons and Ms. Pickles switch roles each week so that the students in each group spend an equal amount of time with each teacher. After this procedure is followed for six weeks, all of the students take the Beginning Level of the *Gates-MaGinitie Reading Tests* (GMRT), which has well established reliability and validity. Each student has a raw score (number correct) on the test. The raw scores are added for each group and divided by the number of students in each group to get a group mean. The means of the two groups are compared.

Analysis

The usual method of comparing group means is *analysis of variance* (ANOVA), a sophisticated statistical procedure that attempts to explain the variation in scores. In a properly conducted true experimental design, the only thing that will cause a difference in performance between groups is the treatment (independent variable), in this case reading or not reading to the children immediately prior to daily reading instruction. Depending upon the outcome of the ANOVA, the researcher can make the argument that reading to the children **caused** improved reading test scores.

As in the Hampton Experiment, the simplest ANOVA involves only two groups: the experimental group and the control group. Sometimes researchers will refer to the number of cells in an ANOVA design. A *cell* is a box that represents a particular group in the experiment. In this case there are two cells with 24 subjects in each one:

Experimental	Control
N=24	N=24

Assume that there are 24 children in each group (cell) and that their raw scores (items correct on the test) are as follows:

Experimental Group: 16 15 22 16 15 20 21 14 22 12 18 20
                     19 20 23 14 19 19 20 21 18 22 19 17

    Mean = 18.42   Standard Deviation = 2.96

Control Group: 21 17 19 13 10 21 16 18 16 15 17 19
                     15 14 17 16 11 16 17 14 18 14 16 18

    Mean = 16.17   Standard Deviation = 2.70

Standard Deviation for the combined groups = 2.83

The difference in performance between the groups is referred to as the *experimental effect*. Clearly, the experimental group outperformed the control group on the standardized test. However, there are several important questions we should ask before we begin recommending this reading procedure for tens of thousands of children.

How big is the experimental effect?

Is the experimental effect reliable? In other words, if we repeated the experiment, what is the probability that we would get the same experimental effect?

Is the experimental effect generalizable?
Is the experimental effect important?

Effect Size

The experimental effect is often referred to as the effect size. However, *effect size* is really the experimental effect you would find if you tested the entire possible population of participants (e.g., all first-graders in the United States). Because of practical limitations (i.e., time and money), almost all experiments involve relatively small samples so that an experimental effect is only an estimation of effect size.

The raw experimental effect in the Hampton example is the simple difference between the experimental and control group means (18.42 – 16.17), 2.25 test items correct. So what? Is an effect size of 2.25 items a lot or a little? One approach to answering this question involves common sense. You could go to the norms tables for the standardized test and see how much difference 2.25 items would make in terms of percentile or grade equivalents. For example, if the mean for the experimental group turned out to be one percentile point higher than the mean for the control group, the Hampton teachers might consider the reading activity not worth the expenditure in instructional time. On the other hand, if the difference were 10 percentile points, they might readily conclude that reading to the children immediately prior to formal reading instruction is highly beneficial and recommend making it an official part of the curriculum at Hampton Elementary.

A more common approach to measuring the size of the experimental effect – and one that can be used with any type of quantifiable assessment – involves stating the difference between the means in terms of standard deviation units. The standard deviation of the reading test scores for all 48 Hampton first grade students in the experiment was 2.83. To convert the experimental effect to standard deviation units you subtract the control mean (16.17) from the experimental mean (18.42) and then divide by the standard deviation (2.83).

$$18.42 - 16.17 = 2.25$$

$$2.25 / 2.83 = .795$$

We can verbalize this by saying that on the average the first-graders in the experimental group performed about three quarters of a standard deviation better on the reading test than the control group. Generally, an effect of .2 standard deviations is considered small; an effect of .4 standard deviations is considered moderate; and an effect of .8 is a whopper. Given the duration and cost of our hypothetical Hampton experiment, an effect of .795 standard deviations would probably be considered very important in terms of curriculum decision making.

Activity 1

Mr. Calhoun, a high school social studies teacher in the Posada School District, teaches world history using multimedia presentations in the experimental class and standard text materials in the control class. Students were randomly assigned to the two classes. On the 100 item mid-semester exam the mean score for the experimental group was 86 and the mean score for the control group was 77. The standard deviation for the exam was 8. What is the size of the experimental effect, and what argument should the social studies teacher be making?

Discussion of Activity 1

The size of the experimental effect is 1.125 standard deviation units [(86 − 77) / 8 = 1.125]. This is a monster effect, and the teacher should be arguing for more multimedia in social studies classes. A word of caution: if Mr. Calhoun treated the groups differently other than in his use of multimedia, he might have been the cause of all or some of the experimental effect. For example, he might have been more enthusiastic and held higher expectations for the experimental group. Experimenter bias of this sort is very common and represents a serious threat to the validity or trustworthiness of an experiment. Note that the Hampton Experiment controlled for the teacher effect by having Ms. Pickles and Mr. Gibbons participate as the teachers with each group for an equal amount of time. This type of control procedure is sometimes referred to as *counterbalancing*.

ANOVA and Statistical Significance

Statistical Significance

In theory, if an experiment is precisely replicated using a fresh set of participants from the population of interest, the same experimental effect should occur. In practice, this is almost impossible with experiments in the social and behavioral sciences. There are the inevitable human sources of error, and sampling from the population of interest is almost never the ideal case where all members of the population (e.g., all children in first grade) are equally available to participate. In addition, the size of the sample influences the reliability of the experimental outcome. For instance, if you were to do the Hampton Elementary experiment using only two children in each group, as a matter of chance selection the groups could easily be very different in terms of the initial reading skills, general maturity, and attitudes of the children.

On the other hand, if 100 children in first grade were randomly assigned to the experimental and control groups, the probability that the groups would be radically different with respect to reading skill, maturity, and attitude would be much lower than if only four children were randomly assigned to the two groups. In any quantitative experiment there is always one question that must be answered: What is the probability that the experimental effect is a fluke? Stated differently, if the experiment were redone under the same conditions, would we get the same results?

If you flip a coin 10 times and do this many times, you will average five heads and five tails. However, there is one chance in 1,024 of getting either heads or tails 10 times in a row. The same thing happens in research. The fact that random sampling is employed doesn't guarantee that the groups are equal with respect to the abilities and other characteristics of experimental and control groups. Observed differences between group means is sometimes just a fluke. A *statistical significance test* is a mathematical calculation of the probability that differences between groups are an accidental result of the sampling procedure. **Beware! In this context the word *significance* does not mean importance.** Significance only refers to the reliability of the statistic and should never be interpreted to mean that the statistic is large, practical, or relevant to a theory. One of the most common blunders in quantitative studies is the misinterpretation of significance testing. In fact, the misuse and misinterpretation of significance testing in psychology and education is so profound and widespread that some well known researchers (e.g., Carver, 1993) have called for its abolition. In addition, Carver (1978), Cohen (1994), and Shaver (1993) have made the case that significance testing is based on false premises and that there are more effective and less ambiguous ways of reporting and interpreting data. For example, reporting means, standard deviations, and effect sizes along with carefully describing every aspect of the experiment.

Analysis of Variance

An ANOVA always includes one or more tests of statistical significance. When there are only two groups, as in the Hampton experiment, the test of statistical significance is called a *t*-Test and is reported in the following manner: $t(46) = 2.75, p < .01$. The purpose of this test is to determine the likelihood that the difference between the group means was caused by sampling error (e.g., the smartest children were coincidentally assigned to the experimental group. The *t* stands for *t*-Test. The number in parentheses (46), sometimes referred to as *degrees of freedom* or (df), is the number of participants in the experiment minus 2, in this case 48 –2. The number 2.75 is called the *t* value. (You can think of the *t* value as a kind of experimental effect size.) The *p* stands for probability; < is the sign for less than; and .01 is a percentage, in this case one percent. The expression $t(46) = 2.60$, $p < .01$ can be verbalized as follows: a *t*-test with 46 degrees of freedom resulted in a *t* value of 2.60, which has a probability of 1% – or one chance in one hundred – of occurring because of sampling error.

In research articles you will typically find statements such as the following: "the difference between the two means was statistically significant at the .01 level." Most researchers consider .05 to be the lowest acceptable level of sampling reliability. Tests of statistical significance should be accompanied by a report of means and standard deviations. Sometimes means and standard deviations are reported in a table, but they may also appear in the text as follows: (M=18.42, SD=2.96). Here is how Mr. Gibbons and Ms. Pickles wrote the statistical results of their experiment.

The mean of the experimental group on the *GMRT* (M=18.42, SD=2.96) was significantly greater, statistically, than the mean of the control group (M=16.17, SD=2.68), $t(46) = 2.75$, $p < .01$.

The *t*-Test used in the Hampton Experiment is used in true experimental designs in which the subjects in a sample have been randomly assigned to two groups. Technically, this is referred to as a *t-Test for the difference between two independent means*.

The *F-test* is another common test of statistical significance associated with ANOVA. It is used when there are more than two cells in an experimental or quasi-experimental design. For example, if Ms. Pickles and Mr. Gibbons wanted to find out if boys and girls were affected differently by the treatment conditions, they could have set up this design:

Design Example X

Treatment Condition

Gender	Experimental	Control
Girls	cell 1	cell 2
Boys	cell 3	cell 4

There are four cells in this design and four groups: girls in the experimental condition (cell 1), girls in the control condition (cell 2), boys in the experimental condition (cell 3), and boys in the control condition (cell 4). In this design there are two factors: treatment condition and gender. A *factor* is a classification of experimental conditions. In this case each factor has two cells. In research jargon this is referred to as a 2 x 2 design, two factors each with two groups. In this case, factor 1 includes experimental and control and factor 2 is gender, which includes boys and girls. A 3 x 2 design would have two factors, but the one factor would have three conditions, for example if there were three treatment conditions. In theory there can be any number of factors and any number of cells in any factor. The *F*-test compares the group means for each factor, which is also referred to as a *main effect*. Look at the hypothetical means in the Design Example Y.

Design Example Y

Treatment Condition

		Experimental	Control	
Gender	Girls	19	16	M=17.5
	Boys	18	15	M=16.5
		M=18.5	M=15.5	

There are eight means in the design: the four individual cell means (e.g., 19 is the mean score for girls in the experimental group), 18.5 is the mean for all students in the experimental condition (boys and girls together), 15.5 is the mean for all students in the control condition, 17.5 is the mean for all girls in both treatment conditions, and 16.5 is the mean of all the boys' scores on the test. In this case the *F*-test would test the difference between the experimental group (M=18.5) and the control group (M=15.5). This would be one of the main effects. The *F*-test would also test the difference between the girls (M=19) and boys (M=16.5). Gender would be another main effect.

In addition, the *F*-test determines whether or not there are any statistically significant interactions. An *interaction* is a condition in which two or more factors combine to produce a special effect in individual cells in the design. In Design Example Z, the means in the margins are identical to the marginal means in the Design Example Y.

Design Example Z

Treatment Condition

		Experimental	Control	
Gender	Girls	21	14	M=17.5
	Boys	16	17	M=16.5
		M=18.5	M=15.5	

However, the individual cell means are quite different from those in Design Example Y. On the surface it appears that girls outperformed boys and that the experimental group outperformed the control group, but a closer inspection reveals that the real action is taking place in cell 1, with the girls in the experimental group. Notice how wrong it would be just to state that the experimental group outperformed the control group considering that the boys in the control group seemed to do a little better than the boys in the experimental group. It would also be odd to argue that the girls did better than the boys given that the boys in both treatment conditions outperformed the girls in the control group. A more enlightening interpretation would be that the experimental treatment had a profound influence on the girls but not the boys. This is an experimental interaction, in this case the interaction between treatment condition and gender.

The interaction in Design Example Z is demonstrated in Figure 1 below. When the lines cross, the interaction is said to be *disordinal*. The lines in Figure 2 do not cross and are referred to as an *ordinal* interaction. An ordinal interaction indicates that a treatment had more impact on one group than another. A disordinal interaction suggests that the treatment affected the groups in different – and possibly opposite – ways.

Figure 1

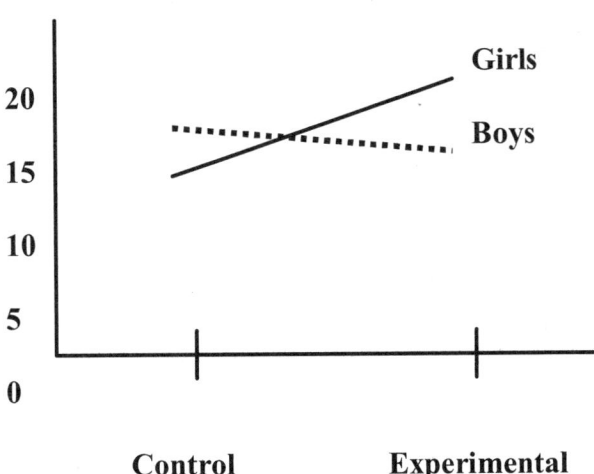

Figure 2

An *F*-test reported in the results section of a journal article looks almost the same as a *t*-Test and has a similar interpretation, for example, $F(3,115)=4.92$, $p<.05$. The only important distinction is that there are two different degrees of freedom represented in parentheses. The first number is the total number of cells in the design minus 1. The second number is the number of participants in the study minus the number of cells. Where all these numbers come from is less important than your ability to recognize a test of statistical significance when you see one and to understand its overall purpose.

Activity 2

If the Hampton Elementary experiment was replicated with the additional factor of gender, and if the results were the same as in Design Example Z, what might be a possible explanation for the interaction? (See Appendix A for a plausible solution.)

Statistically Significant Correlations

Statistical significance is also reported for correlations. The usual format is: $r = .77$, $p<.01$, where r is the symbol for correlation, .77 is the actual correlation, and p refers to the probability that there would be some correlation – not zero – if the same correlational procedure were done repeatedly using different samples of participants. A significance test for a correlation answers the same basic question as t and F-tests: What is the chance that a statistic of this magnitude could occur because of sampling error? In this case if a correlation of .77 has a p value of .01 it means that there is less than one chance in 100 that a correlation this big could occur by chance when there is really zero correlation between the two variables. A p value of .05 means one chance in 20; .001 means one chance in 1000; and .0001 means one chance in 10,000. When a significance test uses a greater than (>) instead of a less than (<) sign, it suggests that the observed effect (differences between group means or a correlation) may be an error. For example, $r = .29$, $p > .05$ means that there is at least one chance in 20 that the observed correlation of .29 could actually be .00.

In most cases, when researchers report that there were no statistically significant effects, it means that the p values for those tests were greater than .05. It is important to remember that the p value does not translate into effect size or importance. When a study includes large numbers of subjects, it is possible to have statistically significant but trivial results. For example, a correlation of .06 might be statistically significant, $p < .0001$, if there were thousands of subjects, but would this result have any practical significance?

Generalizability

Generalizability refers to the trustworthiness or relevance of a study as it pertains to people who were not part of the experiment. In the Hampton Experiment the only participants eligible to be in the experimental or treatment groups were the students at Hampton Elementary School.

The *t*-test was statistically significant, which means that if the experiment were replicated with children from the same population we should expect to find an effect in favor of the experimental group. But what is the population and how can we know that the Hampton first-graders are representative of other first grade students? If you are the principal or a primary grade teacher at a different school, what meaning does the Hampton experiment have for you? Should you adopt their reading strategy because of their experiment? Would you trust the results to be meaningful for your school and your students? Should the results from Hampton generalize to your situation?

One way to gauge the relevance of the study is to imagine that the Hampton children and school are indeed representative of some larger population, of which you and your school may or may not be a part. The way to find out is to read with care the description of the subjects/participants in the study. If you can determine that the school environment and the participants are similar to your own circumstances, it is reasonable to at least consider the results of the study generalizable to your school. This is why it is extremely important for researchers to describe the sample and the conditions of the study.

Activity 3

What additional information about Hampton do you think is necessary in order to gauge the generalizability of the Hampton experiment? (See Appendix A for a possible solution.)

Power

In quantitative research, *power* refers to the capacity of a statistical test to detect an experimental effect. If the power of a *t*-Test or *F*-Test is too low, the researcher runs the risk of concluding that there is no effect when in reality there is. If power is too high, the researcher runs the risk of discovering a small and meaningless effect. There are a number of factors that contribute to power, but the two most important are the size of the population effect and the number of subjects in the study. Imagine that we replicate the Hampton Experiment a thousand times with different groups of first grade students all over the United States. If we collected the effect sizes from all of the studies, the mean would be the effect size for the population. If the effect size is large, it will be easier to detect in any given sample than if the effect is small. The number of subjects also influences the power of a statistical test. The more subjects in the study, the greater the power (Cohen, 1988; Rubin & Babbie, 2005).

How many subjects do I need?

This question surfaces in the design of almost every quantitative study. In some cases the question is crucial because of the time and expense that accrue with each additional subject. Earlier in the chapter, we defined effect sizes in terms of standard deviation units with .2 beings small, .4 being moderate, and .8 being large. We defined the sizes of correlations as follows: .39 or less is small, .40 to .69 is moderate, and .70 or greater is large. The rule of thumb in social science research is that you need 20 subjects per cell in order to have adequate power to find moderate effects. For example, Table 1 shows the size a correlation must be to reach statistical significance $p < .01$ with different sample sizes (Fisher and Yates, 1955).

Sample Size	Minimum Correlation
10	.71
20	.54
30	.35

Assume you have 20 subjects with two sets of scores. If you correlate the scores and the result is a correlation of less than .54, the result will be $p > .01$, which means not statistically significant at the .01 level. Our recommendation is that you use a minimum of 10 subjects per cell or in a correlation if you believe you have a large effect; 20 subjects for a moderate effect; and 50 to find a small effect. It never hurts to have additional subjects if you can afford the time and expense.

At this point you may be saying to yourself: "This is all fine and well but how do I know what the population effect size is so that I can determine how many subjects I need?" The answer is that this is a matter of professional judgment on your part. You must ask yourself two questions:

1. Based on my review of the literature and my own experiences, what effect size do I believe exists in the population of interest?

2. Based on my review of the literature and my own experiences, what is the smallest effect worth finding?

Red Flags in Research Results

You should be suspicious of research results that have one or more of the following characteristics:

The researchers report large numbers of participants but no experimental effect sizes. The power of significance tests is heavily influenced by the number of participants in a study. With hundreds of subjects it is possible to find statistically significant but trivial effects. Never accept statistical significance as a substitute for the size of a correlation or actual differences between group means. Remember, significant doesn't necessarily mean important, relevant, or big.

The researchers report statistically non-significant results but the number of participants in the study is small. If there are fewer than 15 or 20 participants per cell, there may not be enough power in the test to confirm differences even if they actually exist. Method A might be better than Method B, but if there are only 10 people in each treatment group the result of the analyses may be statistically non-significant. When non-significant results are reported, look at the means and standard deviations to see whether or not there is an apparent experimental effect and how large it is. Large differences between means that are statistically non-significant because of small numbers of participants should not be automatically dismissed. The study may need replication with more participants.

The study fails to provide means and standard deviations for groups. An ANOVA without accompanying means and standard deviations – and we've seen a few – is almost certainly the result of shoddy research. Without cell means it is almost impossible to judge the value and accuracy of the research. Means and standard deviations are basic.

The researchers misuse the word significant to mean important. Sometimes authors will do this intentionally to try to convince readers that their research has crucial implications for educational theory or practice; sometimes the mistake is the result of ignorance. Many journals now require authors to use the phrase "statistically significant difference" instead of "significant difference" to reduce the inherent ambiguity of the word significant.

The study reports large numbers of correlations. Some researchers go on what is referred to as a fishing expedition for correlations. This typically happens when a researcher has large data sets, for example from survey research where answers to every item on the survey can be correlated with every other item. Using a conventional p value of .05, you can expect some statistically significant correlations to occur just by chance. Beware of research that includes dozens – or even hundreds – of correlations, especially if they are accompanied by claims of causal relationships.

The researchers use ANOVA with one group of participants, but repeat the analysis over and over again substituting different dependent variables. The problem here is that this procedure can result in hundreds of comparisons of group means, some of which may be statistically significant just by chance. Under these circumstances the researchers' explanations of the results may be nothing more than after-the-fact rationalizations.

The methods section of the study gives skimpy descriptions of participants and experimental procedures. The generalizability of most research is dependent upon thick description of the participants, tests, and activities related to the study. Without this information you can't be at all sure that the results are relevant to your clients.

Activity 4

Go to Appendix B and read "Gender, Ethnicity, and College Students' Responses to the *Strong-Campbell Interest Inventory.*" (See Appendix A for possible solutions.)

Read the abstract on page 151.

Skim the introduction and methods sections on pages 151-152.

Read the analysis and results section on pages 152-153. List the red flags from this section of the study.

_____

_____

Read the discussion section on pages 154-155. In general, how have the red flags you discovered in the results section influenced your trust in the authors' conclusions? To what extent do you believe the results of the study are generalizable? What is the basis for your judgment?

_____

_____

Writing Your Research Report: Results

The *results section* in your research report or thesis will probably be the shortest section in your manuscript. In a simple study the results section may be no more than a paragraph because it is limited to the statistical outcomes of the experiment. The results section should include all pertinent descriptive statistics such as correlations, means, standard deviations, and z-scores. The descriptive statistics should be integrated into the text unless there are many of them, in which case they should be tabled. The results section should also include all tests of statistical significance. Inferences that can be drawn directly from the data should also be included. The following is a possible results section for the hypothetical Hampton Experiment:

The *t*-Test for differences between independent means was statistically significant $t(46) = 2.75$, $p < .01$. Comparison of the means revealed that the experimental group ($M = 18.42$, $SD = 2.96$) was higher than the mean for the control group ($M = 16.17$, $SD = 2.70$). The effect size in the sample was computed by subtracting the control group mean from the experimental mean and dividing by the combined standard deviation $(18.42 - 16.17) / 2.83 = .80$. The results indicate that the reading intervention caused an increase in reading achievement as measured by the *GMRT*.

Reaction Guide

1. Significant differences are important differences.   Agree _____ Disagree _____

2. ANOVA is an exploding star.   Agree _____ Disagree _____

3. It is just as bad to have too many as too few participants in a quantitative study.   Agree _____ Disagree _____

4. Statistical significance tests are overrated.   Agree _____ Disagree _____

5. When a correlation is statistically significant,
   it is unnecessary to report the correlation itself   Agree _____ Disagree _____

Why my choice is confirmed.   Why my choice is not confirmed.

1. _____   _____

2. _____   _____

3. _____   _____

4. _____   _____

5. _____   _____

Chapter 9 Self-Test

True or False

1. _____ A statistically significant effect is an important effect.

2. _____ There is no such thing as a negative effect size.

3. _____ It is possible for an ANOVA to have an interaction but no main effects.

4. _____ If an observed correlation of .90 has a statistical significance value of $p > .05$, the correlation in the population might really be zero.

5. _____ If the difference between two means is 7.4 and the standard deviation of the two groups is 9.2, then the effect size is .80.

Matching

6. _____ Two factors creating an effect when they are combined.

7. _____ A statistical significance test.

8. _____ Results of a study can be applied beyond the sample used in the experiment.

9. _____ A small effect size.

10. _____ Contains four cells.
A. interaction
B. 2 x 2 design
C. .27
D. $t(125) = 8.99, p < .01$
E. generalizability
F. r = 4

Companion Website

Additional resources and chapter activities are located at www.edinboro.edu/press.

10 Research Validity

Anticipation Guide

1. Randomization removes all threats to validity.   Agree _____ Disagree _____

2. Treatment fidelity is a process used in marriage counseling.   Agree _____ Disagree _____

3. If an experiment needs to be replicated, it was probably done wrong in the first place.   Agree _____ Disagree _____

4. A placebo is a phony treatment.   Agree _____ Disagree _____

5. Researchers should be blinded.   Agree _____ Disagree _____

Chapter Rationale

It is often the case that empirical studies published in professional journals cite impressive looking statistics and appear on the surface to establish cause and effect relationships when, in fact, the research designs are so flawed that conclusions of a causal nature are invalid. To be a smart consumer of research in counseling and education it is critical that you are able to make informed judgments regarding the validity of published research.

Objectives

When you have completed this chapter, you should be able to read research in your area of specialization and determine whether or not the authors have made valid and sound arguments for establishing cause and effect relationships. You should also be able to define and identify common threats to the validity of educational and psychological research.

Graphic Organizer

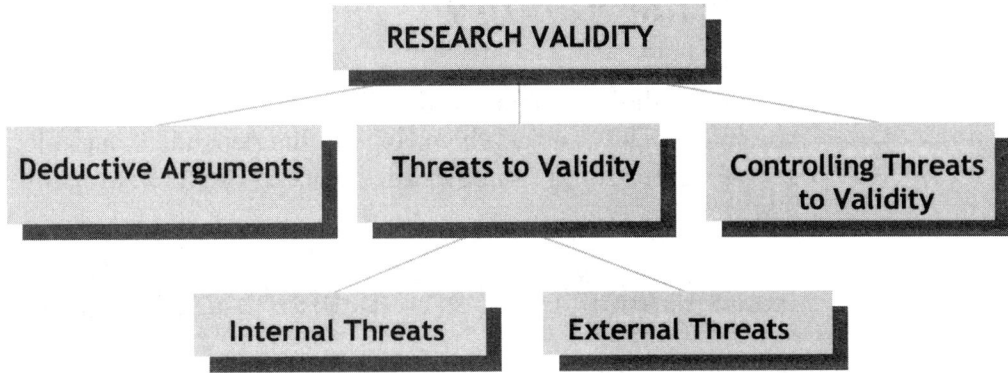

Establishing Cause & Effect

Common purposes for research include description (e.g., surveys that generate descriptive statistics) and prediction (e.g., correlations). However, the most usual purpose of research is to establish cause and effect relationships, typically by asking the question: Will a manipulation of the independent variable cause a change in the dependent variable? For example, if a method of teaching elementary mathematics is the independent variable, and students' scores on a state mandated mathematics test are the dependent variable, will manipulating the method of teaching mathematics cause a change in students' test scores? Or, stated in another way, is Method A more or less effective than Method B with respect to performance on the mathematics test?

The fact that an experiment is set up to compare Method A with Method B does not by any means guarantee that if one treatment group performs better than the other there is proof of causality, and the deductive format of an experiment does not guarantee its validity. To establish causality, all other possible causes of the effect must be ruled out. There are many reasons why researchers falsely assume causality when there are other competing – and in some cases better – explanations for experimental outcomes. We will refer to these competing explanations as *threats to validity*; and there are two types: internal and external.

Internal Validity

Internal validity refers to the likelihood that the independent variable actually caused the change in the dependent variable. The following are some examples of threats to the internal validity of research.

Nonequivalence of Participants / Sampling Effects

Nonequivalence of participants is the granddaddy of threats to internal validity, primarily because it is so widespread. Experimental research designs are based on the assumption that all variation is controlled with the exception of the independent variable. In order to prove that Method A is superior to Method B it is essential to structure the experiment in such a way that only the treatment (independent variable) can be the reason for experimental outcomes. If subjects are not randomly assigned to treatment conditions it is impossible to know whether the outcomes are the result of the treatment or some difference between the groups in Method A and Method B (e.g., intellectual ability or locus of control). In addition, without random assignment of subjects to groups, statistical significance tests are worthless. Randomly assigning participants to treatment conditions doesn't guarantee that the groups will be identical, especially with small groups; but it does ensure that any nonequivalence of participants in treatment groups is statistically predictable. Whenever participants are not randomly assigned to groups in an experimental or quasi-experimental design, it is a threat to validity; and statistical results cannot be trusted unless the researchers give a very thorough description of the groups and provide detailed evidence that the groups are equivalent in all the ways that would be important to the experiment.

Treatment Fidelity

Treatment Fidelity is a botched experiment in which, for example, assessments are administered incorrectly or treatments are not carried out as planned (e.g., one group is given too much time to complete a task). Depending upon the circumstances, treatment infidelity can amount to anything from a benign irritation to the researcher to a fatal flaw in the experiment.

Maturation

Maturation is a threat to experimental validity when physical or psychological changes in the participants are the real cause of a change in the dependent variable. For example, if a group of seven-year-olds are given agility tests at the beginning of second grade, participate in a program designed to improve agility, and are then retested at the end of the school year, it is impossible to know whether improvements are the result of the treatment or the result of natural maturation.

Regression Toward the Mean

Regression Toward the Mean is a measurement phenomenon in which subjects with extreme scores on a test or other evaluation tend to appear less extreme in a second testing with scores moving toward the mean. For example, suppose you weighed all female college students on a large campus and found that 30 weighed less than 80 pounds and 30 weighed more than 250 pounds. If you retested these 60 individuals a year later, it is almost a certainty that the mean weight of the light group will have increased while the mean weight of the heavy group will have decreased. People who fall into extreme measurement categories tend to be unstable in that characteristic and tend to become more average over time. In this case one might expect that some of these people were greatly under or overweight because they were sick and that many of them will have been on diets or in a state of recovery during the intervening year.

Attrition

Attrition refers to participants dropping out of a study. Sometimes this is a threat to the validity of a study because the number of participants becomes so small that it destroys the power of the experiment. However, a more subtle threat occurs when the participants who drop out all have something in common. For example, a college professor believes that a rigorous course in the philosophy of science will improve general intellectual performance. With the permission of the 29 students in his Logic 454 course, the professor administers a valid IQ test to the students. At the end of the course the professor administers the same instrument as a posttest to the remaining 16 students. The difference between the pretest and posttest means will favor the posttest if the students who dropped out of the course were less intelligent than those who remained. The reverse could also be true if the smart students decided to get out of Dodge. In either case, a cause and effect conclusion would be entirely unwarranted.

Activity 1

For each of the following scenarios, check the threats to validity that apply to each. Be prepared to justify your choices. (See Appendix A for our answers; yours might be different and also correct.)

Scenario 1

A researcher hypothesizes that cognitive activities designed to cure letter reversal problems in children with learning disabilities are more effective with young children than with older children. The researcher wishes to make a case for early intervention. The researcher identifies in the school district all children with reading problems that involve letter reversals. Twenty six-year-old children who fall into the target population are randomly assigned to Group A. Twenty eight-year-old children are similarly assigned to Group B. All participants are given a valid pre-test to identify letter reversal problems. The children all participate in a valid reading program that focuses on letter reversals. At the end of one semester the participants are post-tested and gain scores are computed as the dependent variable. Differences between the two groups are large and statistically significant showing huge improvements by the six-year-olds. The researcher concludes that early intervention is more effective with younger than with older children.

_____ Nonequivalence of Participants

_____ Attrition

_____ Maturation

_____ Regression Toward the Mean

_____ Treatment Fidelity

Scenario 2

A physical education teacher wants to experiment with a new method for teaching rope climbing. She asks for volunteers from her 10th grade class and puts them into the experimental group. The rest of the class is taught using the traditional method. The dependent variable will be the time it takes to climb the rope. The means of the two groups will be compared.

_____ Nonequivalence of Participants

_____ Attrition

_____ Maturation

_____ Regression Toward the Mean

_____ Treatment Fidelity

Scenario 3

In an experiment on counseling techniques for heterosexual parents of gay teenagers, 24 sets of heterosexual parents of gay teenagers are randomly assigned to Therapy Technique A or Therapy Technique B for a period of one year. Three counselors from a pool of six volunteers are randomly assigned each of the two methods. Neither of the therapy techniques is at all Freudian. Each counselor is randomly assigned to work with four couples. Unfortunately, one of the counselors in Therapy Technique A has never come to understand that sometimes a cigar is just a cigar and introduces a heavy dose of Freudian analysis into his counseling sessions. At the end of the counseling sessions a valid and reliable measure of gay acceptance on the part of the parents reveals small and statistically nonsignificant differences between the two groups. The researchers conclude that Therapy Techniques A and B are equally effective.

_____ Nonequivalence of Participants

_____ Attrition

_____ Maturation

_____ Regression Toward the Mean

_____ Treatment Fidelity

Scenario 4

A counselor in a challenging urban junior high school develops a program that she believes will improve the self-concepts of students who are struggling readers. Moreover, her conviction is that an increase in positive self-concepts will lead to improved reading ability. The counselor pretests all 300 ninth grade students in her junior high on a standardized reading achievement test and selects the 15 lowest scoring students (mean percentile rank of 3). The teacher implements her self-concept program during the month of October and then retests the 15 students in the experimental program. The results of the posttest show a dramatic rise on the reading test from 3rd percentile to 35th. The counselor concludes that the reading improvement is due to the self-concept program and makes her case to the principal for expanding the program to include the entire ninth grade.

_____ Nonequivalence of Participants

_____ Attrition

_____ Maturation

_____ Regression Toward the Mean

_____ Treatment Fidelity

External Validity

In the search for cause and effect, *external validity* refers to the likelihood that phenomena observed under experimental conditions are relevant in other contexts. Once internal validly has been established (i.e., the independent variable really did cause the experimental effect), one has to ask whether or not the same or similar effects would occur in other places. Is the experiment generalizable? If Method A worked better than Method B in an elementary school in urban Cleveland, would Method A be the best choice for an elementary school in rural Colorado? The following are some examples of threats to the external validity of research.

Generalizability

Generalizability refers to the relevance of a statistic or experimental outcome to environments external to the experiment. To the extent that the results of a study are believable, relevant, and true beyond the participants and specific context of the study, the results are said to be generalizable. From the purist's perspective, a statistical result is only generalizable to the population from which the sample of participants was randomly selected. In reality, random sampling from a target population (e.g., elderly men, gay couples, and gifted children) almost never occurs; researchers are usually forced to use convenience sampling. If you are inclined to be pragmatic, this sampling limitation doesn't necessarily mean that a study in non-generalizable. If there are 50 kindergarten children in an experiment, surely they are representative of some larger population – albeit unknown - of kindergarteners. For this reason it is critical for researchers to provide as much information as possible about participants/subjects so that the consumers of research can make informed judgments about the relevance of the research to their clients, their students, their environments. When researchers fail to provide detailed descriptions of participants and how they came to be involved in the research, it is a serious threat to the external validity of the study because the generalizability of the study is unknown.

A second aspect of generalizability is related to representativeness of the sample and the scope of the treatment conditions. For example, if a study is done with fourth graders, will the results generalize to fifth graders? First graders? Adults? If Methods A, B, and C are being compared, and Method B turns out to be the best of the three, can the researcher claim that Method B is *the* best Method? Suppose there are 99 Methods available?

Researchers frequently over generalize their results. The wise consumer of educational and psychological research will read carefully to ascertain the generalizability of the findings.

Placebo Effects

The word *placebo* originally referred to the Roman Catholic vespers for the dead and had the literal meaning of "I shall please." A medical placebo is like a sugar pill, a treatment that by itself should have no medical consequences but may offer some mental relief to a patient. It is possible for people to experience psychological and physical consequences from a placebo if they believe they are receiving real medication. This is called a *placebo effect*, and it is a serious threat to external validity. For this reason it is not uncommon for ads in magazines promoting new drugs to show the results of experiments that have attempted to control the placebo effect. Typically, results of desired improvements and side effects (such as drowsiness, nausea, and abdominal pain) are reported for two groups: the group taking the new drug and a placebo group. If the experiment is done properly, the subjects do not know what group they are in. It is not unusual for the placebo group to show medical improvement as well as various side effects even though they have received no real medical treatment. By keeping all of the subjects in the dark regarding their group affiliations, the placebo effect is assumed to be evenly distributed in both groups and is, therefore, controlled. If you simply had an experimental drug group and a control group with no placebo, improvements in the experimental group could be caused by the placebo effect. Something almost always works better than nothing.

There are also placebo effects in educational and psychological research. If people believe they are improving in math skills or self-confidence, for instance, because they are part of an experiment – they might just be trying harder – this is a placebo effect. The threat to validity is that when the recommended treatment or program is used outside of the experimental situation it is no longer an experiment. The placebo effect is removed, and clients may not experience the positive effects that characterized the experimental group in the original study.

Hawthorne Effect

The *Hawthorne Effect* is similar to the placebo effect and occurs when participants in a study perform at a higher level than normal because they are part of an experiment. The Hawthorne effect was first observed in conjunction with a study of worker productivity in the Western Electric Company. In one case the researchers wanted to know if increasing lighting would raise productivity. It did. However, the researchers also found that lowering the light increased worker productivity. Participation in the experiment rather than the manipulated lighting caused the changes in productivity. In general, participants in a study will work hard to please the experimenter because they have been identified for special treatment or because the experimental situation is a novelty. Subjects will tend to behave in ways that conform to what they believe are the experimenter's expectations. This is a threat to external validity because when the treatments – whether factory lighting or a new reading program – are tried outside of the experimental context, the magnitude of the treatments may be much lower than what was observed in the experiment.

Experimenter Effects

Experimenter Effects are changes in the dependent variable caused by the attitudes, biases, or other attributes of the person conducting the experiment. This is especially true if the experimenter is in direct contact with the participants and has a set of beliefs about the value of the treatment conditions. Suppose the experimenter is an English teacher who wishes to test the merits of Methods A and B for teaching high school seniors how to write poetry. Further suppose that the teacher will be the instructor for both groups and that she thinks Method A will be superior to B. Perhaps the teacher is unknowingly more enthusiastic with Group A than Group B. Or, it may be that Method A is better suited to this particular teacher's instructional style. In either case a statistical outcome favoring the experimental group could be caused by the experimenter and not by any relevant differences between the two methods of teaching poetry.

Pretest Sensitization

Pretest Sensitization refers to the possibility that performances on a posttest are influenced by whatever students have learned from taking the pretest. Posttest scores might go up because of what the participants learned from the pretest. This is a threat to external validity because in a nonexperimental situation there will be no pretest, which means that treatment outcomes might be different from what was discovered in the original experiment.

Activity 2

For each of the following scenarios, check the threats to external validity that apply to each. Be prepared to justify your choices. (See Appendix A for our answers; yours might be different and also correct.)

Scenario 1

Freedom High School is in a challenging urban environment and has an extremely high dropout rate. Only 11% of the school's graduates go to college. One of the school counselors wants to try a new career counseling program in an effort to encourage Freedom's graduates to continue their education after high school. The counselor manages to get 40 eleventh grade students to volunteer to participate in her study. The students are randomly assigned to the experimental group and a control group. The experimental group goes though the 9-week career counseling program. The control group does not receive career counseling during the study. The dependent variable is a measure of student enthusiasm for attending college. At the conclusion of the study the counselor finds that there is a full standard deviation difference between the groups on the *Attitude Toward College Assessment*, favoring the experimental group. The counselor reports the result as a major success for the new program.

_____ Poor Generalizability

_____ Placebo Effects

_____ Experimenter Effects

_____ Pretest Sensitization

_____ Hawthorne Effects

Scenario 2

A researcher who is interested in teaching keyboarding skills to children in the primary grades arranges to conduct his experiment in a private, nonsectarian school. The school has two classes of second grade children whom the researcher randomly assigns to two keyboarding methods (X and Z), both of which are unfamiliar to the children and the teachers. This is a posttest only design. The researcher provides all of the instruction and is unbiased in his opinions regarding the respective values of the two instructional techniques. After a semester of instruction, Method X proves superior to Z, and the researcher publishes an article recommending X for teaching keyboarding skills in the primary grades.

_____ Poor Generalizability

_____ Placebo Effects

_____ Experimenter Effects

_____ Pretest Sensitization

_____ Hawthorne Effects

Scenario 3

Ms. Chumwinkle tests all of her first grade students' knowledge of phonics and then provides them with intensive phonics instruction for four weeks. The students do not know they are part of an experiment. At the end of the program Ms. Chumwinkle gives the children the same phonics test and calculates the students' gain scores. The scores are very impressive.

_____ Poor Generalizability

_____ Placebo Effects

_____ Experimenter Effects

_____ Pretest Sensitization

_____ Hawthorne Effects

Scenario 4

Mr. Butler is the advisor for the high school chess club and is convinced that students will develop better chess strategies by playing against a computer than by playing against people. There are sixty students in the chess club, and Mr. Butler randomly assigns them to one of four groups: computer group (W), conventional group (X), placebo group (Y), and a control group (Z). Group W plays against the computer; Group X plays against each other; Group Y does special exercises that students are told will make them smarter; Group Z has no treatment. The dependent variable is the number of moves students are able to make before being defeated by Mr. Butler. After all the students have played against Mr. Butler, the mean score of Group W is much higher than any of the means of the other three groups.

_____ Poor Generalizability

_____ Placebo Effects

_____ Experimenter Effects

_____ Pretest Sensitization

_____ Hawthorne Effects

Scenario 5

Yukon Middle School participated along with seven other middle schools in a district wide assessment of a new science curriculum. Four schools were randomly assigned to the new (experimental) curriculum and four were assigned to use the existing (traditional) science curriculum, which had been in use in all eight middle schools for about 10 years. A variety of test scores and demographic data showed that the experimental and traditional schools were quite similar in terms of resources, achievement, and culture. The schools used the assigned curriculum for the entire school year. In May the students in all eight schools took a standardized science achievement test. The results showed a large effect in favor of the experimental science curriculum. The next year the schools in the traditional group switched to the new science curriculum. However, the administration was very disappointed to discover at the end of the year that the science performances of the students had increased no more than the schools using the old curriculum.

_____ Poor Generalizability

_____ Placebo Effects

_____ Experimenter Effects

_____ Pretest Sensitization

_____ Hawthorne Effects

Controlling Threats to Validity

In order to more clearly explain fundamental principles, we have referred repeatedly to Methods A and B, the most basic of experimental designs. Good research designs, however, are almost never as simple as this because added complexity is often necessary in order to control for threats to validity. For example, in Chapter 8 you were introduced to the basic pre-post control group design:

Treatment group: random assignment, pretest, treatment, posttest

Control group: random assignment, pretest, no treatment, posttest

While the research design is straightforward, its bare bones structure makes it vulnerable to several threats to validity.

Activity 3

Check the threats to validity that are built into the basic pre-post control group design.

_____ Nonequivalence of Participants

_____ Attrition

_____ Maturation

_____ Regression Toward the Mean

_____ Treatment Fidelity

_____ Poor Generalizability

_____ Placebo Effects

_____ Experimenter Effects

_____ Pretest Sensitization

_____ Hawthorne Effects

Discussion of Activity 3

Nonequivalence of participants is probably not a threat because participants in this design are randomly assigned to groups. Attrition, maturation, regression toward the mean, treatment fidelity, poor generalizability, and experimenter effects might be threats depending upon the nature of the study, how well the experiment was managed, and how the participant sample was obtained. However, in this design, placebo effects, pretest sensitization, and Hawthorne effects are serious threats. If the experimental group members believe the treatment will affect them, it might, in which case any experimental effect could just be a placebo effect and not the result of the treatment at all. The treatment group could also be influenced to unusual performance because of the novelty of the tasks involved or because of being part of a group that is receiving special attention. In this case, the Hawthorne effect might be causing observed differences between the two groups' posttest scores. Finally, in this design it is always possible that the pretest sensitized the participants to the treatment causing an effect that would not have occurred if there had been no pretest.

Control Groups

In the Activity 3 design, the subjects in the sample are randomly assigned to one of two groups; then the groups are randomly assigned to either the experimental or the control condition. The *experimental group* receives the treatment and the *control group* does not. This is a true experimental design, but it can be improved by adding additional control groups. For example, sometimes subjects in an experimental group perform better just because they are in an experiment and not because of the treatment; this is known as the *Hawthorne Effect*. One way to control for the Hawthorne effect is to create a second control group that receives a *placebo*, a treatment that is unrelated to the purpose of the experiment. Then, if the experimental group outperforms both control groups, the Hawthorne Effect is probably not the cause of any differences in group performances. To control for pretest sensitization, a third control group could be added. The third group is identical to the original control group except that the subjects do not take the pretest. If the mean of control group 3 is not statistically different from control group 1, one could argue that pretest sensitization was not a factor in the performance of the experimental group. The appropriate statistical analysis for this design would be a completely randomized, one-factor ANOVA with four cells:

Cell 1	Cell 2	Cell 3	Cell 4
Experimental Group	Control 1	Control 2	Control 3
Pretest	Pretest	Pretest	
Treatment		Placebo	

In the event of a statistically significant main effect, *post hoc t-Tests* would be used to compare the individual cells with each other.

Replication

Another way to control for threats to validity is through *replication*, redoing the experiment. There are two kinds of replications: exact replication and systematic replication. An *exact replication* duplicates every facet of an experiment. A *systematic replication* is essentially the same experiment but with modifications that rule out certain threats to validity or make the experiments as a group more generalizable. For example, if the first experiment was a basic pre-post control group design, a good systematic replication would involve eliminating the pretest. This would reduce the threat of pretest sensitization. Or, if an experiment derived its participant sample from a private elementary school, the systematic replication might take its sample from a public elementary school. Replications add to the credibility of research because they assist in ruling out chance effects as well as threats to internal and external validity.

Blinding

Threats to external validity (e.g., placebo effects, experimenter effects, and Hawthorne effects) commonly result when researchers' and participants' knowledge of the experiment create outcomes that are mistaken for treatment effects. *Blinding* is any procedure that controls threats to external validity by restricting information to researchers and participants. For example, if participants do not know they are part of an experiment, it will inhibit Hawthorne effects. If participants do not know whether they are in an experimental or placebo group, the researcher can control for placebo effects. If the researcher must evaluate the performances of participants and is blind to which group individuals belong to, it will inhibit experimenter effects. A *double-blind procedure* refers to conditions under which both participants and researchers are blind with respect to assignment of individuals to treatment conditions.

Activity 4

Read "Deconstructing dispositional bias in clinical inference: Two interventions" (Appendix B), concentrating on the methods section. There will be some unfamiliar statistical terminology, and the article may prove challenging for students who are outside the field of counseling. However, you should still be able to use the information from this chapter to answer the following questions.

1. Did the researchers attempt to control for threats to validity? Which threats were addressed?

_____ _____

2. Have the researchers covered all bases, or are there some threats that still remain?

_____

3. Do you believe the results of the study are generalizable? If so, to whom?

_____ _____

4. On a scale from 1 to 10 with 1 being terrible and 10 being excellent, how high would you rate this study for dealing with threats to validity?

_____

Writing Your Research Report: Discussion

The *discussion section* immediately follows the presentation of results. The first order of business is to relate the results to your research questions or statements and draw conclusions. However, the conclusions should only be those you can derive directly from the data after you have taken into consideration all the weaknesses of your study and potential threats to validity. Do your statistical results or qualitative data answer the research question? Do they confirm or disconfirm your research statement? Is method A superior to method B? Can X be predicted from Y? You should also relate your results to the literature review. Are your results consistent with previous research? Do they support one point of view versus another? The discussion section should also include implications for theory and practice. What recommendations would you make to practitioners based on your research? Finally, you are entitled to speculate as long as you clearly distinguish your speculations from data driven results and conclusions.

Rarely is a research report without weaknesses, and it is common practice to include a subsection call *limitations* in which the researcher discusses design flaws or treatment fidelity. For example, the researcher may have been forced to use intact groups, in which case the absence of random assignment is a limitation that should be discussed. It is also frequently the case that a study generates more questions than it answers. Therefore, it is also common to include a subsection called *future research* in which the researcher identifies questions or hypotheses that have emerged from the study.

Reaction Guide

1. Randomization removes all threats to validity.   Agree _____ Disagree _____

2. Treatment fidelity is a process used in marriage counseling.   Agree _____ Disagree _____

3. If an experiment needs to be replicated, it was probably done wrong in the first place.   Agree _____ Disagree _____

4. A placebo is a phony treatment.   Agree _____ Disagree _____

5. Researchers should be blinded.   Agree _____ Disagree _____

Why my choice is confirmed.   Why my choice is not confirmed.

1. _____   _____

2. _____   _____

3. _____   _____

4. _____   _____

5. _____   _____

Chapter 10 Self-Test

True or False

1. _____ Quantitative research is deductive.

2. _____ It is relatively easy to establish cause and effect relationships.

3. _____ The placebo effect and the Hawthorne effect are quite similar.

4. _____ Regression toward the mean is a threat to internal validity.

5. _____ Pretest sensitization is built into the pre-post control group design.

Matching

6. _____ A phony treatment.

7. _____ A threat to validity when the experimenter bungles the intervention.

8. _____ Controls for pretest sensitization.

9. _____ When an experiment has no applicability in the real world.

10. _____ The most serious threat to internal validity.

A. experimenter effects
B. poor generalizability
C. treatment fidelity
D. nonequivalence of participants
E. posttest only design
F. placebo

Companion Website

Additional resources and chapter activities are located at www.edinboro.edu/press.

11 Qualitative Research I: Characteristics, Use & Design

Anticipation Guide

1. Qualitative research is conducted in a laboratory. Agree _____ Disagree _____

2. The researcher serves as the data instrument in qualitative research designs. Agree _____ Disagree _____

3. Science can not be examined through qualitative approaches. Agree _____ Disagree _____

4. Interpretation is important to qualitative analysis. Agree _____ Disagree _____

5. Case study research is generalizable to the greater population. Agree _____ Disagree _____

Chapter Rationale

"As an undergraduate student preparing to be a kindergarten teacher, I was required to do 15 hours of field observation in an elementary classroom and write detailed reflections of what I saw. So, I made arrangements to spend 3 hours a week for 5 weeks in a local kindergarten class. I was so excited for these visits. I couldn't wait to hear the sing-song voices of smiling 5-year olds reciting their ABCs and looking lovingly at the wonders of books and numbers.

The first day I visited, Taylor vomited on his desk and in his lap. This made Kelly cry and sent Jamie into screaming, "Take me home. This place stinks!" Jacob ran to Taylor, peered closely at his desk and announced, "Whoa, Taylor had bacon for breakfast." The rest of the children grabbed their noses with shouts of "UCK, and P.U." With all of this swirling around her, the teacher calmly asked the children to move to the rug area; put Taylor on her lap and began wiping his face with tissues; and sent me to the office for the nurse.

On another day of observation, the Fire Drill alarm was sounded during the math lesson, for which we were using candy worms. As the children lined up to leave the room, Kristy ran desk to desk saving the "poor worms" from the fire. This sent the children into possessive screams of "Hey, those are mine," and "She's stealing my candy." The teacher calmly supervised line formation while directing Kristy to bring the worms to her. Kristy raced forward with the candy worms spilling out of her cupped hands, and the teacher opened her sweater pocket so she could deposit them. The teacher winked at Kristy and led all 25 children and their worms safely out of the building.

At the end of my 5 weeks of observations, I decided that teaching at a middle school was in my future; kindergarten was not. The experience of participating in the kindergarten classroom for a lengthy period of time revealed to me the inner workings of 5-year old children and the demanding task of teaching them (Dawn)."

Numbers can not tell every story. Not all human experiences can be measured, some need to be described. *Qualitative methodology* provides description beyond the numbers because it allows for ambiguity, thriving on data that reflects the complexity and change of a given cultural phenomenon. Telling someone born after 1969 that 500,000 people were at the Woodstock Festival does not begin to convey the complexity of the event or the diversity of the attendants, let alone the historical significance of "Three Days of Peace and Music."

Qualitative methodology allows us to keep it real. Because the natural environment is impacted very little, if at all, during a qualitative study, data gathered provide a subjective reality that is critical to understanding any human phenomenon. Human life is dynamic, evolving with each new experience. There is no manipulation and no control over what will occur in a qualitative study, reflective of life and Forrest Gump's box of chocolates…you never know what you're gonna get. Through a cultural immersion approach, the qualitative researcher experiences life within a group or event, allowing examination from the participants' points of view and remaining open to whatever may occur within the culture. In the kindergarten observation reflections, I had carefully described the events of each day. Through those descriptions I realized that, though some days were calm, many were wrought with interruptions and confusion. I also recognized that the constant needs of young children had to be met by a caring and calm teacher…who didn't mind vomit or sticky candy on her clothing.

In this chapter we will explore the use of cultural immersion through qualitative methodologies, as a means of effective research.

Objectives

When you have completed this chapter, you will know the characteristics, theoretical underpinnings, and advantages of qualitative research. You will be able to describe various qualitative research designs and explain how they all reflect inductive thinking.

Graphic Organizer

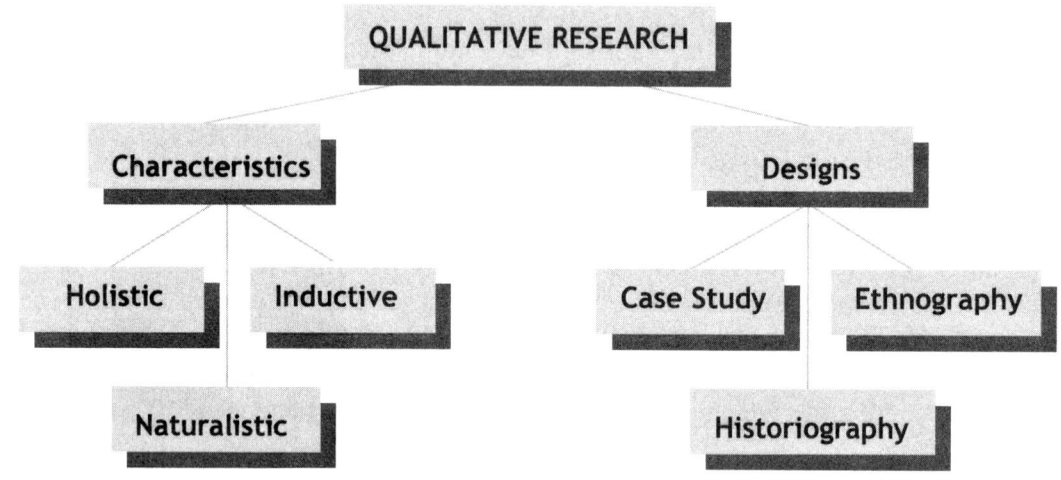

Characteristics of Qualitative Research

"Qualitative research methods were developed in the social sciences to enable researchers to study social and cultural phenomena. Qualitative research methods have been designed to help researchers understand people and the social and cultural contexts within which they live." (Myers, 1997, p. 241)

Qualitative researchers gather detailed information through the observation of real people, places, and events. The three guiding principles of the qualitative method can be identified as describing, understanding, and explaining human experience.

The primary way that qualitative researchers reach conclusions is through inductive reasoning. *Inductive reasoning* leads to a conclusion by observation of specific instances of events. For example, in (1) the conclusion that all the apples in the barrel are rotten is based on three observed instances of rotten apples. However, the truth or falsity of the conclusion cannot be determined absolutely from the observations. It is possible that all of the apples are rotten, but it isn't necessarily true.

> (1) The first apple in the barrel was rotten.
> The second apple in the barrel was rotten.
> The third apple in the barrel was rotten.
> Therefore, all the apples in the barrel are rotten.

Another variation of this type of argument involves predicting an event based on past observations. In the example above, the conclusion might be: Therefore, the fourth apple in the barrel will be rotten. All inductive arguments entail some doubt. You cannot know for sure that the entire barrel of apples is rotten unless you have examined every one of them.

In the evaluation of an inductive argument, it is necessary to decide how much information is required to make a generalization or a prediction. For instance, if you had a barrel of apples and picked out three rotten ones in a row, would you be willing to conclude that the whole barrel was rotten? What about seven apples? Fifteen apples? A hundred apples? Obviously, the more decomposing apples that surface without the appearance of any good apples, the better the evidence for a completely rotten barrel of apples. Inductive arguments are classified as either weak or strong. A *strong argument* has lots of supporting evidence (e.g., 100 rotten apples). A *weak argument* has little supporting evidence (e.g., 3 rotten apples). Qualitative research is primarily inductive in its methods, and the researchers' conclusions can be classified as weak or strong. A qualitative study that has large numbers of systematic observations from multiple sources is likely to be a strong study with believable conclusions.

Activity 1

The following stories have arguments embedded in them. Evaluate each one as deductive or inductive, weak or strong, valid or invalid, sound, or unsound. More than one answer may be required. (See Chapter 4 to review deductive reasoning.)

Scenario 1

Tim is a new marriage counselor who has worked with two couples so far. In a discussion with a veteran of clinical practice, Tim makes the following comment: "I enjoyed working with these couples, marriage counseling is easy."

____ deductive   ____ inductive   ____ weak   ____ strong

____ valid   ____ invalid   ____ sound   ____ unsound

Scenario 2

All students in 10th grade will enjoy reading the *Merchant of Venice* by William Shakespeare. Carlota is a student in 10th grade. So, we should expect her to enjoy the play.

____ deductive   ____ inductive   ____ weak   ____ strong

____ valid   ____ invalid   ____ sound   ____ unsound

Scenario 3

The principal, Ms. Munson, wants to test The Adventure Reading Program for students in second and third grade. There are two classes at each grade level and the school uses a homogeneous grouping procedure in assigning students to classes. The lower achieving classes in second and third grade continue with the old curriculum for the year, and the higher achieving classes get the new phonics program. The curricula are properly implemented and the students are appropriately tested for reading achievement at the end of the year. The students in the new program gain an average of 1.7 grade levels while the students in the old program gain only .6 grade levels. Ms. Munson concludes that phonics programs are superior to other reading programs.

____ deductive   ____ inductive   ____ weak   ____ strong

____ valid   ____ invalid   ____ sound   ____ unsound

Scenario 4

Ms. Harper is the counselor at Harry S. Truman Middle School, which is 10% Latino, 20 % African-American, and 70% White. Students who have significant, negative interactions with teachers are typically referred to Ms. Harper for counseling. For more than a year Ms. Harper has been keeping a systematic and detailed record of these incidents. One of the English teachers, Ms. Langley, has had eight incidents within the last year, all with African-American males. Jimmy Smith is a Black student who will be starting seventh grade at Truman next week. Jimmy has a history of disruptive school behaviors. Ms. Harper is recommending that Jimmy not be placed in any of Ms. Langley's classes because she believes there is a good chance that Jimmy and Ms. Langley will have issues that might otherwise be avoided.

____ deductive ____ inductive ____ weak ____ strong

____ valid ____ invalid ____ sound ____ unsound

Discussion of Activity 1

See Appendix A.

Naturalistic Research

Sometimes referred to as *naturalistic research*, the qualitative process is such that there is serious effort to allow the reality of the events to unfold under observation. The researcher tries to enter the natural, group environment, or culture, with no pre-dispositions, with a mind open to whatever may occur. In this way, the researcher is able to see what people actually do, how they behave in their real world.

The design of a qualitative study emerges as the study proceeds, responding to the natural occurrences without artificial interruption or alteration. The term *discovery* is often used by qualitative researchers who choose a topic of study, then investigate that topic in its natural environment. The use of discovery results in a holistic, or complete, picture of a situational reality. By spending long periods of time within the kindergarten classroom, I was able to see all of what takes place. Reading the teacher's planning book would have shown the planned order of events; Calendar Time, Story, Handwriting, Math. But it would not have allowed me to see children's reactions to surprise interruptions or the teacher's responses to illness and innocent thievery.

The qualitative researcher must examine many pieces of information and then put the pieces together to make a whole. Therefore, the researcher is actually the data gathering instrument. The data gathered takes the form of words and pictures formulated in the researcher's mind. The individual interpretations made are important to the ultimate goal of the research, a complete and detailed description. These descriptions provide, in turn, the opportunity for people unfamiliar with the observed culture to gain understanding of it. Though Dawn had once been a kindergarten child, she needed to view that culture as an adult to truly understand it. Her interpretation as an adult was formulated from the data she gathered via field note observations, interviews, and physical artifacts. Once Dawn was able to review that wealth of data, she could more clearly see what was needed to be a successful kindergarten teacher and that there were more appropriate alternatives for her.

Activity 2

Select an event which occurs commonly in your day. The event could be your daughter's soccer practice or your bus commute to work or your lunch hour in the break room. Sit back and observe that event, without participating in it, for 15-20 minutes. Take detailed notes on what you see, hear, and smell. Write quickly and constantly; try not to miss anything. After your observation, read your notes carefully.

Which of your senses did you use the most in this observation? _____

Identify three things you discovered that you were not aware of prior to this observation?

_____

What were some of the surprises?_____

Why do you think you saw them for the first time during this activity?_____

Did seeing this event through careful observation, change any ideas or opinions you had about the culture in operation? What was changed and how?

_____

As we become comfortable in our own culture, we often move through our daily events paying little attention to what is happening around us. Focusing on the details of those events can reveal interesting language and behaviors that change our understanding and interpretation of our own cultural reality.

Qualitative Research Designs

The field of qualitative research is growing quickly. As a process, qualitative research has come to represent an expanding collection of research strategies used in the social sciences. It is beyond the scope of this text to educate you completely about all of them, but there are commonalities among qualitative approaches that should be considered.

*Human experience is the focus. All qualitative research is intended to gain understanding of the lives of the people under study.

*The research occurs in uncontrolled, natural environments. All qualitative research is conducted in the places where people live their lives. There are no laboratory settings and no controlled treatments, but rather non-intrusive observations of the natural unfolding of natural human events.

*Results are holistic. A complete picture of a human event is the desired outcome of all qualitative research studies. Specific variables are not separated from the whole of the event because an overarching view of the phenomenon under study is anticipated.

*Data is rich in detail, relying on language descriptors instead of numbers. Language provides the information that allows qualitative researchers to learn about human behavior and to communicate what has been learned. The complexity of human life is conveyed through descriptive terms and narrative text.

*Data is gathered over a lengthy time period spent with the subjects. Qualitative researchers join the culture which they are studying by spending time with the members and getting involved with them. Researchers become a part of the culture by their frequent and deep immersion.

Beyond the general shared characteristics of various qualitative research strategies, there are three distinct approaches that are commonly used in many professional areas of human study. These approaches have unique purposes and guidelines for implementation that allow for address of specific social research needs.

Case Study

Case Study provides opportunity for a researcher to examine a phenomenon in great depth by limiting focus to a single case example of that phenomenon. The subject of a case study could be a single life event, one specific environment, or an individual person. The goal of the case study method is to provide a detailed and complete description of one case that accurately reflects the natural occurrence of the case phenomenon. Case studies generally do not attempt to address entire cultures, nor do they strive to generalize their results to a broader population than the one studied directly. Having said that, the most famous case studies are often those that do result in new, important theories with broad applications. For example, the Swiss psychologist Jean Piaget conducted case studies of his own children, watching their actions and reactions over the course of their childhoods. Piaget used his observations to construct a theory of cognitive development that revolutionized thinking in child development.

Usually conducted over a longer period of time, the case study involves an in-depth study that results in a vast amount of collected information. The case study often collects data from field documents, archival records, personal interviews, direct observations, and physical artifacts. Further, these data are considered through complementary description of the contexts in which they took place. The case study researcher works to achieve a holistic understanding of a particular social situation, so the final data is reported in narrative format, telling the story of the phenomenon examined.

Ethnography

Ethnography was developed by anthropologists, who often referred to it as field research, as a way to describe human culture. Each group of people, each culture, has its own rules, procedures, traditions, and language that set it apart from all other groups. Ethnography provides for detailed examination of the way a particular group of people lives, so the characteristics that are unique to the group can be uncovered.

By spending a great deal of time in a group and systematically gathering information through note taking of observations, transcripts of conversations, and physical artifacts, ethnographers attempt to interpret the community of the people, coming to an understanding of their way of life (Lancy, 1993). Further, this data is gathered in a non-invasive manner. The researcher becomes a part of the culture without impacting the operation of the culture. Immersion in this way, allows the research to periodically disengage from the phenomenon and fade from the view of the participants. Becoming invisible, in a sense, allows the researcher to build a factual description of the natural behaviors that occur within the social interactions of the culture.

George Spindler was an American anthropologist who pioneered the use of ethnographic methodology in education. Exploring the transmission of culture, Spindler identified the diverse and common ways in which children across a wide range of cultural systems are educated. The data described basic educational approaches that were consistently used throughout the cultural systems (Spindler, 1997).

Historiography

Historiography involves a systematic collection and evaluation of information about past events. This research relies on the use of *archival data*, written documentation most often found in museums, libraries or private collections.

Because of their reliance on the collected evidence of others, historical researchers must check their information carefully, comparing data across multiple sources for accuracy and authenticity. This multi-faceted collection creates the need for researcher interpretation of data to develop reasonable explanations of past events. Though historiography must be focused through careful reasoning and supported by a broad spectrum of evidence, subjective and creative analyses of data are necessary to interpret the multiple sources and diverse perspectives which are used.

David Wolff (1999) examined 80 year-old archived documents from the former Soviet Union to provide an authentic accounting of the Cold War. Much of this evidence was under lock and key, requiring permission from high level politicians and cooperation from both countries. After years of reading and comparing, reviewing and contrasting, Wolff was able to explain the events surrounding the development of this period in world history.

The Dynamic Nature of Qualitative Research

Human experiences are diverse and dynamic. People, environments, and resulting culture are in constant states of adaptation and accommodation. To truly understand a human phenomenon, one must look for the subtle clues that reveal themselves under scrutiny. Numbers can not explain the complexity of a kindergarten classroom or the culture of an adolescent peer group. Test scores can reveal performance on a specific characteristic, but if you want to understand a human event, you must watch and listen. And if you want to share your understanding with others, you must use words. Qualitative methods provide the means by which this type of discovery can occur.

Activity 3

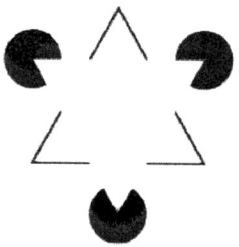

This is a Kanizsa Triangle.

Describe it using only numbers. _____

Describe the Kanizsa triangle again, using only words.
_____

The Kanizsa triangle is an optical illusion.

Why must it be explained with words instead of numbers?
_____

Why are the numbers of minimal importance in an explanation of this optical illusion?
_____

Discussion of Activity 3

Though you may have initially thought that the number 3 was going to play a critical role in describing the Kanizsa Triangle, you now realize that there is much more involved in this design than the creation of triangles. Shapes, shape placement and color are important elements to your explanation. Without the use of language rich with nouns and adjectives, I can only wonder what you may produce when trying to replicate this optical illusion.

Reaction Guide

1. Qualitative research is conducted in a laboratory.   Agree _____   Disagree _____

2. The researcher serves as the data instrument in qualitative research designs.   Agree _____   Disagree _____

3. Science can not be examined through qualitative approaches.   Agree _____   Disagree _____

4. Interpretation is important to qualitative analysis.   Agree _____   Disagree _____

5. Qualitative research is generalizable to the greater population.   Agree _____   Disagree _____

Why my choice is confirmed.   Why my choice is not confirmed.

1. _____   _____
2. _____   _____
3. _____   _____
4. _____   _____
5. _____   _____

Chapter 11 Self-Test

True or False

1. _____ Qualitative research strives to explain human behavior.

2. _____ Ethnography is designed to objectively examine ethnic groups.

3. _____ Historical research requires creative interpretation of data.

4. _____ There are three qualitative research designs.

5. _____ Language is the data form for qualitative research results.

Matching

6. _____ naturalistic

7. _____ holistic

8. _____ interpretive data

9. _____ ethnography

10. _____ deductive

A. viewing the entire picture
B. inductive and subjective
C. real world environment
D. objective research
E. cultural immersion

Companion Website

Additional resources and chapter activities are located www.edinboro.edu/press.

12 Qualitative Research II: Data & Analysis

Anticipation Guide

1. Interviews should be very structured and formal.　　　Agree _____　Disagree _____

2. Field notes are only for observing outdoor events.　　　Agree _____　Disagree _____

3. Triangulation allows you to present data in a triangular shape.　　　Agree _____　Disagree _____

4. Research participants can help you draw conclusions from your research data.　　　Agree _____　Disagree _____

5. Researcher bias is unavoidable when drawing conclusions from qualitative data.　　　Agree _____　Disagree _____

Chapter Rationale

When you think of research, you may recall an early school-room science experiment involving a worm, push pins, and a scalpel. Your teacher probably gave you a sheet of graph paper, a pen, and a list of questions about the number of segments on the worm's body; the length of the worm; or even the number of hearts (10, by the way). So you poked and prodded the worm, counted and measured the appropriate body parts, and wrote numbers within the squares of the graph paper; and when the numbers were entered, you had completed your research.

What your teacher may not have known however, was that later that day, you and your friends talked about how sticky the worm felt, how the smell reminded you of garbage, and why it shouldn't be acceptable to kill worms in the interest of 7th grade science.

To fully know what her young researchers learned from dissecting the earthworm, the science teacher would have been well-served to listen in on this conversation. The qualitative data revealed during the discussion of the feel and the scent of the worm, as well as the ethics of animal dissection, provide important insights into the learning that had occurred beyond the numerical data requested.

Because not all valuable information can be reflected in numbers, it is important to consider other data sources. Qualitative research methods rely on those other sources, so understanding their application can allow you to go beyond the numbers and tell the rest of the story.

Objectives

When you have completed this chapter, you will know the characteristics of qualitative research data. You will understand various qualitative data types and how best to employ them. And you will be able to design a disciplined approach to data analysis, examining the need for formulating decisions supported by evidence.

Graphic Organizer

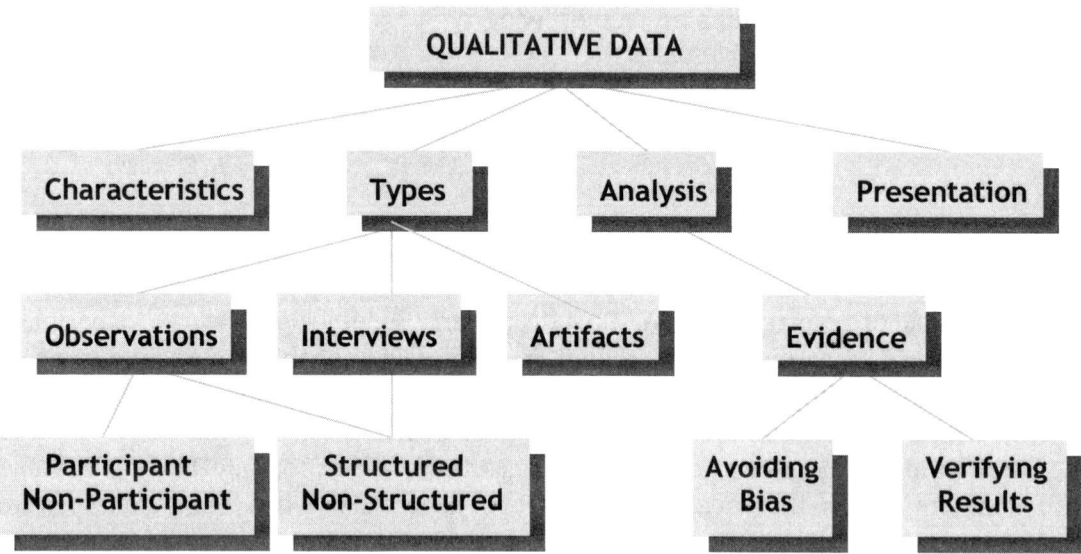

Characteristics of Qualitative Data

Qualtitative research provides "richly detailed accounts of human experience" (McGrath & Kulka, 1991). For example, when the students were discussing their worm dissection experience, they recounted the feel and the smell of the worm as well as their beliefs about the social and political ramification of the dissection itself.

Data can be defined as the preliminary information researchers collect from the event they are studying. Data are the evidence of what has been seen and heard, providing clues to the meaning behind the actions and words. The purpose of qualitative data is to reveal the participants' understanding of the culture or event. There is no search for finite answers or undeniable truth.

Qualitative research has to be proven by the data collected, so the data must be authentic and true to the event under study during the time in which it is being studied. Because it is collected over long periods of time, qualitative data can get lost or damaged quite easily, so careful planning of data collection and sticking to the plan are crucial.

It is important to note that qualitative data is interpretive, at least partly due to the fact that the qualitative researcher is the data instrument. The qualitative researcher tends to become subjectively immersed in the subject of study, allowing for rich and detailed data that reflects the researcher's interpretation. This human instrument is unique to qualitative data, but common to all quailtative data types, as you will soon see.

Methods of Data Collection

There are many variations among qualitative data collection techniques, but all take some form of words, pictures, or objects as artifacts. Whether using observations, interviews or artifact collections, you, as a qualitative researcher, will become intimately involved in the data you are gathering.

Observations

Observations involve watching and listening to events as they naturally unfold, then recording what was seen and heard. Using vision and hearing, the researcher focuses attention on the phenomenon under study, gaining "first hand information in a naturally occurring situation" (Burns and Grove, 1999 p. 358). Awareness of all that occurs, allows the researcher, serving as the observer, to fully absorb the complexity of human behavior. Good observations are labor intensive, requiring hours of concentration and focus and containing as much detail as possible. Good observations also avoid interfering with the natural phenomenon, resulting in research that is valid, an authentic and accurate picture of the behavior.

Recorded observations are often referred to as field notes because they are created in the field while the events occur. It is easier to record what is seen than to accurately recall what is seen, so observers write detailed records, making note of the obvious, as well as the more subtle, events unfolding during the observation period. This entails vigilant attentiveness and furious writing. The 7th grade science teacher's observations of student behaviors during the worm dissection may have included such comments as: "Christine never touched the worm" or "Jon complained a lot" or "Eric told his group all answers" or "Carrie frowned during the entire lab." These field notes can reveal information about the students that numerical responses on the graph paper cannot, if the science teacher wants to know.

Observation data collection techniques can take the form of structured and methodical plans or unstructured and flexible. Both techniques are useful depending on the needs of the research study.

Unstructured Observations

Unstructured observations usually occur at the onset of a field trip to help narrow the focus of the investigation. The researcher takes notes on behaviors that are thought to be interesting, forming opinions and making evaluations during the process. This type of observation can result in a wealth of information because it is not restricted by predetermined focus; however, much of the information gathered is discarded during the analysis process. The science teacher walking around the room watching and listening to the general hum of aspiring scientists would be using unstructured observation.

Structured Observations

Structured observations implement a data gathering procedure that is developed before entering the culture. This allows the researcher to collect data in a systematic and structured manner, giving the data focus and ultimately making it more useful. The observer's attention must be narrowly focused on only the variables which have been selected, and an organized plan can help establish and maintain that focus.

*Preparing field note sheets on which to write the observations helps to keep them organized. Include headings on each sheet for the date, time, place, and subjects of the observation. Include a line on the bottom of each sheet for the observer's signature upon completion of that observation.

*Preparing guiding questions to direct the observation creates an efficient structure for gathering meaningful data. Print the questions clearly near the top of the field note sheets for frequent reference during the observations. Some observers prefer lined note sheets to increase legibility of the handwritten notes, but computers, especially laptops, are certainly acceptable replacements for pen and pencil, in most situations.

Structured observations are directed by guiding questions. The more specific the questions, the more appropriate the observation data. Just jotting notes of what is seen or heard does little but add confusion to data. These notes must have a focus. If the science teacher's objective was to see students' natural behavioral reactions during a dissecting lab, the previous field notes would be appropriate. If the science teacher's objective was to determine who the social leaders were in the class, those notes would be helpful. But, if the science teacher's objective was to determine who could appropriately complete a prescribed laboratory report, the observation notes are relatively worthless.

Highly structured observations could involve the use of checklists, simply counting how many times a predetermined event occurs. Teachers commonly use checklists in observing classroom behaviors such as discipline infractions, homework submissions, and attendance. It is worth noting that reducing the observation data to the counting of behaviors, may more appropriately qualify it as quantitative data than qualitative.

Example of an observation sheet:

> **How do students respond to the worm dissection laboratory?**
>
> **Who assumes a leadership role?**
>
> Class Period _____   Date _____
>
> <u>Notes</u>

Observation data collection formats can fall along a continuum from unstructured to highly structured. The combination of a planned focus and detailed, narrative information serves the purpose of many social science researchers who attempt to understand the full complexity of human culture.

*   *
_____
Unstructured   Highly Structured

There are two types of observation data collection techniques which qualitative researchers must understand before heading to the field.

Participant Observations

Participant observations involve a high degree of participation in the phenomenon under study by the researcher. Serving as the research instrument, the observer has a role as a member of the culture, taking part in the activity which is being observed. The science teacher is an appropriate participant observer because of the natural role as a member of the culture. It is important that observers are careful not to attract undue attention to themselves so they don't influence how people behave and so the observation remains neutral. Had the science teacher stopped at each lab station, peered at the individuals and written in a black notebook, students may have adjusted their behaviors, knowing they were under scrutiny.

Non-participant observations

Non-participant observations require that the researcher remains detached from the phenomenon under study. There is no, or at least minimal, interaction with the people being observed. Non-participant observers attempt to be as unobtrusive as possible. Sometimes tools such as remote audio and video recorders or even two-way mirrors allow a researcher to observe without participating in the culture at all. The science teacher might have used a non-participant observer role by remaining at the front podium to watch and take notes, detached physically from the students and giving the impression of being uninvolved in their culture.

These two data collection techniques can complement each other and be used together, so just as with the format of the observation, you might think of these as placed on a continuum. The participant observer becomes immersed in the culture, assuming a participatory role and blending in with the members. The non-participant observer avoids entry into the culture, remaining detached and separate for the events taking place around him. Sometimes, there is a need to move away from the polar ends of the continuum, assuming some of the characteristics and behaviors of both observer types. Our science teacher was a participant observer as a regular and accepted member of the class culture, but was a non-participant observer by not taking an active role in the actual dissection activity with one or more student lab groups. This position between the distinct roles of observation types was necessary to maintain the natural environment, and therefore minimize the chance for artificial student behaviors.

*   *
_____

Participant Observer   Non-Participant Observer

The types of observation formats and the roles of the researcher observer can be combined to best meet the needs of the cultural phenomenon under study. Consideration of the specific intent of the research and the limitations or possibilities of the natural environment will allow the researcher to employ observation data collection techniques that are productive and efficient. In our science classroom, there are many observations that could occur, and each would serve a different purpose.

Worm Dissection Lab	Participant	Non-Participant
Structured	Students take notes to learn about each others' reactions to touching the worm	University student visitor takes detailed notes to explain the types of student misbehaviors seen
Unstructured	Students take notes about the lab experience	University student visitor takes notes about the class

Activity 1

This activity requires 30-45 minutes, each day, over 3 days to complete, so plan accordingly. Remember, qualitative research requires an investment of time and energy. You are going to serve as an observer; first as an unstructured, non-participant observer then as a structured, non-participant observer, and finally as a structured, participant observer.

1. Select an arena with which you are unfamiliar. For example, if you aren't much of a sports fan, attend local high school sporting events. If you don't frequent a local church, attend services. As long as the arena involves a large collection of people and an event that is not known to you, you may choose.

2. During your first visit, position yourself closely to, but not as a central part of the people at the event. Select 3–5 people to observe. Quietly observe and take notes describing the people you've chosen.

3. Create an observation sheet labeled with the guiding questions, "What emotions are revealed by the participants?" "What are some of the causes of these emotions?"

4. During your second visit, position yourself at a central point within physical contact of 3-5 people at a similar event (for example, another high school game or the next church service). Communicate superficially with these people. You can smile at them or say "Hello," but avoid full conversations. Again, observe and take notes addressing the guiding questions.

5. During your third visit, position yourself within a group of 3-5 people at the same event. Communicate in a direct and personal manner. Ask questions, participate in conversations, share your popcorn or song book. Again, observe and take notes addressing the guiding questions.

6. Save your notes for the follow-up activity under Data Analysis, later in this chapter, but look at them now in the order they were collected. Draw two or three general conclusions about the use of the three observational data collection techniques based on the information you gathered. Which technique did you find most useful? Why was it most useful?

Interviews

Interviews involve face-to-face attempts to obtain information in the form of verbal responses from one or more respondents. It is a conversation. The goal of interview data is to reveal opinions, attitudes and perceptions which people in the culture hold.

Similar to observations, the interviewer is part of the data instrument. As a data collection tool, interviews can reveal information that is unobtainable in any other way. Participants in an interview are often willing to be candid in their comments, allowing the researcher to gain a truer picture of the phenomenon under investigation. One tip to maximize the success of your interview is to spend time in the culture before interviewing any participants. These preliminary visits allow people to become familiar with your presence and help you gain some level of understanding of them and the culture in which they are operating.

Interview data collection techniques can take the form of structured and methodical plans or unstructured and flexible, similar to the opportunities for observations. Both techniques are useful depending on the goals of the research study.

Structured interviews

Structured interviews are used once hypotheses or research questions have been determined. The interview questions are standardized and consistent in both their presentation and purpose. These key questions, sometimes called probes, are used to focus responses to the research question and to encourage expansion of short or incomplete responses. If multiple respondents are used, each receives the same questions in the same order. As students were dissecting their worms, the teacher could have asked questions of individuals such as, "What is one thing you have learned during this lab experience?" or "What is one change you think would improve this lab experience?" to gather information about the effectiveness of the lab and direction for adjustments in future classes.

Unstructured interviews

Unstructured interviews are more flexible than structured interviews as their goal is to engage participants in conversation about the issues under examination. The researcher may begin with specific questions, but is ready to respond to the directions in which each participant may travel. This responsive technique allows for the investigation of topics that the researcher may not have considered prior to the interview as well as uncover information that may not have been revealed within the framework of predetermined questions. Multiple respondents are permitted to digress from the researcher's original attention, sometimes offering unique knowledge or special insight that increases the researcher's understanding. The science teacher could have asked various students the question "How do you feel about using live animals for scientific study?" to initiate a conversation about the ethics of animal dissection and to develop understanding of adolescent perceptions of this social issue.

Activity 2

Identify a person whom you know, but not intimately, and secure her permission to engage in a discussion about a specific topic. You could choose a newly hired colleague, a co-worker in another department, or a new neighbor. Select a topic that allows for descriptive responses, but one that is not politically or culturally offensive. During your first discussion, ask the question, "What do you think about...?" Listen carefully to her response, prodding gently to encourage thorough descriptions, but not directing her answer.

1. Take notes during the interview that reflect their responses; save these for later.

2. What was the most difficult part of conducting the interview? Did you get the information you wanted? Did you get information that surprised you? What information did you want, but did not receive?

3. How might a structured interview have changed the information you received? Would you have rather used a structured interview or the unstructured format? Why?

Artifacts

Artifacts are typically pieces of printed materials, but can include objects, photographs, video tapes, paintings, music, and even clothing. Often times, artifacts are not used as the primary data source, but rather provide ancillary information. They provide context that enhances the researcher's understanding of the culture. Qualitative researchers will often gather artifacts in conjunction with interview and observation data to allow for *triangulation*, collecting data from multiple sources. In gathering artifacts for the earthworm lab, students could consider including the dissected worms, the prepared slides of worm organs, photographs of the worms, and the final written lab report. This use of multiple data sources encourages systematic analysis and reduces opportunity for subjective analysis.

Artifacts can be personal belongings of individual members of the culture or official materials owned by the group at large. Not all materials found within a given culture are appropriate data pieces. When considering the worm dissection lab, appropriate artifacts may include the dissected worms, but would not include the Bunsen burners stored on the back tables. Artifacts should represent the phenomenon under study and provide evidence of that particular event.

Activity 3

Refer to "Qualitative Evaluation Methods Applied to a High School Counseling Center" (Appendix B) to complete this activity.

1. Explain two of the reasons that these researchers chose qualitative methodology for this study.

2. Describe the use of triangulation in this study.

Data Analysis

I once had a professor who told me that analyzing qualitative data was like panning for gold. The gold miner first scoops a pan full of water and sediment, mixed in a muddy mess. Then he moves the pan quickly in a circular motion, swirling the water over the pan's edge, and watching closely as the sediment separates itself from the water. The heavier sediment falls into the center of the pan while the gold flakes and pieces rise to the top. The shimmer of the gold eventually reveals itself to the observant miner, who carefully pulls the gold aside and discards the unworthy sediment. A diligent and persistent miner may even find the elusive gold nugget.

Qualitative data analysis involves organizing what you have seen, heard, and read so that you can make sense of what you have learned. Working with the data, you create explanations, post hypotheses, develop theories, and link your story to other stories. To do so, you must "categorize, synthesize, search for patterns, and interpret the data" you have collected. (Glesne & Peshkin, 2002, p.127). Unlike quantitative data which can be decoded through various mathematical computations, qualitative data must be sifted and reviewed through personal interpretation supported by evidence. Just as persistent sifting of river sediment can reveal gold, when analyzed well, your data will reveal understanding of the phenomenon and allow you to convey that understanding to others.

The purpose of qualitative data analysis is to discover the views and perceptions of the people from which the data was taken, so the researcher must temper personal reactions to the data. Though interpretation is important to qualitative data analysis, this interpretation must be well-supported by the factual information gathered. If I observe several students frowning, closing their eyes, and holding their noses during a dissection lab, I wouldn't necessarily interpret this data as adolescents with bad attitudes. I would consider the possibility that the students are uncomfortable with the task for a plethora of reasons and continue my observations to identify those reasons. Analysis of the observed event, during the event, allows me to draw initial conclusions, then reenter the phenomenon for confirmation, clarification, or redirection of those initial decisions.

Qualitative data analysis does not wait until the research study ends, it occurs continually during the study. Consistent and frequent reflection on the observed behaviors while they are underway is important to valid interpretations. The researcher must use a string of decisions during data collection to encourage effective data analysis. After noticing that a student is frowning during the worm lab, it would be appropriate to alter my observations to focus on facial expressions of other students. This alteration of focus allows me to see a cultural phenomenon unfold…the natural, unrehearsed reactions of adolescents. I am, in effect, analyzing the initial data I receive – the frowning – and using my analysis to redirect my data collection procedure.

Much of qualitative data analysis does occur at the conclusion of the event when the researcher steps away from the environment and looks closely at the evidence. This is a time for careful and cautious scrutiny of observation notes, interview responses, video tape recordings, and all other data collected during the inquiry. Analyzing data at this time is the last step before drawing conclusions about what the researcher has learned. It must be approached with attention to detail and awareness of connections and discrepancies.

One of the most important aspects of qualitative data analysis is identifying themes or patterns of language and behavior, often called *domains* or *domain representations*. Though it can seem daunting, and is a time and attention challenge, you already have some experience analyzing qualitative data. Just as you arrange your kitchen cupboards or tool shed, you will arrange your qualitative data. You will look at everything you have and note commonalities and patterns that emerge. Then you establish a coding system that represents those commonalities and patterns.

When I look at all of the "stuff" in the earthworm experiment, I see that the teacher has placed everything into 3 groups.

Lab Tools	*Report Supplies*	*Supporting Materials*

Within these 3 groups, I notice further similarities and differences among the items, so I can make groups within the teacher's original groups. Now, I have 7 groups in 3 areas of the science room…it's getting messy.

Lab Tools	*Report Supplies*	*Supporting Materials*
Dissecting Tools	**Quadrille Paper**	**Hygiene Products**
Observation Tools	**Blue Pens**	**Clean Up Supplies**
	Computers	

I look at the 7 groups in the 3 areas of the room and note more specific characteristics, so I can further divide items. This division of items results in 15 groups within the 7 larger groups in the 3 areas of the science room … I'm drowning in organization!

Lab Tools	*Report Supplies*	*Supporting Materials*
Dissecting Tools	**Quadrille Paper**	**Hygiene Products**
Dissecting Board		Hand Sanitizer
Dissecting Pins	**Blue Pens**	Gloves
Scalpel		
Tweezers	**Computers**	**Clean Up Supplies**
Tongs	Desktops	Paper Towels
Earthworms	Laptops	Sealable bags
		Spray Cleaner
Observation Tools		Air-Sick bags
Magnifying Glass		
Safety Glasses		

The coding used for the earthworm lab data analysis indicates that the culture of this science room revolves around operation and use. Initial categories of Lab Tools, Report Supplies, and Supporting Materials established the common patterns which had been observed when reviewing the details and subtle characteristics of all of the *data pieces,* the individual bits of information. These categories provided the *context codes*, the large categories for all subsequent data organization. Within those context codes, other patterns emerged and were coded as *situation codes* because they reflected specific situations that occurred within the context code; Dissecting Tools and Observation Tools were situation codes within the context code of Lab Tools.

Qualitative data analysis is interpretive, but always supported by the evidence gathered. Decisions about what data means are not arbitrary or completely subjective. The piles into which the researcher placed items were determined by interpretation of the data about the individual items. Perhaps, you would have put all glasses in one pile, without differentiating between the Magnifying Glasses and Safety Glasses because you use them both for observation during the lab. Since your decision is supported by the data, it is a valid interpretation. Placing all Glasses in the same pile as Computers however, is not supported by the data, since Computers are not used in the process of Observation during the lab.

Some of you may welcome the age of technology because it is providing versatile computer programs to assist you with qualitative data analysis. Software such as Atlas/ti, The Ethnograph v5.0, Qualrus, or Transana can help you manage your qualitative data. The programs will code, sort, and even identify relationships among the data entered. They can help to automate and speed up some analysis tasks giving quicker access to the data. It is worth noting that there reigns great debate about the use of computer analysis with qualitative data. Concerns include the possibility that researchers will be removed from the on-going analysis that is important during data collection because they will wait to enter the observation field notes into the computer software program after all the observations are completed. Another concern addresses the complex mental processing that the human brain provides in filtering subtle nuances of any environment; this has not yet been replicated by a computer program and so is missing when qualitative data enters the sterile environment of a computer's bits and bytes (Winsome St. John, 2000).

Activity 4

You need to return to the data collected in completion of Activity 1 of this chapter. Review the observation field notes taken, considering the commonalities or patterns of behavior that emerge. Arrange your notes within appropriate context codes. Remember that you may not use every note you have because not all behaviors will share commonalities or fit into patterns; humans vary within every culture, so you may have an exception that you will not include for this activity. Now that you have groupings under context codes, subdivide the data within each of the context code groups into situation codes, but leaving them still within their original context code groups. Step away for your work for awhile. When you return, carefully examine your codes and your placement of data within those codes. Rearrange as you deem appropriate.

1. What was the most difficult part of this analysis?

2. How often did you change your mind about your codes? Your data placement?

3. Now that you can see your data pieces organized through your codes, what general observation can you make?

Drawing Conclusions Through a Disciplined Process

"Although distinctly different from quantitative statistical analysis both in procedures and goals, good qualitative analysis is both systematic and intensely disciplined". (Frechtling & Sharp, 1997). As Chapter 11 of this text explained, the goal of qualitative research is to gather, analyze, and present genuine data that provides an authentic view of the selected human event under study. Once you have conducted a solid analysis of the data, you must draw conclusions that allow you to communicate your findings.

Drawing conclusions from the qualitative data gathered "is not a question of an artist's giving shape to seamless, inchoate material, but of an intense observer's scrupulous recording of naturally-occurring social interactions from which patterns are inferred and interpreted." (Miles & Huberman, 1984, p. 20). Employing the scientific characteristics of systematic, rigorous, disciplined, analytical, and critical decision-making, allows the qualitative researcher to draw conclusions that are well supported by the evidence gathered.

Evidence Supported Decisions

Miles and Huberman (1984) emphasize the importance of examining qualitative conclusions for "their plausibility, their sturdiness, their confirmability – that is, their validity." (p. 11) *Validity* in this instance refers to the strength of the data conclusions as reflected in their ability to withstand scrutiny. Valid conclusions are defensible and supported by the strong data.

Avoiding Bias

It is virtually impossible to draw conclusions from qualitative data that are completely without bias. As we discussed in Chapter 11, qualitative researchers serve as data instruments, filtering incoming data through their eyes and ears. Because of this intense and personal involvement in the data, conclusions drawn are inevitably influenced by the researcher's perspectives and predispositions. These biases however, can be confronted and minimized.

One way to avoid bias is to think critically about what your data is saying. Your data is the evidence that you have about the human phenomenon under study, so pay careful attention to it. Evaluate this evidence in light of the initial research question. Consider where the evidence points and what conclusions will be supported by that evidence.

Another consideration for drawing unbiased conclusions is to analyze your evidence from many angles. Look for possible flaws in your reasoning by checking for subtle assumptions or one-sided interpretations. Follow your line of reasoning to see if it is logical and supported by your data. Be on guard for language that can be misinterpreted.

And finally, to address the potential bias of your conclusions, encourage the reader to consider the authenticity of your decisions. In the presentation of the conclusions you are making about your data, inform the reader of your perspectives and any predispositions you may have had about the data. This supports the reader as a critical consumer of the research.

Verifying Results

As we have discussed, interpreting qualitative data can be subjective, so it is critical to verify your conclusions. By taking precautions to confirm your conclusions you improve the validity of the study you have just conducted. Steps to this verification process include:

*Repeated review of data

*Input from Others

As you begin to draw conclusions about your data, review the evidence you have. Check that each of your conclusions is well grounded in the information you recorded and analyzed. If you have multiple data sources, perhaps observations, interviews, and artifacts, consider their consistency. Do they provide evidence that steers your conclusion in one direction or does their evidence seem conflicting and inconsistent? Cross-check your data pieces to verify the conclusions to which they seem to be leading you. Compare and contrast the data, looking for emerging meanings to support your conclusions. Do not hurry this repeated review.

Revisit your evidence as many times as you feel necessary to be secure in the conclusions you are making.

Once you have made your conclusions, step away for a time. Allow the process to settle in your mind and on the computer monitor. When you go back to what you've written you may see things a bit differently. This can cause you to reconsider your initial conclusions. Don't shy away from this re-evaluation, but use it as an opportunity to validate or to reexamine your conclusions.

Another opportunity to improve the strength of your qualitative research conclusions is to share your results with others. These can include other researchers or some of the participants of your study. Researchers who have experience in qualitative methodologies can provide an objective response to your conclusions based solely on the evidence you provide. They are not influenced by relationships built with participants or predispositions to the initial creation of the research question.

Participants in your study can tell you if you have accurately recorded their feelings, actions, or intentions. They can react to the conclusions you have drawn based on their ownership of the human event studied. They are not influenced by the potential for publication or promotion, but instead react to the honest representation of their culture.

Though you do not want others to be the deciding factors in your research conclusions, they may assist you in seeing something that was hidden without their input.

Conclusions in qualitative research are not conveyed in numbers or through statistical analyses as in quantitative methodologies. Qualitative research relies on the language of the culture represented. Using words can often convey a clearer picture of human phenomena, but careless use of language can also create unrealistic reports and misinterpretations of events. As the previous chapters have shown, conducting meaningful qualitative research is difficult. It requires discipline, structure, time, and energy. Drawing solid, defensible conclusions also requires discipline, structure, time, and energy. The qualitative process must be sound and your conclusions must be authentic. "Unless you can convince your audience that the procedures you used did ensure that your methods are reliable and that your conclusions are valid, there is little point in aiming to conclude a research study ... Short of reliable methods and valid conclusions, research descends into a bedlam where battles are won only by those who shout the loudest." (Silverman, 2001, p. 254)

Activity 5

Refer again to "Qualitative Evaluation Methods Applied to a High School Counseling Center" (Appendix B) to complete this activity.

1. Explain the domain analysis process used by these researchers.

2. How do these authors use the available literature to assist them in forming conclusions from their data?

3. Beyond drawing conclusions based on the data gathered, these researchers provide an opinion about the application of the conclusions to others, specifically to "co-workers and colleagues." How do they support their opinion? Is their opinion well-grounded? Explain your response.

4. How do these authors encourage the reader to consider the authenticity of the conclusions drawn from this study? What do they ask readers to "do" with this study?

Data Presentation

Just as the researcher analyzes qualitative data during the data collection process, the way in which the qualitative data will be presented is developed during the data analysis process. As data patterns emerge during analysis, there must be a means to contain them. Tables, matrices and other graphic representations are the tools used to hold the data as the researcher organizes it. Sometimes analysis of the data requires the researcher to reconsider the codes used and even the data placement within those codes. When there are changes in data organization, the content of the graphic is modified to reflect that new understanding.

Tables are often used when data details are to be presented. There are as many table forms as there are qualitative researchers, but generally tables provide display of the data as reflected in the context codes and situation codes employed during analysis. Tables of some observable data, including frequency of events, provide listings within the codes.

Table 1

Observations of Actions During Earthworm Lab

Collaborative Set-Up	

Verbalization	Recognition of Quantity of Items
	    Students questioning need
	    Teacher responding
	Interaction with Earthworms
	    Students talking to worms
	Interaction Between Teacher and Students
	    Humor
	    Complaints
	    Students – Abuse of worms
	        Request excusal from lab

Physical Actions	Play-Acting with Tools
	    Students fencing with scalpels
	    Students placing magnifying glasses on peers
	Teacher Redirecting Behaviors
	    Writing students' names on board
	    Serious warnings

Tables of interview responses provide *domain representations* of data collected. These domains result from observed commonalities, or patterns, among the responses given during the interviews. The researcher explains the context of the interview within the title of the table, Observations of Actions During Earthworm Lab, then identifies the domain within the table, Collaborative Set Up, and divides the domain into broad categories, Verbalization and Physical Actions, finally providing detail about the observation data, Play-Acting with Tools, to support the domain.

Table 2

Teacher Interview Data Following Earthworm Lab

A Beneficial Experience

Science Content
        "Students made excellent observations about the organs."
        "They applied the scientific method pretty well."

Social Awareness
        "I'm always glad when students question the ethics of dissection."
        "The discussion about the cycle of life was a surprise, but valuable."
        "We'll see what they decide is a good substitute for the earthworms."

Relationships
        "Most of them complain about being assigned partners, but 9 times out of 10, it works out."
        "The partner rotations in labs seem to create a friendlier class of students."
        "Students talk to each other in here, but I wonder if they connect with those same people in any other part of their social lives."

Matrices use symbols to demonstrate specific behavioral characteristics, often positioned in opposition, such as positive or negative. The multiple dimensions of an event can be clearly represented within a matrix. The title of the matrix table explains the context and focus of the observation. The behavior categories are determined during analysis of the specific observation data. The specific behaviors are then assigned to the students who demonstrated the behaviors and described through placement within the behavior categories and by symbols representation the behavior type.

Table 3

Matrix of Student Participation in Worm Dissection

Student	Facial Expression	Verbalization	Active Involvement
1	+	+	+
2	–	0	+
3	–	–	–
4	+	+	0
5	–	0	+

+ = perceived as positive at least twice by the observer
– = perceived as negative as least twice by the observer
0 = demonstration perceived fewer than twice by the observer

Table 4

Frequency of Verbal Communication Types
During Earthworm Lab

	Students	Teacher
Humor	17	6
Questioning	31	25
Complaints	4	0
Correction	8	11

Regardless of which graphic presentation you use for your data, it should be guided by the concept you want to convey. All components of the data presentation are important from the title of the graphic to the details contained within. It is through the data presentation that researchers move the process of collecting, organizing, and interpreting information, to the communication of the research findings.

Activity 6

Return to the data you collected for Activity 1 and analyzed for Activity 3. Select the format that you feel is most appropriate for presenting your data results. Then create the presentation.

The ultimate goal of qualitative researchers is to gather, analyze, and present authentic data that convey the true meaning of a given human phenomenon. The qualitative data process is truly reflective of the holistic intent of qualitative research as the collection, analysis, and presentation steps meet and overlap, converge and digress. Just as human events unfold before our carefully observing eyes and ears, qualitative data presents itself and the phenomenon it represents.

Reaction Guide

1. Interviews should be very structured and formal.   Agree _____   Disagree _____

2. Field notes are only for observing outdoor events.   Agree _____   Disagree _____

3. Triangulation allows you to present data in a triangular shape.   Agree _____   Disagree _____

4. Researcher bias is unavoidable when drawing conclusions from qualitative data.   Agree _____   Disagree _____

5. Research participants can help you draw conclusions from your research data.   Agree _____   Disagree _____

Why my choice is confirmed.   Why my choice is not confirmed.

1. _____   _____

2. _____   _____

3. _____   _____

4. _____   _____

5. _____   _____

Chapter 12 Self-Test

True or False

1. _____ Qualitative research has to be proven by collected data.

2. _____ Qualitative data analysis reveals the perceptions of the people studied.

3. _____ Coding systems are usually based on color or size.

4. _____ Matrices are used to show opposing characteristics of behavior.

5. _____ Computer programs are not appropriate for qualitative data analysis.

6. _____ Analyzing qualitative data requires strict structure.

7. _____ The research question should guide the research conclusions.

8. _____ Research conclusions should be made quickly, to react to the human event immediately.

Matching

9. _____ artifacts

10. _____ field note

11. _____ guiding questions

12. _____ domains

13. _____ triangulation

14. _____ inchoate

15. _____ qualitative validity

16. _____ evidence

17. _____ bias

A. used to direct the observation data
B. personal belongings or official group materials
C. recording of observations during the event

D. using multiple data sources together

E. themes of patterns of language and behavior

F. the arrangement of qualitative data in linear fashion

G. unclear, unformed

H. strength of data conclusions

I. data

J. predisposition; pre-formed opinion

Companion Website

Additional resources and chapter activities are located www.edinboro.edu/press.

13 Multimethod Research

Anticipation Guide

1. Adhering to one research method is important for valid results.   Agree _____   Disagree _____

2. Numerical data is the best for drawing defensible conclusions.   Agree _____   Disagree _____

3. Multiple perspectives help teachers understand students   Agree _____   Disagree _____

Chapter Rationale

M&M candies were created for a special group of people who needed something beyond the basics they were receiving. M & Ms were first sold to U.S. GIs serving overseas during World War II (1941-1945). The soldiers couldn't get chocolate from home because it melted into its paper wrapper during shipment, significantly changing the flavor. Enclosing the chocolate in a hard candy shell provided the best of both worlds; the chocolate that soldiers craved arrived safe and sound in a wrapping that enhanced its flavor.

It is common sense that different research projects would require different research methods and that methods used should be chosen on the basis of the information sought. The traditional quantitative approach is not always appropriate to examining individuals, groups, or school cultures. The qualitative approach is not effective for measuring, testing hypotheses, or analyzing data statistically. A multimethod approach provides a research design option that capitalizes on the strengths of both quantitative and qualitative strategies and limits their weaknesses, providing a way to learn more completely about issues in which we are interested.

Objectives

At the completion of this chapter you will be aware of the use of multimethod research designs and the characteristics of multimethod research that set it apart from both quantitative and qualitative research. You will examine design strengths and weaknesses.

You will also consider times when and ways in which multimethod research can be appropriately used.

Graphic Organizer

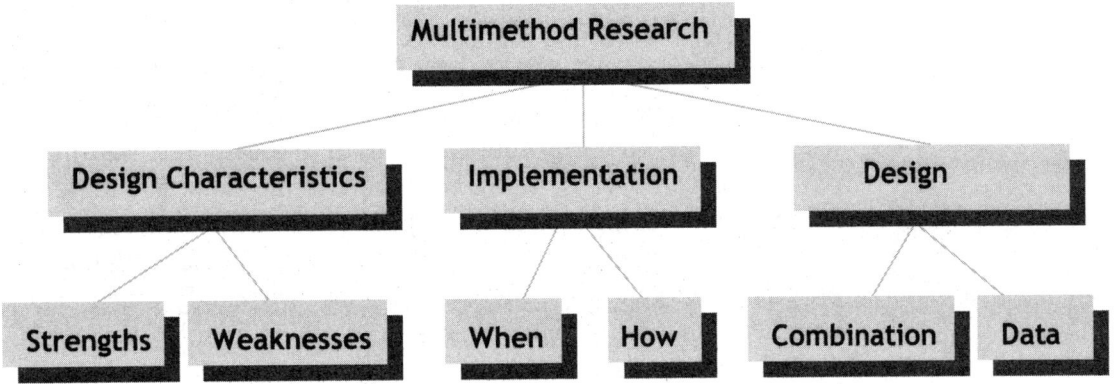

What is Multimethod Research?

To compare multimethod research to M&M candies is not a stretch. Just as M&M's provided a complete treat for soldiers in distant lands, multimethod research can provide complete answers to the research questions you want to answer about your students and their learning. Let's suppose you are in charge of the math tutoring program at your high school, and your superintendent wants to know if the program is working. You consider the word, "working" and decide that it could mean the following: Are the students in the program learning math? Do the students in the program enjoy math? Do the students in the program enjoy the program? Have math scores improved on the state math assessment? Answers to any one of these questions could tell the superintendent about an aspect of the tutoring program, but answers to all of these questions would give the superintendent a much more complete understanding of any success the math tutoring program may be fostering.

Multimethod research is a research method that combines aspects of quantitative and qualitative approaches into one research study. Multimethod research allows for the collection and analysis of many, diverse data sets to provide a detailed description of an educational phenomenon. Multimethod research can provide stronger evidence, more detailed description, a fuller understanding by using numbers and words in combination.

Because you are already familiar with the concerns and values inherent in qualitative and in quantitative research designs, you can probably see that combining the designs may minimize the weaknesses in each and enhance their strengths. If students say they hate math tutoring, but test scores for students who participate in the tutoring program are consistently higher than for students who don't participate, a teacher wants to know why students hate the program. The test scores seem to indicate the tutoring is working in some ways; but there is more to the story, and more test scores are not going to tell it. Supporting student math test scores with student comments about their experiences in the math tutoring program answers the question "is it working" much more completely than the numerical scores alone would do. Asking students about their feelings can add insight and understanding about the tutoring program that could direct change to increase its effectiveness. Multimethod research would include examination of the student test scores and student perceptions or opinions to provide answers to the superintendent's question. Collection and analysis of both quantitative and qualitative data is the key component of multimethod research.

Activity 1

Describe a time when you tried to understand poor student performance but never really figured it out. What information would have helped you gain clear understanding of a student who performed poorly and why?

___

___

___

___

___

Discussion of Activity 1

Educators are frequently called upon by parents and others to explain students' lack of success. Many times those explanations are based solely on number of assignments completed or not completed, recorded tests scores, or discipline infractions. Having information that describes a student's telling behaviors, such as falling asleep in class or frequently asking to leave class to use the restroom; or information that has been given by the child such as "I never go to sleep before midnight because that's when Mommy gets home" or "We don't have breakfast at my house" can support the numerical information educators try to use. Being able to see and understand the whole child and communicate that understanding to others is important to his or her success in school.

The Multimethod Researcher

The goal of a multimethod design is to allow for a thorough examination of an educational event or issue. The use of multiple perspectives is a strength of educators' daily decision making behaviors. When you want to know the whole story and not just one piece of the story, a multimethod design may provide you with the research tool necessary. It is important to recognize though, that a multifaceted examination of any-thing is more demanding than a monofaceted look.

Multimethod designs often require more time and energy than single method designs as the researcher must collect and analyze multiple sets of data, use different approaches to collect data, and analyze data in different ways. The multimethod researcher must decide which data, both qualitative and quantitative will work together to answer the research question fully. Will the diverse data sets complement each other? What data will address all aspects of the research question? How will the data be combined to respond to the research question? Data collection often requires several data collection events that may include testing, interviewing, and/or observing, and data analysis usually requires multiple analyses of the data as the researcher considers how the varied sets are connected to each other and to the research question.

The multimethod researcher must also be well-versed in both qualitative and qualitative methodology so as to be able to implement both appropriately within the multimethod design. The combination of methodologies must be determined in light of the research question to be answered and the best parts of each methodology for that question must be selected thoughtfully. There are infinite ways to combine research methodologies, but the multimethod researcher must determine the combination that is most appropriate for their own research question. Each multimethod study is unique to its researcher's decisions about intent, procedures, data, and reporting. And each design relies on the competence of the researcher. Designing multimethod studies can, however, become second nature as educators realize that the best way to answer questions about student learning is to use both numbers and words.

> The classroom is a constantly changing environment with complicated issues and complex participants. One-dimensional research approaches are sometimes insufficient to address these environments. Quantitative and qualitative techniques are compatible and can improve the ability of educators to answer the questions posed to them. "Researchers need not adhere to either approach, but should freely choose a mix of attributes from both paradigms in searching for a richer understanding of learning environments" (Fraser & Tobin, 1991, p. 47).

Multimethod Research Designs

As noted earlier there are an infinite number of ways in which qualitative and quantitative methodologies can be combined. Multimethod is gaining quickly in popularity among educational researchers and is influenced by the unique characteristics of those researchers and their research goals. But there are some guidelines to understanding multimethod research designs that can provide you with a structure for creating your own approach.

All multimethod research involves mixing components of the separate methodologies of qualitative and quantitative approaches in some fashion. Sometimes this mixing results in sequential combination of methodologies and other times it results in concurrent combination of methodologies. Snyder (2006) describes sequential combinations as explanatory or exploratory. Explanatory designs have a focus on quantitative methods/data complemented by qualitative methods/data. Exploratory designs are initiated with qualitative methods/data followed by quantitative methods/data. Triangulation designs allow the multimethod researcher to gather quantitative and qualitative data at the same time, so that both data sets are given similar emphasis.

Multimethod research design allows you great flexibility in examining issues of concern to you. This flexibility however, does not mean your research approach can be successful without structure and careful planning. Referring to one of the three general designs may help you in creating an approach that is appropriate to your needs and that uses sound research practices.

We believe that the appropriate selection of qualitative and quantitative research design components is the future of social science research. At the same time, we acknowledge that multimethod studies do not provide ideal solutions for all research questions: Just as M&M's will not be the candy of choice for those of you who don't like chocolate.

Activity 2

Read the article, "Exploring the links between critical literacy and developmental reading" (Appendix B). Respond to the following.

1. What is the first research question posed by the author? _____

   _____

   _____

2. Did this question require quantitative or qualitative data? _____

3. Explain why that type of data is appropriate to the question. _____

   _____

   _____

4. What specific data was used? _____

5. How was the data presented? _____

   _____

6. What is the second research question posed by the author? _____

   _____

   _____

7. Did this question require quantitative or qualitative data? _____

8. Explain why that type of data is appropriate to the question. _____

9. Describe the researcher's use of purposive sampling. What sample was used? Why was it an appropriate sample for this study?

Writing Your Research Report: The Abstract

Writing a good abstract is always a challenge because it requires the researcher to summarize the entire report in only 120 words. The abstract should include the following components in order:
The topic or problem under investigation

- A description of the participants, e.g., age, gender, special characteristics

- Experimental or qualitative methods and procedures, including names of assessments

- Means, standard deviations, and results of statistical significance tests

- Findings, conclusions, and implications

The abstract should be succinct and easy to read so that other scholars will be able to determine its value in their reviews of the literature. Rather than trying to create the perfect abstract at a single writing, begin by composing two to four sentences for each of the major components of the abstract. Concentrate on developing a paragraph that tells the story of your research. Then, check the length of the paragraph. It will probably be too long. Eliminate redundancies and less important information until you have an abstract of appropriate length. Guidelines are available on pages 12–15 of the *Publication Manual of the AmericaPsychological Association.*

Reaction Guide

1. Adhering to one research method is important for valid results. Agree _____ Disagree _____

2. Numerical data is the best for drawing defensible conclusions. Agree _____ Disagree _____

3. Multiple perspectives help teachers understand students Agree _____ Disagree _____

Why my choice is confirmed.   Why my choice is not confirmed.

1. _____   _____

2. _____   _____

3. _____   _____

Companion Website

Additional resources and chapter activities are located www.edinboro.edu/press.

References

American Educational Research Association (2007). Research Ethics Web site. Retrieved November 22, 2007, from http://www.aera.net/aboutaera/?id=717.

American Psychological Association (2007). Research Ethics & Regulations for Human Subjects Web site. Retrieved November 22, 2007, from http://www.apa.org/science/research.html.

Barker, J., Bernard, D., Cappabianca, L., Dahlstrand, J., Maguire, J., Meredith, B., & Rewers, P. (2004). Increasing student engagement rate. In D. M. Snodgrass & K. M. Adams (Eds.). *Instructional leaders in an era of data-driven decision making* (pp. 35-39). Edinboro, PA: Edinboro University Press.

Bradbury, R. (1953). *Fahrenheit 451*. New York: Del Ray.

Brown, B. H., Richards, H. C., & Wilson, C. A. (1996). Pet Bonding and Pet Bereavement Among Adolescents. *Journal of Counseling & Development, 74*, 505-509.

Bruning, J. L., & Kintz, B. L. (1997). *Handbook of computational statistics* (4th ed.). Glenview, IL: Harper Collins.

Burns, N., & Grove, S. (2007). *Understanding nursing research* (4th ed.) Philadelphia: W. B. Saunders.

Carver, R. P. (1978). The case against statistical significance testing. *Harvard Educational Review, 48*, 378-399.

Carver, R. P. (1993). The case against statistical significance testing, revisited. *Journal of Experimental Education, 61*, 287-292.

Chen, M., Froehle, T., & Morran, K. (1997). Deconstructing dispositional bias in clinical inference: Two interventions. *Journal of Counseling and Development, 76*, 74-81.

Cohen, J. (1988). *Statistical power analysis for the behavioral sciences* (2nd ed.). Mahwah, NJ: Erlbaum.

Cohen, J. (1994). The earth is round ($p<.05$). *American Psychologist, 49*, 997-1003.

Einstein, A. (1905). *Zur Elektrodynamik bewegter Körper* [On the electrodynamics of moving bodies]. *Annalen der Physik, 17*, 891-921.

Fisher, R. A., & Yates, F. (1949). *Statistical tables for biological, agricultural, and medical research*. New York, NY: Hafner.

Frechtling, J., Sharp, L., (1997). User-Friendly Handbook for Mixed Method Evaluations. Directorate for Education and Human Resources. Retrieved November 23, 2007, from http://www.ehr.nsf.gov/EHR/REC/pubs/NSF97-153/START.HTM#TOC.

Frostig, M. (1963). Marianne Frostig Developmental Test of Visual Perception. Palo Alto, CA: Consulting Psychologists Press.

Gates, A. I. (1926). A study of the role of visual perception, intelligence, and certain associative processes in reading and spelling. *Journal of Educational Psychology, 17,* 433-445.

Gay, L. R., Mills, G. E., & Airasian, P. (2005). *Educational research: Competencies for analysis and applications* (8th ed.). Upper Saddle River, NJ: Prentice Hall.

Glesne, C., & Peshin, A. (1992). *Becoming qualitative researchers.* White Plains, NY: Longman.

Heatwole, C. M. (1998). Robust feedback control of flow-induced structural radiation of sound. *Dissertation Abstracts International,* 58 (09), 5068B. (UMI No. 9808454)

Heyerdahl, T. (1950). *Kon-Tiki.* Chicago, IL: Rand McNally.

Krathwohl, D. R. (2004). *Methods of educational and social science research: An integrated approach* (2nd ed.). Long Grove, IL: Waveland Press.

Lancy, D. F. (1993). *Qualitative research in education: An introduction to the major traditions.* New York: Longman.

Lesley, M. (2001). Exploring the links between critical literacy and developmental reading. *Journal of Adolescent & Adult Literacy, 47,* 180-189.

Maurer, D. W. (2003). *Whiz mob: A correlation of the technical argot of pickpockets with their behavior pattern.* Lanham, MD: Rowman and Littlefield.

McGrath, J. E. & Kulka, R. (1991). *Judgment calls in research: An unorthodox view of the research process.* Newbury Park, CA: Sage Publishing.

McKenzie, J. D., & Goldman, R. (2005). *The student guide to MINITAB® release 14.* Boston: Pearson Education.

Micceri, T. (1989). The unicorn, the normal curve, and other improbable creatures. *Psychological Bulletin, 105,* 156-166.

Miles, M., & Huberman, A. (1984). Drawing valid meaning from qualitative data: Toward a shared craft. *Educational Researcher, 13*(5), 20-30.

Muray, P. V., Levitov, J. E., Castenell, L., & Joubert, J. H. (1987). Qualitative evaluation methods applied to a high school counseling center. *Journal of Counseling and Development, 65*, 259-261.

Myers, M.D. Critical Ethnography in Information Systems. In A.S. Lee, J., Liebenau, & J. I. DeGross (Eds.). *Information Systems and Qualitative Research* (pp 276-300). London: Chapman and Hall,

Myers, M. D. (2007). Qualitative research in information systems, MISQ Discovery web site. Retrieved November 22, 2007, from www.qual.auckland.ac.nz.

Newton, I. (1687). *Philosophiae Naturalis Principia Mathematica*. London, Imprimatur. *Publication manual of the American Psychological Association* (5th ed.). (2001). Washington, DC: American Psychological Association.

Rubin, A., & Babbie, E. R. (2005). *Research methods for social work*. Florence, KY: Thomson Wadsworth.

Shaver, J. P. (1993). What statistical significance testing is, and what it is not. *Journal of Experimental Education, 61*, 293-315.

Silverman, D. (2001). *Interpreting qualitative data: Methods for analyzing talk, text and interaction* (2nd ed.). London: Sage Publications.

Spindler, G. D. (1997). *Education and cultural process: Anthropological approaches* (3rd ed.). Long Grove, IL: Wavelength Press.

Stahl, S. A., Duffy-Hester, A. M., & Stahl, K. A. D. (1998). Everything you wanted to know about phonics (but were afraid to ask). *Reading Research Quarterly, 33*, 338-355.

Tomlinson, S. M., & Evans-Hughes, G. (1991). Gender, ethnicity, and college students' responses to the Strong-Campbell Interest Inventory. *Journal of Counseling and Development, 70*, 151-155.

Winsome St. John, P. (2000). The pros and cons of data analysis software for qualitative research. *Journal of Nursing Scholarship, 32*, 393-397.

Wolff, D. (1999, October). Coming in from the cold. *Perspectives Online*. Retrieved November 22, 2007, from http://www.historians.org/perspectives/issues/1999/9910/9910ARC.CFM.

Glossary of Terms

Absolute value – the value of a number without reference to its sign (+ or -)

Accounting for variance – in correlational research it is r^2, the percentage of score fluctuations in one variable predictable based on a second variable

Achievement test – an instrument that measures an individual's knowledge or skill

Action research - a form of applied research, designed to resolve practical problems and immediate concerns at a local level

Analysis of variance (ANOVA) – a statistical procedure designed to explain the variation in scores in an experimental or quasi-experimental design

Applied research – utilizes the knowledge and theories of natural and social sciences to solve real world problems or to create new products

Aptitude test – an instrument that measures potential or predicts future performance

Artifacts – printed materials and objects that assist in the documentation of qualitative observations

Attrition – any process or event that results in the loss of subjects in an experiment

Baseline – measures of pretest performance, commonly used in single subject designs

Blinding – any procedure that controls threats to external validity by restricting information to researchers and participants

Case study – an in-depth qualitative study of a single example of a phenomenon

Chi square – a statistic used to determine whether or not the observed frequencies in a contingency table are a chance event or the result of some systematic relationship between nominal variables

Class mob – a group of pickpockets that target affluent victims

Cognitive test – an instrument designed to measure intellectual abilities

Completely randomized control group design – a quantitative method in which subjects are randomly assigned to experimental and control groups and conditions are randomly assigned to groups

Concurrent validity – validity established through correlation with another test that already has established validity

Construct validity – the extent to which an assessment adequately measures the domain of knowledge claimed by test developers

Context codes – large categories of organized data in a qualitative study

Control group – in quantitative studies, any group that does not receive the experimental treatment

Convenience sampling – the selection of an experimental sample based on ease and availability

Correlation – a statistic that is computed from two sets of data and indicates the extent to which one variable is predictable based on the other

Correlation fallacy – the belief that if two variables are correlated, then one must be causing the other

Correlation matrix – a chart or grid that shows the correlation between each variable and all the other variables in the grid

Correlational coefficient – a statistic that indicates the strength of a correlation in a sample

Criterion-referenced test – an assessment in which performances are compared against a fixed standard and not against the performances of other individuals

Counterbalancing – a control measure designed to eliminate experimenter bias and other threats to validity in an experimental design

Data – pieces of information that are used as a basis for reasoning or calculation

Data pieces – bits of information in a qualitative study

Data set – a group of numbers that have not yet been converted into a statistic

Deductive reasoning – a form of argumentation in which a set of premises leads to a conclusion

Degrees of freedom – in a *t*-Test, the number of participants in the experiment minus 2

Dependent variable – the assessment in a quantitative design

Description – the inventory, chronology, or representation of a phenomenon

Descriptive statistic – a number that summarizes or describes a set of numbers

Disordinal interaction – when two or more factors combine to produce a special effect in individual cells in an experimental or quasi-experimental design, a plot of cell means shows that the treatment had different effects on different groups

Domains – themes or patterns that emerge in a qualitative study

Double-blind procedure – a quantitative process in which both participants and researchers are ignorant with respect to assignment of individuals to treatment conditions

Effect size – an estimate of the experimental effect if the entire possible population served as subjects

Equivalent forms reliability – the correlation between two assessments designed to have identical outcomes when administered to the same group

Ethnography – the study of cultural patterns in natural settings

Exact replication – an experiment in which the methods are a duplication of the methods in a previous experiment

Experimental group – the subjects who receive the treatment in a quantitative design

Ex Post Facto design – "from a thing done afterward", a design in which there is no systematic manipulation of an independent variable

Experimental effect – in true experimental designs, differences caused by the treatment

Experimenter effects – changes in the dependent variable caused by the attitudes, biases, or other attributes of the person conducting the experiment

Explanation – incorporates the description and prediction of phenomena and states why the phenomena occurred

External validity – refers to the likelihood that phenomena observed under experimental conditions are relevant in other contexts

Face validity – a determination of validity based on common sense, professional knowledge, and logic

Factor - a name given to an independent variable in an ANOVA

F-test – the statistical significance test used when there are more than two cells in an experimental or quasi-experimental design

Generalizability – refers to the trustworthiness or relevance of a statistic or experimental outcome to environments external to the experiment

Grift – to engage in criminal activity

Hawthorne effect – an observed experimental effect that results, not from any treatment, but because subjects are part of an experiment

Historiography – the systematic collection and evaluation of information about past events

Independent variable – the method, intervention, or treatment designed to modify the dependent variable

Inductive reasoning – a from or argumentation that leads to a conclusion through the accumulation of pieces of evidence

Instrument – any structured process for collecting data

Interaction – a condition in which two or more factors combine to produce a special effect in individual cells in an experimental or quasi-experimental design

Internal consistency – an estimate of reliability based on the extent to which parts of a test correlate with each other and the total test score

Internal validity – the likelihood that the independent variable actually caused the change in the dependent variable

Interval variable – a set of numbers reflecting a scale in which the order of the numbers is mathematically meaningful and the intervals between the numbers on the scale are identical

Interviews – face-to-face procedures for obtaining information in the form of verbal responses from one or more respondents

Jug mob – a low class mob

Magnitude of the correlation – its size or strength

Main effect – the experimental effect for a factor in ANOVA

Maturation – a threat to validity when physical or psychological changes in the participants over time are the real cause of change in the dependent variable

Mean – the arithmetic average of all scores in a data set

Measurement – the quantification of experience

Measures of central tendency – the mean, median, and mode, which provide information about the center of a distribution of scores

Median – the middle score in a data set

Methodology – the participants, instrumentation, and procedures for collecting data and the design for analyzing the data in a study

Mob – a team of pickpockets

Mode – the most frequently occurring score in a data set

Multimethod research – a research method that combines aspects of quantitative and qualitative approaches into one research study

Multiple regression – or multiple correlation, is a statistical procedure in which several variables are used to predict the performance of another variable

Naturalistic research – qualitative procedures in which the researcher allows the reality of events to unfold under observation without manipulation or interference

Negative correlation – a coefficient that demonstrates the extent to which higher scores on one variable predict lower scores on a second variable

Nominal Variable – a set of numbers or other symbols that sub-classify objects or events into one or more categories

Non participant observation – a qualitative technique in which the researcher remains detached from the phenomenon under study

Nonequivalence of participants – the assumed result in a quasi-experimental design because subjects have not been randomly assigned to groups

Norm-referenced test – an instrument that compares an individual's performance with the performances of a group of individuals who have already been assessed

Normal curve – also referred to as a bell curve, a perfectly symmetrical distribution of scores

Norming group – in the development of a norm-referenced, standardized test, it is the group to which the performances of individual test-takers in the future will be compared

Null hypothesis – a research statement which posits no relationship or differences between variables

Observed frequency – with respect to Chi square, the number of observations in one cell in a contingency table

Observations – in qualitative research, watching and listening to events as they naturally unfold, then recording what was seen and heard

Ordinal interaction – a plot showing that an experimental effect is more powerful for one group than for another

Ordinal variable – – a set of numbers reflecting a scale in which the order of the numbers is mathematically meaningful and the intervals between the numbers on the scale are unequal or indeterminate

Participant observations – data collected while the researcher interacts with the culture being observed

Passage dependence – a condition in reading comprehension tests in which answers to questions can only be obtained through the reading of the text

Passage independence – a condition in reading comprehension tests in which answers to questions do not require reading the text

Pearson r – a correlational statistic used when both variables use ratio or interval scales

Percentile – a point on a scale from 1 to 99 showing the percentage of scores that fall below that point (e.g., a score with a percentile of 33 means that 33% of scores in the distribution fall below that score)

Perfect Correlation – +1 and -1, which occur when one set of scores is perfectly predicted by a second set of scores

Placebo effect – an observed experimental effect caused by the participants' expectations about the treatment rather than by the treatment itself

Population – refers to the complete set of humans, animals, plants, or objects that share a common characteristic or set of characteristics

Positive Correlation - a coefficient that demonstrates the extent to which higher scores on one variable predict higher scores on a second variable

Positivism – the belief that reality exists and that it is the researcher's task to define and describe that reality

Posttest only design – a research design that tests only after the treatment (no pretest)

Power – the capacity of a statistical significance test to detect an experimental effect

Power test – an instrument in which speed of completion is a significant factor in performance

Prediction – the ability to forecast phenomena based on systematic observations

Predictive validity – the ability of an instrument to predict events or behaviors in the future

Pretest sensitization – a threat to validity that occurs when performances on a posttest are influenced by whatever students have learned from taking the pretest

Pretest-Posttest single group design – an experimental design in which one group is tested, administered the treatment, and then tested again

Pure research – sometimes referred to as "hard" or "fundamental" research – it is designed to advance knowledge for the sake of knowledge, without regard for practical applications

Qualitative research – the inductive, nonmathematical, naturalistic collection of narrative and visual data and artifacts to explain cultural phenomena

Quantitative research – the deductive examination of phenomena by counting and measuring, usually with the assistance of instrumentation

Quasi-experimental research design – a quantitative study in which random assignment of subjects to groups is impossible

Randomization – techniques designed to ensure that the selection of subjects in a sample is free from bias that might lead to false conclusions

Range – the difference between the highest and lowest scores in a data set

Ratio variable – a set of numbers reflecting a scale in which the order of the numbers is mathematically meaningful, the intervals between the numbers on the scale are identical, and the scale includes a true zero

Raw scores – numbers in a data set that have not been used to create a statistic

Regression line – a straight line drawn through a two-variable scatter plot such that the total distance of all plots from the line is less than with any other straight line that can be drawn

Regression toward the mean – a measurement phenomenon in which subjects with extreme scores on a test or other evaluation tend to appear less extreme in a second testing, with scores gravitating toward the mean

Reliability – a measure of the extent to which an instrument is consistent and dependable

Replication – the redoing of an experiment either exactly or with some planned variation

Research – any discovery procedure that requires the systematic collection of data

Research question – a query that guides scientific investigation and data gathering

Research statement – a statement that guides scientific investigation and data gathering

Sample – a subset of individuals, items, or events selected to represent a population

Set – another term for a group

Simple random sampling – a selection process in which all individuals in a population have an equal and independent chance of being selected

Situation codes – sub-classifications of context codes

Situational variables – unexpected events that occur during a study and which may influence the fidelity of the research

Skewed distribution – data that are not distributed symmetrically

Skin the pokes – the action of emptying wallets and pocketbooks of valuables and money

Snowball sampling – a selection process in which the researcher selects a sample and then uses those individuals to recruit additional participants

Sound argument – one that is valid and in addition contains only true premises

Split-half reliability – a measure of internal consistency derived from correlating the results of two assessments that have been created from a single instrument

Stall – a pickpocket whose job is to distract the victim while another pickpocket takes the wallet or purse

Standard deviation – the square root of the variance

Standardized test – an assessment with a uniform set of procedures

Statistic – a summary or descriptive number that is created from a group or set of numbers

Statistical significance – the probability that a correlation or experimental effect is the result of sampling error

Statistical significance test – a mathematical calculation of the probability that differences between groups are an accident and not the result of the treatment

Statistics – a set of procedures for describing, analyzing and interpreting quantitative data

Stratified random sampling – a sampling procedure ensuring that individuals in the population who share a certain characteristic will be represented in the study

Structured interview – an interview in which questions are standardized and consistent in both their presentation and purpose

Structured observations – observations derived from data gathering procedures developed in advance with guiding questions

Systematic replication - an experiment in which the methods are a duplication of the methods in a previous experiment but with a planned variation (e.g., age of subjects)

Test-retest reliability – the correlation between two separate administrations of a test with the same group of individuals

Threats to validity – competing explanations for causality in experimental designs

Transformed score – one in which the numerical value of the raw score is changed into a number that shows the relationship of raw scores to each other

Treatment Fidelity – the extent to which the methodology of an experiment is conducted as planned

Triangulation – in qualitative research, the use of alternative sources of evidence to support a conclusion

T-score – standardized score with a mean of 50 and a standard deviation of 10

TIDS – factors that influence reliability: time, items, difficulty, and scope

Unstructured interview – a flexible, exploratory, qualitative data collection process without predetermined focus

Unstructured observations – observations made without predetermined focus

Valid argument – one in which the conclusion follows logically from the premises even if the premises are false

Validity – the extent to which an instrument measures what it claims to measure

Variable – in quantitative research, a concept with numerical representation

Variance – the dispersion of scores within a data set

Z-score – a statistic with a mean of 0 and a standard deviation of 1, it shows in standard deviation units where a raw score falls relative to the mean in a distribution

Appendix A
Answers to Self-Tests &

Chapter 1: Structure of Social Science Research

Self-Test
1. F
2. T
3. F
4. T
5. F
6. A
7. B
8. D
9. E
10. C

Chapter 2: Research Topics, Questions, & Statements

Self-Test
1. F
2. T
3. T
4. T
5. F
6. A
7. E
8. C
9. D
10. B

Activity 2

1. The question is unclear, violating the SMEC principle of clarity.

2. The question is too broad, violating the SMEC principle of scope.

3. The question is not researchable.

Activity 4

1. Research statements

2. The authors are stating what they expect to find based on evidence presented in the introduction.

3. Yes

Chapter 3: Review of the Literature

Self-Test
1. F   6. A
2. F   7. D
3. F   8. C
4. F   9. B
5. F   10. E

Chapter 4: Overview of Quantitative Research

Self-Test
1. T   6. D
2. F   7. A
3. T   8. A
4. F   9. D
5. T   10. B

Activity

1. Premises and conclusion

Premise 1: Segregation leads to racial hostility.

Premise 2: Self-segregation during lunch and recess is still segregation.

Premise 3: Cross-racial incidents of verbal and physical aggression are indications of racial hostility.

Premise 4: Reductions of cross-racial aggression indicate a reduction in racial hostility.

Premise 5: The experimental design will establish that reductions in racial hostility are caused by the experimental desegregation program.

Premise 6: The schools will properly implement the program.

Conclusion: Therefore, reductions in incidents of cross-racial aggression demonstrate the effectiveness of the program.

2. Valid

3. Sound

4. Individual perceptions

Chapter 5: Descriptive Statistics

Self-Test	1. F	6. D	11. 15	16. 190
	2. T	7. A	12. 7	17. 13.57
	3. F	8. B	13. 13	18. 3.68
	4. F	9. C	14. 7	19. 1.35
	5. T	10. E	15. 5	20. 4

Activity 3B

Variance = 71.06

Chapter 6: Correlation

Self-Test	1. T	6. C	11. -4.5	16. .98
	2. T	7. A	12. 17	17. 42
	3. F	8. F	13. 5.4	18. Straight line
	4. F	9. B	14. -38	19. -1
	5. F	10. E	15. 5.4	20. 100%

Activity 2

1. .40

2. .88   -.71   .55   -.16

3. 7%

4. .66

Chapter 7: Measurement

Self-Test	1. T	8. F	15. F	22. D
	2. F	9. F	16. G	23. A

3. F	10. F	17. D	24. D
4. F	11. C	18. I	25. B
5. F	12. A	19. J	
6. F	13. B	20. H	
7. F	14. E	21. B	

Activity 1

1. ordinal
2. interval
3. nominal
4. ratio

Activity 2   r = .79

Activity 3   r = .74

Activity 4   r = .77

Activity 5

1. Yes, considering the length of the article, the authors have an extensive discussion of reliability and validity of their assessments.

2. All of the coefficients in the first table on page 10 are correlations between the K-TEA and other well known reading assessments. The authors are using these correlations to establish concurrent validity of the K-TEA. Does the WRAT actually measure reading comprehension?

3. A correlation of .68 is moderate and accounts for only 46% of the variance in the scores in the two tests. With over half of the variance unaccounted for, we do not view this as a strong validity coefficient. Is the WRAT a valid measure of reading comprehension?

4. Assuming that one approach is better than the other, 60 days is a very brief period of time to expect measurable results. The teachers in the schools may have been different in their teaching skills, or some of the regular classroom teachers might not have embraced inclusion.

5. The last sentence is completely inconsistent with the outcomes of the study. There were no statistically significant differences in achievement in the two settings, yet the authors went on to recommend an increase in the number of inclusive classrooms in the school district. As an exercise in deductive reasoning, this would be like saying:

> All men are mortal.
> Socrates is a man.
> Therefore, Socrates is immortal.

Their conclusion didn't follow from the premises of the study, which makes the argument invalid.

Chapter 8: Quantitative Methods

Self-Test
1. T   6. D
2. F   7. C
3. T   8. A
4. F   9. F
5. T   10. B

Activity 1

1. Snowball
2. Simple Random
3. Convenience
4. Stratified Random

Activity 2
1. Purposive
2. Scholastic Reading Inventory
3. No
4. Marzano strategies
5. No
6. No
7. Unknown
8. Yes
9. Causal conclusions are inappropriate when there are no experimental controls or randomization procedures.

Activity 3

Step 2. 120
Step 3. 11,200,000
Step 4. 200
Step 5. 1,800
Step 6. 1,600

Step 7. 2,560,000
Step 8. 307,200,000
Step 9. 27.43
Step 10. .229
Step 11. .48

Activity 4

This is an ex post facto design and not a true experiment. There are no treatment conditions.

Chapter 9: Analyses of Variance

Self-Test
1. F   6. A
2. T   7. D
3. T   8. E
4. T   9. C
5. T   10. B

Activity 2

One possibility is that the literature read to the students was so oriented to the interests of girls that the boys failed to benefit from Mr. Gibbons and Ms. Pickles reading to them.

Activity 3

There are many missing pieces of information. Here are a few of them:

What were the reading levels of the children at the time of the experiment?
What reading program(s) is being used at Hampton?
What philosophy guides the teachers, e.g., phonics, whole language?
What literature was selected for the experimental group?
How many years have Ms. Pickles and Mr. Gibbons been teaching?
Do the teachers have master's degrees?
What is the ethnic composition of the school?
What percentages of children at Hampton are in free or reduced lunch programs?

Activity 4

Red Flags: Skimpy sample description, repeated ANOVAs, no reported effect sizes

Generalizability: This is a post hoc study laid out as an experimental design. We do not believe the results are generalizable because of the convenience sampling and lack of sample description. It seems to us the authors did a lot of speculating based upon large numbers of statistical tests that may have permitted chance differences.

Chapter 10: Research Validity

Self-Test
1. T   6. F
2. F   7. C
3. T   8. E
4. T   9. B
5. T   10. D

Activity 1

Scenario 1: Nonequivalence of participants and maturation
Scenario 2: Nonequivalence of participants
Scenario 3: Treatment fidelity
Scenario 4: Regression to the mean

Activity 2

Scenario 1: Placebo, experimenter, and Hawthorne effects
Scenario 2: Poor generalizability
Scenario 3: Pretest sensitization
Scenario 4: Experimenter effects
Scenario 5: Hawthorne effects

Activity 4

1. Yes, nonequivalence of participants, treatment fidelity, placebo effects, Hawthorne effects, and experimenter effects
2. Generalizability
3. Yes, white counselor trainees in large master's degree programs
4. 9

Chapter 11: Qualitative Research I: Characteristics, Use & Design

Self-Test   1. T   6. C

2. F   7. A
3. T   8. B
4. F   9. E
5. T   10. D

Activity 1

Scenario 1: inductive, weak

Tim has worked with two couples and it's been easy. His conclusion that his future experiences in marriage counseling will be the same is an example of a weak inductive argument. It is similar to the "rotten apple" argument.

Scenario 2: deductive, unsound

If it were true that all 10th grade students enjoy reading the Merchant of Venice, then it would follow that Carlota would as well. However, the premise about all 10th grade students is almost certainly false. This is a valid deductive argument but it is unsound because it has a false premise.

Scenario 3: deductive, invalid, unsound

The key here is in realizing that this is quantitative research because Ms. Munson is comparing groups using a formal assessment. This makes it a deductive argument, which in this case is both invalid and unsound. Ms. Munson seems to begin with a premise that she can determine something about student performance and curriculum by contrasting low achieving with high achieving students. In addition, her conclusion is unrelated to the data or the conditions under which it was collected. The conclusion does not follow from the premises. The experiment was not about testing the value of phonics programs in general. This would be like saying:

> All phonics programs are great.
> Reading Adventure is a phonics program.
> Therefore, we should increase the budget for the school library.

Scenario 4: inductive, strong

Ms. Harper has documented eight instances of African-American students having problems with Ms. Langley, and her fear that Jimmy could be number nine seems reasonable under the circumstances. This is a strong inductive argument.

An alternative interpretation is that Ms. Harper's reasoning is deductive in nature:

> Ms. Langley has issues with African-American male students.   (Premise)

Jimmy is an African-American male student.   (Premise)
Therefore, Ms. Langley might have issues with Jimmy.   (Conclusion)

In this interpretation the answers to the activity would be deductive, valid, and unsound. The first premise is questionable.

Chapter 12: Qualitative Research II: Data & Analysis

Self-Test
1. T
2. T
3. F
4. T
5. F
6. F
7. T
8. F
9. B
10. C
11. A
12. E
13. D
14. I
15. J
16. H
17. G

Activity 3

1. "Thoughtful social scientists and researchers have raised significant questions about the limitations of quantitative data."

The validity and reliability of standardized measures could be compromised by the potential conflict of the two goals of the study.

Qualitative methodology would "provide a richer and more comprehensive data base from which recommendations could be generated."

2. Data was gathered from three sources. Using two research teams provided "cross-verification of conclusions."

Activity 5

1. Responses to the interviews were analyzed by the two interviewers. They identified similarities and discrepancies in responses to the interview questions within and across the groups. Recurring themes in responses were identified and categorized. All data was analyzed in the same manner by two research teams.

2. They located published research that had results consistent with this study.

3. The researchers speculate that there may be insufficient trust among colleagues for this type of evaluation to be conducted by the employees themselves and that an outsider's perspective is needed to maintain objectivity. They support this notion by referring to anthropological paradigms.

4. The authors present their procedures and their results in detail. They support their conclusions with literature and defend their approach. However, they also identify limitations to their study and make suggestions for alternate procedures that could be used in future, similar studies. Readers are asked to "consider using qualitative methodologies" in their own research, and to review the authors' data, relying on their own perspectives and allowing for "identification of patterns in the data" from those perspectives.

Chapter 13: Multimethod Research

Activity 2

1. What happens when students enrolled in a basic skills reading course experience critical literacy as an entrance into academic modes of discourse?

2. Qualitative (using a qualitative interpretive method) Quantitative (norm-referenced test scores and surveys)

3. The question broadly asks for "what happens." This will require detailed description of events. Some of what happens may be reflected in measurable skills so test scores and surveys may be valuable.

4. Qualitative – interest inventories; responses to literature; writing samples, focus group interviews and class discussions (through linguistic coding) Quantitative – norm-referenced test scores (Nelson-Denny) and surveys

5. In detailed textual descriptions; in graphs and figures

6. To what extent do the students enrolled in this course construct or begin to construct themselves as readers and writers through the means of critical reflection and critical literacy pedagogy?

7. Both

8. Some of the reading behaviors are measurable (counts of specific behaviors), but descriptions of student interview responses are also needed.

9. The researcher used 22 students enrolled in her literacy course because they all were investigating critical literacy for the first time. They were an appropriate sample because they met the research question subject criteria; all college students and all enrolled in a basic literacy course.

Appendix B
Supplemental Readings

Pet Bonding and Pet Bereavement Among Adolescents

Brenda H. Brown, Herbert C. Richards, and Carol A. Wilson

> The authors studied adolescent-pet bonding and bereavement following pet loss. Three hypotheses were entertained: (a) Adolescents who are highly bonded to a pet experience more intense grief when it dies than do those less bonded; (b) degree of bonding, when measured by self-disclosure, is greater for girls than for boys; and (c) intensity of bereavement is greater for girls than for boys. To test the hypotheses and provide descriptive data about bonding to various species, 55 adolescents who had recently experienced pet death were administered background questionnaires, Companion Animal Bonding Scales (Poresky, Hendrix, & Mosier, 1987), Pet Attitude Scales (Poresky, Hendrix, & Mosier, 1988), and Texas Inventory of Grief Scales (Faschingbauer, 1981). Results supported the hypotheses. Suggestions for counselors are offered.

Most children and adolescents at one time or another express a strong desire to own a pet (Kidd & Kidd, 1985; Salmon, 1982). Pets offer affection, intimacy, and unconditional love—all qualities essential for the emotional health and sense of well-being of children (Blue, 1986; Levinson, 1980). For many adolescents, pets serve as silent counselors, best friends, and even surrogate siblings (Arehart-Treichel, 1982; Beck & Katcher, 1983). Although many counselors now recognize the prominent role played by animals in the emotional lives of young people (Barker, 1993), there has been little empirical investigation of the counseling implications of pet death (Sharkin & Bahrick, 1990).

Evidence is accumulating, however, that children develop strong emotional attachments to their pets (Rynearson, 1978; Nieburg, 1981). Such attachments can be as intense as the emotional bonds between people (Katcher & Rosenberg, 1979; Voith, 1985). Once such a bond has formed, the loss of a beloved animal, as that of a family member, is traumatic. For many young people, their first experience with death is that of a pet. It is hardly surprising, then, that pet death is the most frequently reported stressor among preadolescents (Greene & Brooks, 1985). Although not as well researched, adolescents also seem to form strong bonds with animals. For them, bonding provides an anchor during the tumultuous years of puberty—a steady, reliable source of affection in a life filled with insecurity and rapid change.

It is a common observation that a period of bereavement follows the loss of a loved one, whether animal or human. As far as grieving is concerned, there is little difference between loss of human beings and that of pets (Levinson, 1981; Nieburg, 1981). In fact, Quackenbush and Graveline (1985) argued that loss of a pet can evoke the same sequence of psychological reactions as those observed by Kübler-Ross (1969): denial, anger, bargaining, depression, and acceptance. "So, in many ways, you can expect to grieve for your pet as you would for a human family member" (Quackenbush & Graveline, 1985, p. 34). For adolescents and children alike, bereavement can be intense and lengthy when such a bond is broken (Stewart, 1983).

There are, of course, individual differences in the degree to which someone bonds with an animal. It seems plausible to suppose that intensity of bonding strongly influences the course of bereavement following a pet's death. For young adolescents, many of whom are in the midst of great emotional upheaval, the link between bonding and bereavement should be especially evident. Therefore, the major hypothesis of this investigation is that the strength of the bond between an adolescent and his or her pet will predict the intensity of bereavement following the loss of the animal.

Evidence also shows that bonding, as assessed through self-report, varies according to sex. Kidd & Kidd (1985), for example, found that 94% of the children they surveyed said that they loved their pets, but the boys in their sample reported loving their pets to a significantly lesser degree than did the girls. Interestingly, these same boys described giving and receiving affection from their pets as often as girls did. The boys may have loved their pets as much as the girls, but were less willing to disclose their feelings. Perhaps the reluctance of boys to be so forthright is dictated by a cultural tradition in which men are expected to be less expressive. Whatever the explanation for these effects, a secondary hypothesis of the study is that the degree of bonding, at least when measured by self-disclosure, will be greater for girls than for boys.

The purpose of the current study is twofold: (a) Descriptive data about pet ownership among adolescents and the degree of bonding occasioned by various types of animals is examined, and (b) Test results are reported for the following hypotheses:

1. The intensity of the bond between an adolescent and a pet will predict the intensity of bereavement following the loss of the animal. That is, adolescents who are highly bonded to a pet will experience more intense grief when it dies than will those less bonded.
2. The degree of bonding, at least when measured by self-disclosure, will be greater for girls than for boys.
3. As a logical consequence of Hypotheses 1 and 2, intensity of bereavement will be greater for girls than for boys.

METHOD

Participants

A total of 55 adolescents (27 boys and 28 girls) between the ages of 12 and 17 years participated in the study. These young people lived in rural and small city environments within a 150 square mile area encompassing parts of northwestern Maryland, southern Pennsylvania, and eastern West Virginia. Most were middle class; all but 4 were White. They had all experienced the death of a pet within the year previous to the study.

Procedure

Young people were recruited from local 4-H and Boy Scout organizations, 9th- and 10th-grade classes at area high schools, and referrals from friends and colleagues (none of the potential participants was known to any of the investigators, however). The senior investigator spoke privately to each about conditions for participation, invited him or her to join the study, and administered a prescreening instrument.

Prescreening. To avoid recording spuriously high levels of grief following pet loss, it was important to minimize the effects of other stressful life events. For this reason, each potential participant was screened with the modified Adolescent Life Change Event Scale (ALCES). The ALCES is a 24-item, self-report measure of stress that has been validated for individuals ranging in age from 12 to 29 years (Forman, Eidson, & Hagan, 1983). Items consist of a rank-order listing of potential life changes that are known to be stressful (pet loss is ranked 11th). Anyone who marked any item more stressful than pet loss was excluded from participation in the study.

Data collection. After the prescreening, those who remained in the study were given the instrument package and provided with directions for completing it. They were also provided with consent forms to be signed by a parent or guardian and stamped, addressed envelopes for returning completed questionnaires.

Measures

Companion Animal Bonding Scale (CABS). The CABS provides a sensitive "assessment of self-reported behavior indicative of the establishment of a bond between a person and an animal" (Poresky, Hendrix, & Mosier, 1987, p. 744). The CABS has been validated for college and high school students (ranging in age from 14 to 47 years); reliability estimates (internal consistency) ranged from .77 to .82 for those samples.

The CABS consists of eight items that ask about a variety of human-animal interactions (e.g., "How often were you responsible for your pet's care?" "How often did you hold, stroke, or caress your pet?" "How often did you sleep near your pet?"). Each item is scored on a 1 to 5 Likert scale (*always* = 5 to *never* = 1), and a total score is obtained by summing across items.

Companion Animal Semantic Differential. This instrument, also referred to as the Pet Attitude Scale (PAS), was designed to assess "the respondent's perception of a childhood companion animal" (Poresky, Hendrix, Mosier, 1988, p. 257). The PAS is internally consistent (alphas as high as .90 have been reported), and it is correlated with the CABS ($r = .54$).

The PAS consists of 18 bipolar, semantic differential word pairs (e.g., beautiful–ugly, kind–cruel, trusting–fearful). To express how they feel about their pets, respondents are instructed to place a check in one of six spaces between word pairs. To reduce acquiescence response set, eight of the items are directionally transposed—that is, the positive adjective appears on the right rather than on the left. Each item is scored so that a higher number indicates a more positive attitude. Total PAS scores, are obtained by summing across the 18 scales. As with the CABS, higher PAS scores indicate stronger bonding.

Bereavement. The Texas Revised Inventory of Grief (TRIG) is a self-report measure that "permits rapid evaluation of the extremity and nature of an individual's personal reaction to bereavement" (Faschingbauer, 1981, p. 2). Reliabilities of TRIG subscales have been found to range from .70 to .90.

As a warm-up, respondents rate the closeness of their relationship to a pet (e.g., "closer than any relationship I've had before or since with a pet," "closer than most relationships I've had with other pets") and whether the animal's death was expected, unexpected, slow, or sudden. The main body of the TRIG is divided into three parts. The first includes eight items about feelings and actions immediately following the pet's demise (e.g., "I found it hard to do my school work or chores well after my pet died"). Respondents register their reactions on 5-point Likert scales (ranging from *completely true* to *completely false*). Items are scored 1 to 5; higher scores indicate more grief. A total (called a "past" score) is obtained by summing across the eight items.

The second part features 13 statements about present feelings (e.g., "I still want to cry when I think of my pet who died"). As with the first, 5-point Likert scales are used to assess levels of grief. A total (called a "present" score) is obtained by summing across the 13 items. As with the past scale, higher scores indicate higher levels of grief. Past and present scores tend to be moderately correlated (in our study, the correlation was .59, $p < .001$), and a reliable total score can be obtained by summing across the two scales.

The third part contains three true-or-false questions. Respondents are asked whether they feel grieved about the pet who died, whether they are now functioning as well as before the death, and whether they believe they have the same illness as the pet.

After completing the TRIG, respondents were thanked and invited to write down any special thoughts and feelings.

Background information and consent form. Each participant filled out a demographic questionnaire that asked about age, sex, race, education level, religious affiliation, type of pet (e.g., cat, dog, horse), date of the animal's death, family income, and number of other pets and people in the household. A document explaining the nature of the study, the rights and obligations of participants, and a place for parents or guardians to sign for permission to participate was also included.

Preliminary Analyses

Bonding scale reduction. The CABS and PAS yield scores that are incommensurate, but they are intended to measure the same underlying construct. With this in mind, the two bonding scales were reduced to a single continuum:

First, to confirm the notion that the CABS and PAS measure the same construct, the correlation between the two scales was computed. In accord with expectations, the two bonding scales were positively intercorrelated ($r = .48$, $p < .001$). This correlation is similar to the one ($r = .54$) reported by Poresky et al. (1988).

Second, means and standard deviations were obtained for the two scales. Based on these statistics, raw scores were converted to standardized t scores. Third, composite bonding scores were obtained by adding CABS t scores to PAS t scores.

Finally, to create groups of nearly equal size, respondents were ranked according to composite bonding score. The 18 highest scorers were classified as "high bonders" (bonding group = 3); the 18 lowest as "low bonders" (bonding group = 1). The remaining 19 were classified as "medium bonders" (bonding group = 2).

Grief scale reduction. The combined grief scores were obtained by summing the past and present Texas Revised Inventory of Grief (TRIG) scores. In addition, the two warm-up items on the TRIG ("closeness" and "suddenness") were scored on 5-point scales, with higher scores indicating greater closeness or greater suddenness.

Descriptive data and validating correlations. Means and standard deviations for the bonding scales (CABS and PAS), grief scales (Past and Present), closeness to pet, suddenness of death, and the TRIG (third part) items (really grieved, now functioning well, and same illness as pet), are shown in Table 1. These same statistics for background information questionnaire items also are presented.

To check the validity of bonding group (BG) classifications and combined grief scores (Grief), correlations were obtained with all the measures listed in Table 1. If the combined grief scale is valid, it was deemed logical that this scale would be positively correlated with all the bonding and TRIG measures except "now functioning well" (i.e., individuals experiencing more grief probably grieve longer and, as a consequence, are less likely to be "now functioning well"). As can be seen in Table 1, all correlations with grief are positive and significant. It also was anticipated that some measures would be more correlated with bonding and others with grief. For example, it was logical to suppose that ratings of closeness would be more correlated with bonding than with grief, although both would likely be positive. Overall, the pattern of correlations support the validity of the BG and grief scales.

In closing this section, it is interesting to find age negatively correlated with grief, the only significant link with the background indexes. Apparently, older children grieve less following pet loss, or perhaps they admit to grieving less than their younger counterparts.

RESULTS

The first hypotheses was that adolescents who are highly bonded to a pet will experience more intense grief when it dies than those less bonded. Because the TRIG yields two correlated scores (past and present grief), a multivariate analysis was conducted to test this hypothesis (Tabachnick & Fidell, 1983). A three-group multivariate analysis of variance of the two TRIG scales yielded a significant Wilks's lambda (.662, $p < .01$). As an aid to interpreting this result, three univariate tests of the same design were conducted on the two TRIG and combined grief scales (Cooley & Lohnes, 1971). All three analyses yielded significant F-ratios, $F(2, 52) = 4.02$, $p < .04$, for past; $F(2, 52) = 12.75$, $p < .01$, for present; and $F = 11.07$, $p < .01$, for combined grief. The univariate tests are not independent (the pooled within-group correlation was .50), and judgments about respective effects on the individual scales should be avoided. Means and standard deviations of the grief scales as a function of bonding group are shown in Table 2. Collectively, the results supported the first hypothesis. Mean differences favoring high bonders are evident on all three TRIG scales.

To test the notion that bonding (second hypothesis) and grief scores (third hypothesis) are higher for girls than for boys, the data were sorted according to sex. As with the first analysis, there were two correlated dependent variables for each comparison. Two Hotelling T tests, one for each hypothesis, yielded significant results, $T(2, 52) = .168$, $p < .05$, for the bonding scales; $T(2, 52) = .269$, $p < .01$, for the grief scales. Means, standard deviations, and univariate t-ratios are shown as a function of sex in Table 3.

As with the first hypothesis, the second and third were supported by the data. Significant differences in the predicted direction were found for all the bonding and grief scales. Especially strong effects were evident on the PAS and the present subscale of the TRIG. There can be little doubt that girls score higher than do boys on both the bonding and grief scales.

DISCUSSION

The results support all three hypotheses of the study. As shown in Table 2, mean differences in grief scores between high and low bonders are substantial (especially on the present scale of the TRIG) and in the direction predicted by Hypothesis 1. These findings accord well with our initial ideas and, assuming the bonds of affection between person and animal are similar in kind to those between humans, with the broader literature on attachment (Bowlby, 1980). As far as adolescents are concerned, the data also support Raphael's (1983) assertion that loss of a pet can be of paramount importance to an adolescent. "If his pet has been a valued source of attachment, as well as serving symbolic needs, he is likely to grieve and mourn for him." (p. 146). Taken at face value, our results suggest that attachment and bereavement go hand in hand.

The data also support our conjecture about girls tending to form deeper bonds with their pets than do boys (Hypothesis 2). As can be

TABLE 1

Means, Standard Deviations, and Correlations of Selected Measures With Bonding Group Classification and Combined Grief Scale

Measure	M	SD	Bonding Group	Grief
Bonding scales				
CABS	25.33	6.33	.73**	.35**
PAS	97.76	10.25	.66**	.49**
Grief scales				
TRIG (Past)	20.35	7.75	.35**	.83**
TRIG (Present)	42.33	12.21	.57**	.94**
Additional TRIG items				
Closeness to pet	3.71	1.05	.33**	.31*
Suddenness of death	3.16	1.36	−.13	.30*
Really grieved	1.83	0.38	.24*	.36**
Now functioning well	1.88	0.32	−.01	−.40**
Same illness as pet	1.04	0.19	.00	.27*
Demographic questionnaire				
Age of respondent	15.25	1.58	−.17	−.37**
Household size	4.00	0.96	−.22	.00
Number of pets	4.35	5.49	.00	.11
Pet was replaced	1.56	0.50	.05	.05

Note. Underlined correlations are expected to be higher than corresponding nonunderlined entries. CABS = Companion Animal Bonding Scale. PAS = Pet Attitude Scale. TRIG = Texas Revised Inventory of Grief.
*$p < .05$. **$p < .01$.

TABLE 2

Means and Standard Deviations of the TRIG Scales as a Function of Bonding Group

	Bonding Group							
	Low ($n = 18$)		Medium ($n = 19$)		High ($n = 18$)		Total	
Grief Scale	M	SD	M	SD	M	SD	M	SD
Past	17.67	8.01	19.16	7.35	24.28	6.61	20.35	7.75
Present	34.11	12.81	41.68	8.29	51.22	8.98	42.33	12.21
Combined	51.78	18.73	60.84	14.14	75.50	12.26	62.67	17.89

Note. TRIG = Texas Revised Inventory of Grief.

seen in Table 3, bonding score means are in the predicted direction and statistically significant, but the distributions overlap. Many boys in our sample scored high on the bonding scales; some girls scored low. The following comment written by a 15year-old boy is eloquent testimony that boys as well as girls can develop strong bonds with a pet:

> Well, my bunny Peter CottonTail (Pete) was 14 years old.... He and I would sleep on my uncle's couch in the garage. He was the first pet to belong totally to me. I cared for him... I loved Pete. I have nothing now but memories & photos.

Counselors would be well advised to avoid inferring too much about pet bonding on the basis of gender alone.

Our findings also support the notion that girls express more grief than boys do following pet death (Hypothesis 3). Again referring to Table 3, it can be seen that grief score means, like bonding score means, are in the predicted direction and the differences significant. On the present scale of the TRIG, the difference is nearly a full standard deviation—a result that supports the conclusions of Kidd and Kidd (1985) cited earlier. These results also help explain why Quackenbush and Glickman (1984) found that 79% of the 138 young people seeking therapy for pet bereavement were female. Still, there is substantial overlap, and many boys grieve just as deeply over the loss of their pets. Moreover, sex differences may be explained in more than one way. It is not known, for example, whether boys truly experience less grieving or, because of cultural expectations, admit less grieving on questionnaires (Stoddard & Henry, 1985).

Perhaps some of the most useful insights of this study emerged from informal observations and comments written on questionnaires rather than from the quantitative data. When visiting families, it was common for parents to express relief that their son or daughter "had someone to talk to." A 16-year-old girl wrote, "I think it is great that you are this interested in the feelings of people that have lost pets." Another 17-year-old girl added, "I would just like to thank you for doing this project. It really does mean a lot to me knowing that someone is interested in this subject." The major implication for counselors, then, is to treat pet loss and the grief such loss engenders seriously—as seriously as loss of a family member.

Another useful insight emerges from comments about the role of open expression of grief and burial rituals. One youngster wrote about how the family left the veterinarian's office with their euthanized dog and drove to their minister's home to request that he say a prayer over the body. The preacher invited them to bring their deceased pet into the chapel to be placed at the base of the altar. As the family prayed, the minister read scripture and said a closing prayer. The pet was buried beneath its favorite bush in the family's backyard. As other authors have pointed out (e.g., Quackenbush, 1982; Stewart, 1983), a ceremony may help to bring closure to the grieving process.

Based on the literature and our own findings, the following recommendations are offered for counselors dealing with young people who have lost a pet:

1. As with any grieving person, understand and accept the genuineness of the bereavement.
2. Because society tends to ignore, discount, or trivialize the impact of pet loss, some adolescents may repress their feelings (Sharkin & Bahrick, 1990). It is therefore important to provide validation that such feelings are normal (Carmack, 1985).
3. Explain the typical stages of grief, and how they relate to the death of a pet.
4. Recognize that a young person will likely find little social support in dealing with the loss of a pet. Alert friends and family to the necessity of providing such support.
5. Explore the depth of the bond that existed with the pet to better understand the grief being experienced.

In concluding this discussion, an important limitation of this research should be mentioned. The geographical area where the data were collected yielded homogenous (nearly all White) samples that do not represent the cultural diversity of the nation as a whole. Customs, traditions, and socioeconomic differences elsewhere, especially in urban areas, might mitigate against the anthropomorphic revering of animals so common among our participants. Before counselors in less homogenous settings apply our recommendations, it is important to replicate this research in more culturally diverse geographical regions.

TABLE 3

Means, Standard Deviations, and *t*-ratios of the Companion Animal Bonding Scales (CABS), Pet Attitude Scales (PAS), and TRIG Scales as a Function of Sex

Scale	Boys ($n = 27$)		Girls ($n = 28$)		*t*-ratio
	M	SD	M	SD	
Bonding scales					
CABS	23.85	6.72	26.75	5.69	−1.73*
PAS	93.89	12.88	101.50	4.56	−2.90**
Bonding Composite	93.88	20.35	105.89	11.02	−2.71**
Grief scales					
TRIG (Past)	18.63	8.45	22.00	6.74	−1.64*
TRIG (Present)	36.70	11.88	47.75	9.99	−3.74**
Combined Grief	55.33	17.53	69.75	15.44	−3.24**

Note. TRIG = Texas Revised Inventory of Grief.
*$p < .05$, one-tailed test. **$p < .01$, one-tailed test.

REFERENCES

Arehart-Treichel, J. (1982). Pets: The health benefits. *Science News, 121*, 220-223.

Barker, S. B. (1993). Pet owners no longer grieve alone. *American Counselor, 2*, 26-31.

Beck, A. M., & Katcher, A. H. (1983). *Between pets and people.* New York: Putnam.

Blue, G. F. (1986). The value of pets in children's lives. *Childhood Education, 24*, 85-89.

Bowlby, J. (1980). *Attachment and loss: Vol. III. Loss, sadness and depression.* New York: Basic Books.

Carmack, B. J. (1985). The effects on family members and functioning after death of a pet. *Marriage and Family Review, 8*, 149-161.

Cooley, W. W., & Lohnes, P. R. (1971). *Multivariate data analysis.* New York: Wiley.

Faschingbauer, T. R. (1981). *Texas Revised Inventory of Grief.* Houston, TX: Honeycomb.

Forman, B. D., Eidson, K., & Hagan, B. J. (1983). Measuring perceived stress in adolescents: A cross validation. *Adolescence, 18*, 573-576.

Greene, A. L., & Brooks, J. (1985, April). *Children's perceptions of stressful life events*. Poster presented at the biennial meeting of Society for Research on Child Development, Toronto, Canada.

Katcher, A. H., & Rosenberg, M.A. (1979). Euthanasia and the management of the clients' grief. *Compendium on Continuing Education for the Small Animal Practitioner, 2,* 177-122.

Kidd, A. H., & Kidd, R. M. (1985). Children's attitudes toward their pets. *Psychology Reports, 57,* 15-31.

Kübler-Ross, E. (1969). *On death and dying*. New York: Macmillan.

Levinson, B. M. (1980). The child and his pet: A world of nonverbal communication. In S. A. Corson & E. O. Corson (Eds.), *Ethology and nonverbal communication in mental health*. Oxford: Pergamon.

Levinson, B. M. (1981). Human grief in the loss of an animal companion. *Foundation of Thanatology: Archives, 9,* 5.

Nieburg, H. A. (1981). Pathologic grief response to pet loss. *Foundation of Thanatology: Archives, 9,* 7.

Poresky, R. H., Hendrix, C., & Mosier, J. E. (1987). The Companion Animal Bonding Scale: Internal reliability and construct validity. *Psychological Reports, 60,* 743-746.

Poresky, R. H., Hendrix, C., & Mosier, J. E. (1988). The Companion Animal Semantic Differential: Long and short form reliability and validity. *Educational and Psychological Measurement, 48,* 255-260.

Quackenbush, J. E. (1982). The social context of pet loss. *Animal Health Technician, 3,* 333-337.

Quackenbush, J. E., & Glickman, L. (1984). Helping people adjust to the death of a pet. *Health and Social Work, 9,* 42-48.

Quackenbush, J. E. & Graveline, D. (1985). *When your pet dies: How to cope with your feelings*. New York: Simon & Schuster.

Raphael, B. (1983). *The anatomy of bereavement*. New York: Basic Books.

Rynearson, E. K. (1978). Humans and pets and attachment. *British Journal of Psychiatry, 131,* 550-555.

Salmon, A. (1982). Montreal children in the light of the test of animal infinities. *Annals Medico-Psychologiques, 140,* 207-224.

Sharkin, B. S., & Bahrick, A. S. (1990). Pet loss: Implications for counselors. *Journal of Counseling & Development, 68,* 306-308.

Stewart, M. (1983). Loss of a pet—loss of a person. In A. H. Katcher & A. M. Beck (Eds.), *New perspectives on our lives with companion animals*. Philadelphia: University of Pennsylvania.

Stoddard, J. B., & Henry, J. P. (1985). Affectional bonding and the impact of bereavement. *Advances, 2,* 19-28.

Tabachnick, B. G., & Fidell, L. S. (1983). *Using multivariate statistics*. New York: Harper & Row.

Voith, V. L. (1985). Attachment of people to companion animals. *Veterinary Clinics of North America, 15,* 289-295.

Brenda H. Brown *is a counselor at Frederick High School in Frederick, MD.* **Herbert C. Richards** *is a professor of educational psychology at the Curry School of Eduction, University of Virginia.* **Carol A. Wilson** *is a postdoctoral fellow in the Department of Psychology, University of Utah. Correspondence regarding this article should be sent to Brenda H. Brown, Frederick High School, 650 Carroll Pkwy., Frederick, MD 21701.*

Gender, Ethnicity, and College Students' Responses to the Strong-Campbell Interest Inventory

SAUNDRA M. TOMLINSON and GWENDOLYN EVANS-HUGHES

In this study we investigated the career interest patterns of White American, African American, and Hispanic students attending a summer orientation program at a predominantly White university. A total of 77 students completed the Strong-Campbell Interest Inventory (SCII). Responses were analyzed by gender and ethnicity. The results indicated a gender effect for the Realistic theme. There were no ethnic differences in responses; there was, however, an interaction effect for gender and ethnicity on the Artistic theme and on the two special scales of the SCII: Academic Comfort (AC) and Introversion-Extroversion (I-E). Implications of the findings are discussed.

Este estudio investiga la distribución del interés por una carrera de estudiantes Anglo-Americanos, Afro-Americanos, e Hispanos que asisten a un programa de orientación durante el verano en una universidad que es en su mayor parte anglo-sajona. Setenta y siete estudiantes respondieron a el inventorio Strong-Campbell Interest. Se analizaron las respuestas según género y etnia. Los resultados indicaron un efecto de género para el Tema Realista. No había diferencias étnicas en las respuestas, a pesar de eso, había un efecto de interacción entre género y etnia en el Tema Artístico, y en las dos Escalas Especiales de SCII: Academic Confort e Introversión-Extroversión. Se discuten las implicaciones de los resultados.

A traditional approach to career decision making requires that a student conduct an accurate self-assessment, which includes an identification of personal attributes such as interests, abilities, and values. Counselors often use a variety of information-gathering techniques to aid in the assessment process. The Strong-Campbell Interest Inventory (SCII; Hansen & Campbell, 1985) was rated among the most preferred or frequently used career assessment instruments in college counseling centers (Engen, Lamb, & Prediger, 1982; Zytowski & Warman, 1982). Kapes and Mastie (1988) cautioned that popularity of an instrument should not be confused with effectiveness for a particular need.

Men and women tend to respond differently to occupational interest inventories (Fitzgerald & Betz, 1983). Men are more likely to prefer realistic, investigative, and enterprising occupations, whereas women prefer social, artistic, and conventional occupations (Gottfredson, Holland, & Gottfredson, 1975). Holland (1975) suggested that such preferences exist because of the incorporation of social and occupational sex typing in the Holland types. White, Kruczeck, Brown, and White (1989) used the SCII to investigate occupational stereotyping among college students and found a decline in the degree to which students stereotyped occupations according to gender. Their data, however, indicated that the SCII contained occupations that were in favor of stereotyping masculine fields.

The development of vocational types results from several genetic, cultural, personal, and environmental forces (Holland, 1985). Life history experiences, as measured by the Biographical Questionnaire (Owens & Schoenfeldt, 1979) were found to account for as much as 35% of the variance in the vocational interests of college students (Eberhardt & Muchinsky, 1982).

Gender and family background were among the life history influences found to affect the development of social, investigative, and enterprising typologies (Smart, 1989).

The relationship between race-ethnicity and career assessment instruments remains a focus of concern. African American college students are reported to show career interest patterns and career choice patterns in social occupations (Doughtie, Chang, Alston, Wakefield, & Yom, 1976; Hager & Elton, 1971). This tendency to manifest higher interest in occupations with social themes is further indicated by the underrepresentation of African Americans, Hispanics, and Native Americans in realistic and investigative academic majors and occupations (Bayer, 1972; Smith, 1975, 1980). Although Holland (1975) did not address the role of race in his theory, he noted that this does not mean that race differences have no influence on vocational behavior.

The psychometric validity of career assessment instruments with Black Americans and other "visible racial/ethnic group" members—referring to Black, Hispanic, Asian, Native American—(Cook & Helms, 1988) has been strongly questioned (Carter & Swanson, 1990; Smith 1983; Williams, 1982). Carter and Swanson (1990) suggested that the interest patterns of Blacks reveal differences in the formation, meaning, and expression of interests as compared with the interest patterns of Whites. Other studies have reported that interest inventories are in fact invalid with Blacks (Cameron, 1970). Borgen and Harper (1973) found that interest inventories may be valid with Black collegians with reasonably strong academic backgrounds, and cautioned the use of interest inventories with individuals that differ from the norm sample.

Academic Comfort (AC) is one of the special scales of the SCII that has received both positive and negative support. Academic

Comfort is an indictor of interests that predicts persistence in an educational environment (Swanson & Hansen, 1985). Women generally score higher on AC than do men (Hansen & Campbell, 1985; Swanson & Hansen, 1985). The AC scale has been moderately correlated with grade point average, strongly related to educational level, and positively related to educational goals (Swanson & Hansen, 1985). Because of the recent charges concerning the validity of career assessment instruments with "visible racial-ethnic group" members, one might question the use of such a scale as a measure of persistence in educational settings for multicultural populations.

Cheatham (1990) posed two questions that are fundamental to a discussion of multiculturalism and counseling: (a) Do current career development and choice theories and standardized assessments presume an understanding and appreciation for the valued experiences of all of "societies co-cultures?" (b) Are sociocultural and sociohistorical distinctions relevant to the client incorporated into counseling practice? In light of these current challenges to the relevance of traditional or etic approaches of career development and choice across gender and ethnicity, in addition to issues concerning the validity of career assessment instruments—with specific reference to the Strong Vocational Interest Blank (SVIB) and the SCII (SCII; Carter & Swanson, 1990)—it is imperative that counselors explore the meaning, experiences, history, and culture that have shaped the interest patterns of students.

The application of Holland's theory with a multicultural sample is limited. Few data have been generated using the SCII with a diverse multicultural sample. Much of the previous research with the SCII and college students has focused on sex typing of occupational preferences and validity studies (Hansen & Swanson, 1983; Spokane, 1979; Whitton, 1975). Few studies have attempted to assess the career interest patterns of a racially-ethnically diverse group of college men and women in the early stages of career awareness and exploration.

The purpose of our study was (a) to assess the career interests of a multicultural student group and (b) to determine the relationship of gender and ethnicity to measured interest patterns. Of particular interest in this study were the response patterns by gender and ethnicity on the two special scales of the SCII: the Academic Comfort (AC) scale and the Introversion-Extroversion (I-E) scale. The following null hypothesis was tested: There are no differences, by ethnicity and gender, in the career interest patterns of incoming college students.

METHOD

Participants

Participants were 77 students enrolled in a summer orientation program at a large, predominantly White, eastern public university. The purpose of the summer program was to acclimate incoming first-year students to university life. The majority of the participants were African American, consisting of 12 White Americans (7 men and 5 women), 51 African Americans (17 men and 34 women), and 14 Hispanic Americans (8 men and 6 women). The composition of the Hispanic sample was predominantly Puerto Rican (86%). The age range of the participants was 17 to 25 years, with an age median of 18 years.

Procedure

Students were administered the Strong Campbell Interest Inventory of the Strong Vocational Interest Blank within the first 2 weeks of their arrival at the university. A career counselor from the Office of Career Services administered the inventory to the students in a group setting. The counselor explained the purpose of the inventory and answered all questions. Participation was voluntary. The participants received no course credit for completing the SCII. Each student was assured confidentiality.

Instruments

The Strong-Campbell Interest Inventory of the Strong Vocational Interest Blank (Hansen & Campbell, 1985) is a 325-item scale designed to measure an individual's (a) occupational interests, (b) interest in various leisure activities, and (c) interest in working or living in a variety of environments. The 1985 edition features 264 scales including 6 General Occupational Themes (GOT), 23 Basic Interest Scales (BIS), 207 occupational scales, 2 special scales and 26 administrative indexes (Hansen, 1986). A respondent is asked to answer "like," "indifferent," or "dislike" to each of the listed occupations, school subjects, occupational activities, leisure activities, types of people, and his or her own characteristics.

General Occupational Themes. The GOT scales are organized within Holland's theoretical premise of personality and work environments (Holland, 1966, 1976, 1985). Holland's six orientations are R, I, A, S, E, C (Realistic, Investigative, Artistic, Social, Enterprising, and Conventional). The GOT scales are the most general of the SCII scales (Borgen, 1988). They are cited as especially useful with individuals beginning to think about careers as well as in helping counselors to choose counseling techniques that match client preferences (Hansen, 1984). The median of test-retest reliability coefficients of the GOT over 2 weeks is .91 (Hansen & Campbell, 1985).

Academic Comfort and Introversion-Extroversion. The special scales of the SCII are the AC scale and the I-E scales. The AC is a measure of academic persistence and has a test-retest reliability of .91 for 2 weeks (Hansen, 1986). The I-E scale reflects a tendency for people to have interests toward ideas and things (introverted) or toward others (extroverted). The test-retest reliability of the I-E scale is .91 for 2 weeks (Hansen, 1986).

ANALYSIS AND RESULTS

Table 1 summarizes the means and standard deviations for the GOT scale for men and women. This allows for a quick comparison to the General Reference Sample (Hansen & Campbell, 1985). For women, social, enterprising, and conventional interests are

TABLE 1
Means and Standard Deviations of Dependent Measures by Sex

Scale	Men (n = 32)		Women (n = 45)	
	M	SD	M	SD
Realistic	41.6	9.0	35.4	7.1
Investigative	41.6	10.5	36.8	8.2
Artistic	40.5	10.9	41.3	9.5
Social	42.8	12.7	49.0	10.2
Enterprising	49.1	11.6	49.1	11.6
Conventional	49.5	11.1	47.8	10.2
AC	27.2	16.6	28.5	11.6
IE	52.5	14.2	52.5	10.9

Note. AC = Academic Comfort Scale. IE = Introversion-Extroversion Scale.

average; realistic, investigative, and artistic interests are low in comparison with employed men and women in all six of the GOT types. For men, enterprising and conventional interests are average, and realistic, investigative, artistic, and social interests are low or moderately low in comparison with employed men and women. These findings are generally consistent with previous research with college students (Apostal, 1991).

A 2 (Gender) × 3 (Ethnicity) analysis of variance (ANOVA) was performed on each mean GOT scale score: Realistic, Investigative, Artistic, Social, Enterprising and Conventional. Only a significant main effect for gender was found for Realistic, $F(1, 71)=11.05$, $p<.01$. Higher realistic interests were reported by men ($M=41.6$, $SD=9.0$) than were reported by women ($M=35.4$, $SD=7.1$). Table 2 summarizes the data by gender and ethnicity.

There were no significant main effects for ethnicity; there was, however, a significant interaction effect for gender and ethnicity for Artistic, $F(2, 71)=3.87$, $p<.05$. African American women were less likely to prefer artistic themes ($M=40.03$, $SD=10.07$) than were African American men ($M=44.18$, $SD=10.05$). This interaction is displayed graphically in Figure 1.

The academic comfort mean score for the sample was 27.9 ($SD=13.9$). People with high school diplomas and people with associate or vocational-technical degrees score about 34 and lower and between 35 and 44. As a group, women in this study scored only slightly higher ($M=28.5$, $SD=11.61$) than did men ($M=27.2$, $SD=16.7$). A 3 (Ethnicity) × 2 (Gender) ANOVA revealed no significant main effects for ethnicity or gender, but there was a significant interaction effect between these factors, $F=(2, 71)=3.45$, $p<.05$. African American men scored higher on the AC scale ($M=32.65$, $SD=18.1$) than did African American women ($M=27.18$, $SD=12.17$). This finding suggested that African American men were more comfortable and satisfied with their educational experience than were African American women. Results of this interaction are depicted in Figure 2.

During the preliminary analysis of the data, we noticed that 49% of the interpretive reports suggested a "flat" or undifferentiated interest profile. We speculated a relationship between type of profile (undifferentiated, differentiated) and AC scale scores for this sample. To investigate this speculation, a t test was calculated. The results suggested a significant effect, $t(76)=4.01$, $p<.001$. We then questioned whether this difference was the result of differentiated versus undifferentiated interests or whether the differences noted reflected low interest, general lack of interest,

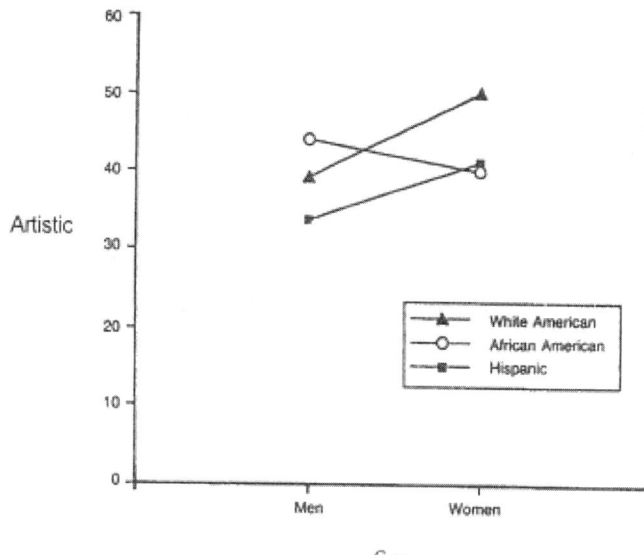

FIGURE 1
Interaction of Sex and Ethnicity on Artistic

or interests that were not tapped by this scale. To examine this assumption, we summed the six GOT theme scores, resulting in a total score for each student. This total score was correlated with AC using a Pearson correlation. The results indicated a relationship of .61, $p<.001$, which may suggest that the flat or undifferentiated profile reports for this group might reflect low interest in the items measured by the inventory.

We performed a 3 (Ethnicity) × 2 (Gender) ANOVA with the I-E mean scale scores as the dependent measure. The main effects were not significant; only the interaction effects were found to be significant, $F(2, 76)=3.52$, $p<.05$. Figure 3 depicts the results of this interaction. Examination of the mean scores by ethnicity and gender revealed that African American women scored higher in the introverted direction ($M=54.0$, $SD=10.2$), whereas African American men scored lower on the I-E scale, or in the direction of extroversion ($M=48.8$, $SD=12.6$). This finding suggested that African American men expressed greater preference in working in people-oriented environments than did African American women.

TABLE 2
Means and Standard Deviations of Dependent Measures by Ethnicity and Sex

	White American				African American				Hispanic			
	Men (n=7)		Women (n=5)		Men (n=17)		Women (n=34)		Men (n=8)		Women (n=6)	
Scale	M	SD	M	SD	M	SD	M	SD	M	SD	M	SD
GOT												
Realistic	42.1	7.8	34.0	2.3	42.3	10.4	36.0	7.9	39.6	7.3	33.3	3.7
Investigative	42.7	5.4	40.6	5.6	43.5	13.2	36.2	8.8	36.5	4.4	36.5	6.7
Artistic	39.3	13.6	50.2	2.4	44.2	10.1	40.0	10.1	33.9	7.3	41.3	5.5
Social	40.6	12.8	53.6	10.6	45.8	12.2	48.5	10.5	38.5	13.7	47.8	7.9
Enterprising	48.3	13.5	44.8	13.1	49.1	11.7	46.4	12.1	49.8	11.1	38.3	8.0
Conventional	50.6	9.1	41.8	4.1	48.9	11.7	49.6	10.1	49.8	12.9	42.7	11.8
AC	27.7	15.2	36.0	7.7	32.6	18.1	27.2	12.2	15.1	7.0	29.5	9.5
IE	53.3	17.2	39.0	9.6	48.8	12.6	54.0	10.2	59.9	13.4	55.5	9.0

Note. GOT = General Occupational Themes (Holland Themes), AC = Academic Comfort Scale, IE = Introversion-Extroversion Scale.

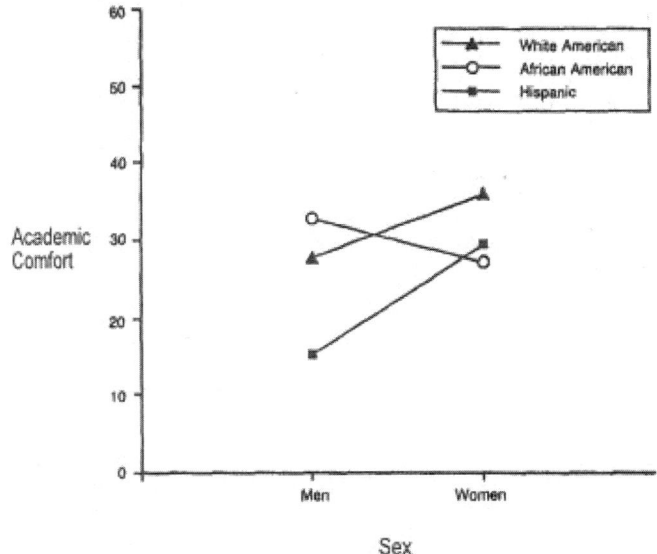

FIGURE 2
Interaction of Sex and Ethnicity on Academic Comfort

DISCUSSION

This study attempted to gather data on the career interest patterns of racially-ethnically diverse college men and women in the early stages of career planning. The findings in this study seem to support previous research suggesting that gender may influence Holland typologies. Men reported significantly higher realistic interest than did women. This finding is consistent with recent research with college students (Apostal, 1991). Contrary to previous findings (Fitzgerald & Betz, 1983; Smart, 1989), there were no significant gender differences for the Investigative, Social, Enterprising, and Conventional typologies. There were no significant ethnic differences in career interests.

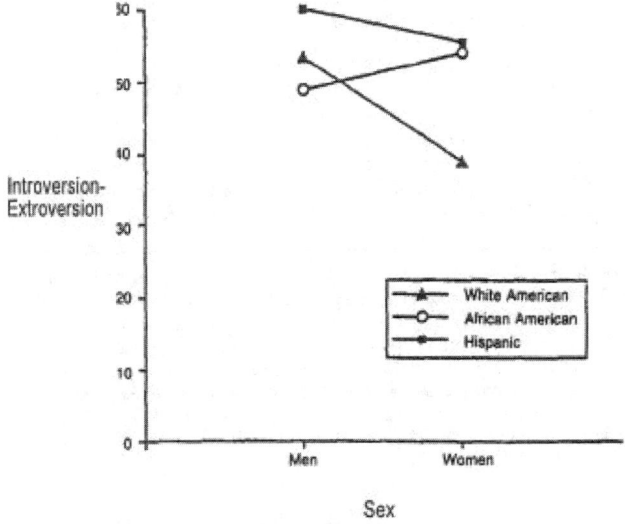

FIGURE 3
Interaction of Sex and Ethnicity on Introversion-Extroversion

Interesting to note was the interaction of gender and ethnicity on the Artistic theme. Research suggests that women are more likely to be Artistic types as compared with men. The general pattern of interests for Hispanic and White women in this study followed this assumption. For African Americans, however, men reported a higher preference for artistic interests than did women. African American men were more likely to be Artistic than were African American women.

The overall AC scores for this group were low. Hansen and Campbell (1985) stated that AC is related to educational expectations for first-year college students; they noted, however, that low scores do not indicate an inability to successfully complete college-level work. White and Hispanic women tended to score higher on AC than did White and Hispanic men. This finding was consistent with other research examining gender and academic comfort (Hansen & Campbell 1985; Swanson & Hansen, 1985). The findings for African Americans, however, differ from previous research. A gender and ethnicity interaction effect revealed that African American men scored higher on the AC scale than did African American women. One might question if this finding was a result of social desirability or whether African American men in this environment were more satisfied with their educational experience, reflecting higher levels of academic persistence as compared with African American women. Because of the generally low scores on this measure, it is difficult to interpret this finding. Further research investigating the relationship between academic comfort and persistence with multicultural populations in varying collegiate environments is needed.

Hansen and Campbell (1985) reported that there are no gender differences on measures of I-E. Men and women have similar scores, with women having a slight tendency to score lower on the I-E scale, or in the extroverted direction, reflecting a tendency toward people-oriented occupations. A Gender × Ethnicity interaction revealed that African American women scored higher on the AC scale, or in the introverted direction, as compared with African American men. The mean scores suggested that African American women were more likely to prefer working with a combination of interests involving people, ideas, and things, whereas African American men were more likely to prefer working with others or in people-oriented occupations. Figure 3 profiles the group scores by gender and ethnicity on the I-E scale. White and Hispanic women expressed greater preference in the extroverted direction, as compared with White and Hispanic men. White women were most likely to prefer people-oriented occupations, scoring lowest on I-E, as compared with the other gender-ethnic groups. Hispanic men scored the highest on I-E and lowest on AC. Hansen and Campbell (1985) suggested that I-E scores may reflect a student's ability to interact and relate to others. People who score under 40 are often the leaders of their peer group; scores over 60 may reflect social discomfort or shyness. These findings may be important for the individual that scores low on AC and high on introversion. This information may be useful in helping students to understand the interrelationship between personal development and career development.

The large number of students whose profiles reflected low interests is an area of concern in this study. A question remains about whether the SCII tapped into the "experience" of these students. Perhaps the post hoc investigation examining differentiated and undifferentiated profiles will provide direction for future research.

Several limitations are apparent in this study. The participants were predominantly African American. Although the African American sample may have been sufficiently large, the White and Hispanic samples were small. This limitation may have resulted in low statistical power, preventing true differences in ethnicity and gender to emerge. Therefore, it is questionable whether or not the findings in this study can be generalized. A larger sample of participants would allow for a thorough investigation of response differences on the SCII as a function of gender and ethnicity. These findings, however, may help to identify important questions for research.

Research examining the career interest patterns of diverse students is limited. The effectiveness of the SCII with visible racial-ethnic group members remains an inconclusive, yet critical issue. This study served as an initial investigation examining gender and ethnicity and the interaction of these variables on the SCII. In light of the limitations, this study does provide support for the notion that gender and ethnicity may serve to influence career interest and choice. To the extent that the results are valid and generalizable, the findings emphasize the importance of life history and background variables in career development. Further research is warranted to delineate the role of gender and ethnicity in vocational decision making.

REFERENCES

Apostal, R. A. (1991). College students' career interests and sensing-intuition personality. *Journal of College Student Development, 32,* 4-7.

Bayer, A. L. (1972). The Black college freshman: Characteristics and recent trends. *American Council of Education Reports, 8,* 1.

Borgen, F. (1988). The Strong-Campbell Interest Inventory (SCII). In J. T. Kapes & M. M. Mastie, (Eds.), *A counselor's guide to career assessment instruments* (pp. 123-126). Alexandria, VA: The National Career Development Association.

Borgen, F. H., & Harper, G. T. (1973). Predictive validity of measured vocational interests with Black and White college men. *Measurement and Evaluation in Guidance, 6,* 19-26.

Cameron, H. K. (1970). The Jensen controversy: II. Cultural myopia. *Measurement and Evaluation in Guidance, 3,* 10-17.

Carter, R. T., & Swanson, J. L. (1990). The validity of the Strong Interest Inventory with Black Americans: A review of the literature. *Journal of Vocational Behavior, 36,* 195-209.

Cheatham, H. E. (1990). Africentricity and career development of African-Americans. *The Career Development Quarterly, 38,* 334-346.

Cook, D. A., & Helms, J. E. (1988). Visible racial/ethnic group supervisees' satisfaction with cross-cultural supervision as predicted by relationship variables. *Journal of Counseling Psychology, 33,* 268-274.

Doughtie, E. B., Chang, W. C., Alston, H. L., Wakefield, J. A., Jr., & Yom, B. L. (1976). Black-White differences in vocational preference inventory. *Journal of Vocational Behavior, 8,* 41-44.

Eberhardt, B. J., & Muchinsky, P. M. (1982). Biodata determinants of vocational psychology: An integration of two paradigms. *Journal of Applied Psychology, 67,* 714-727.

Engen, H. B., Lamb, R. R., & Prediger, D. J. (1982). Are secondary schools still using standardized tests? *The Personnel and Guidance Journal, 60,* 287-290.

Fitzgerald, L. F., & Betz, N. E. (1983). Issues in the vocational psychology of women. In W. B. Walsh & S. M. Osipow (Eds.), *Handbook of Vocational Psychology* (pp. 83-159). Hillsdale, NJ: Erlbaum.

Gottfredson, G. D., Holland, J. L., & Gottfredson, G. B. (1975). The relationship of vocational aspirations and assessments to employment reality. *Journal of Vocational Behavior, 7,* 135-148.

Hager, P. C., & Elton, C. F. (1971). The vocational interests of Black males. *Journal of Vocational Behavior, 1,* 153-158.

Hansen, J. C. (1984). *User's guide for the SVIB-SCII.* Stanford, CA: Stanford University Press.

Hansen, J. C. (1986). Strong Vocational Interest Blank/Strong-Campbell Interest Inventory. In W. B. Walsh & S. H. Osipow (Eds.), *Advances in vocational psychology: Vol 1. The assessment of interests* (pp. 1-29). Hillsdale, NJ: Erlbaum.

Hansen, J. C., & Campbell, D. P. (1985). *Manual for the SVIB-SCII* (4th ed.). Palo Alto, CA: Consulting Psychologists Press.

Hansen, J. C., & Swanson, J. L. (1983). Stability of interests and the predictive and concurrent validity of the 1981 Strong-Campbell Interest Inventory for college majors. *Journal of Counseling Psychology, 30,* 194-201.

Holland, J. L. (1966). *The psychology of vocational choice.* Waltham, MA: Blaisdell.

Holland, J. L. (1975). The use and evaluation of interest inventories and simulations. In E. E. Diamond (Ed.), *Issues of sex bias and sex fairness in career interest measurement* (pp. 19-44). Washington, DC: National Institute of Education.

Holland, J. L. (1976). The virtues of the SDS and its associated typology: A second response to Prediger and Hansen. *Journal of Vocational Behavior, 8,* 349-358.

Holland, J. L. (1985). *Making vocational choices: A theory of vocational personalities and work environments.* Englewood Cliffs, NJ: Prentice-Hall.

Kapes, J. T., & Mastie, M. M. (Eds.). (1988). *A counselor's guide to career assessment instruments* (2nd ed.). Alexandria, VA: The National Career Development Association.

Owens, W. A., & Schoenfeldt, L. F. (1979). Toward a classification of persons [Monograph]. *Journal of Applied Psychology, 65,* 569-607.

Smart, J. C. (1989). Life history influences on Holland vocational type development. *Journal of Vocational Behavior, 34,* 69-87.

Smith, E. J. (1975). Profile of the Black individual in vocational literature. *Journal of Vocational Behavior, 6,* 41-59.

Smith, E. J. (1980). Career development of minorities in nontraditional fields. *Journal of Non-White Concerns, 8,* 141-156.

Smith, E. J. (1983). Issues in racial minorities' career behavior. In W. B. Walsh & S. H. Osipow (Eds.), *Handbook of vocational psychology: Vol. 1. Foundations* (pp. 161-222). Hillsdale, NJ: Erlbaum.

Spokane, A. R. (1979). Occupational preference and the validity of the Strong-Campbell Interest Inventory for college men and women. *Journal of Counseling Psychology, 26,* 312-318.

Swanson, J. L., & Hansen, J. C. (1985). The relationship of the construct of academic comfort to educational level, performance, aspirations and prediction of college major choices. *Journal of Vocational Behavior, 26,* 1-12.

White, M. J., Kruczeck, T. A., Brown, M. T., & White, G. B. (1989). Occupational sex stereotypes among college students. *Journal of Vocational Behavior, 34,* 289-298.

Whitton, M. C. (1975). Same-sex and cross-sex reliability and on current validity of the Strong Campbell Interest Inventory. *Journal of Counseling Psychology, 22,* 204-209.

Williams, R. L. (1982). *Psychological tests and minorities.* Washington, DC: U.S. Government Printing Office.

Zytowski, D. G., & Warman, R. E. (1982). The changing use of tests in counseling. *Measurement and Evaluation in Guidance, 15,* 147-152.

Saundra M. Tomlinson is an assistant professor of counseling psychology in the Department of Educational Psychology at Rutgers–The State University of New Jersey, New Brunswick. Gwendolyn Evans-Hughes is a developmental specialist in the Office of Career Services and a doctoral candidate in the Program in Counseling Psychology at Rutgers–The State University of New Jersey, New Brunswick. Correspondence regarding this article should be sent to Saundra M. Tomlinson, Department of Educational Psychology, Graduate School of Education, Rutgers–The State University of New Jersey, 10 Seminary Place, New Brunswick, NJ 08903.

Reprinted with permission of the American Counseling Association

Deconstructing Dispositional Bias in Clinical Inference: Two Interventions

Mei-whei Chen, Thomas Froehle, and Keith Morran

In this study, the authors examined the effectiveness of instruction in attribution processes and practice in empathic perspective taking in deconstructing dispositional bias of counselor trainees. Videotaped stimulus cases and a clinical attribution scale were used to assess the treatment effects when compared with a placebo control condition. Results revealed significant differences among groups. Counselor trainees receiving either of the 2 interventions showed significantly lower dispositional bias in responding to videotaped clinical cases than did their counterparts in the placebo condition. The study points to a need for a paradigm shift from a person-focused to a system-focused approach in counseling practice. Implications also point to the need for including critical thinking and empathic experiencing in clinical training

A call for appreciating the role that social and political contexts play in contributing to client problems echoes throughout the counseling literature (Albee, 1986; Aubrey & Lewis, 1983; Cassel, 1976; Sue, 1990; Thomas, 1996; Tomm, 1990). Most recently, this perspective has been framed in a social constructionist language, implying that client problems are co-constructed (Gergen, 1985, 1994; McNamee, 1996; White, 1989). This position acknowledges the importance of sociological contextualization, asserting that mental health conditions are not discrete phenomena but are more fundamentally grounded within the social matrix. Elements within the system such as social estrangement, powerlessness, poverty, exploitation, and oppression often spawn or exacerbate mental health problems.

Still, mental health counselors often focus primarily on problems within individuals while overlooking the interaction effect between the person and his or her environment (Gergen, 1990; Gergen & Kaye, 1992; Parry & Doan, 1994). Operating under this bias, counselors attribute clients' problems predominantly to dispositional factors and overlook the situations in which clients' problems are embedded (Batson, 1975; Dumont & Lecomte, 1987; Langer & Abelson, 1974; Wills, 1978). These dispositional factors often include personal traits, attitudes, moods, and temperament. For example, Wills (1978) showed that clinicians often regard their clients as irresponsible, evasive, or resistant as a result of personalistic attributions. They often construe clients' statements about personal feelings and circumstances as self-serving in nature. A history of deprivation, family neglect, and debilitating discouragement experienced by the individual seeking help may not be given the importance it deserves. This tendency for counselors to infer personal defects and to neglect contextual forces invites inferential errors (Dumont & Lecomte, 1987).

Because making inferences is a central element in clinical judgment, accuracy is necessary for effective treatment (Witkin, 1982). The foundation of the counseling profession is a preventive and developmental philosophy. Grounded on this foundation, counselors are presumed to make causal inferences that reflect how individual factors and the social–political context interplay in precipitating and maintaining clients' mental health problems. Unfortunately, there is little support for this assumption. Research has indicated that irrespective of the circumstances, clinicians are inclined to make dispositionally based judgments when making clinical inferences (Gambrill, 1990; Snyder, Shenkel, & Schmidt, 1976). In a study reported by Langer and Abelson (1974), clinicians judged a videotaped interviewee to have more dispositional problems when the interviewee was labeled as a "patient" than when the same person was labeled as a "job applicant." In another study in which a client's problem was constructed to be situational, trained helpers perceived the client's problem to be more dispositional than did nonprofessionals (Batson, 1975). Research also indicates that helpers are more likely to make dispositional attributions when presented with a list of referral resources oriented toward changing individuals than when presented with those oriented toward changing the environments. For example, when helpers were given a list

---

Mei-whei Chen is an assistant professor in the Department of Counselor Education at Northeastern Illinois University. Thomas Froehle is a professor in the Department of Counseling and Educational Psychology at Indiana University. Keith Morran is a professor in the Department of Counseling and Educational Psychology at Indiana University–Purdue University at Indianapolis. Correspondence regarding this article should be sent to Mei-whei Chen, Department of Counselor Education, Northeastern Illinois University, 5500 North St. Louis Avenue, Chicago, IL 60625-4699 (e-mail: M-Chen@neiu.edu).

of resources including a mental hospital, residential treatment center, and mental health clinic to which referrals could be made for clients, they were more likely to judge clients' problems as dispositional than when given referral resources such as community coalition, career information center, ombudsman, and sounding board (Batson, Jones, & Cochran, 1979).

Clinical judgments that focus extensively on the clients' disposition may hinder clients from examining means for acting on their circumstances. Such judgments can discourage the development of a sense of competence and self-worth, which in turn may translate into feelings of powerlessness (Furman & Ahola, 1989; Tomm, 1989). Counseling effectiveness can potentially diminish as a result of counselors' dispositional inferences and judgments.

The question then arises: Why are counselors so inclined to make dispositional judgments? Findings from classical social cognition research point to three mechanisms that contribute to this bias. First, as social perceivers, counselors are influenced by the *correspondent inference mechanism* whereby they infer that an individual's behavior corresponds to an underlying characteristic of that person (Jones & Davis, 1965). Second, like other social perceivers, counselors fall victim to *fundamental attribution error* (Ross, 1977) by inferring broad personal dispositions and expecting consistency of behavior across widely dissimilar situations. Third, *the actor-observer effect* leads the observer (in this case the counselor) to attribute causality to a dispositional quality of the actor (i.e., the client) even though the latter tends to attribute his or her own behavior to situational factors (Jones & Nisbett, 1971; McArthur, 1972; Nisbett, Caputo, Legant, & Marecek, 1973).

Another mechanism that may contribute to dispositional bias is associated with counselors' role characteristics. First, when in the role of observers, counselors tend to see the client as the figure in their perceptual orientation while viewing the client's situation as the ground. During the causal attribution process, this person-as-figure condition invites a heightened focus on the client (Batson, O'Quin, & Pych, 1982). Indeed, easy availability of information about the client and limited access to information concerning the client's circumstances often entice counselors to make dispositional attributions (Gambrill, 1990). Second, in their role as helpers, counselors are influenced by the medical model that views sickness as residing within the person (Tomm, 1990). Consequently, counselors can be more remedial in focus and direct more of their attention toward changing clients rather than toward changing the problem environment. This tendency operates in strong accord with the prevailing social norm that encourages adaptation to the social environment rather than changing that environment.

Because perseverance in clinical judgments is strengthened by confirmatory hypothesis testing and self-fulfilling prophecies, bias in clinical inferences tends to persist over time regardless of conflicting information (Ross, Lepper, & Habbrad, 1975). That is to say, bias mechanisms tend to foster both the development and the perseverance of dispositional inferences. Given this reality, it is imperative that counselor educators and clinical supervisors seek ways to alter this bias in counselor trainees.

As prevalent and potentially damaging as dispositional bias is to clinical inferencing, it has not been carefully scrutinized (Dumont & Lecomte, 1987). Systematic research exploring the efficacy of alternative interventions against this bias is essential. The present study was an attempt to address this void, rooted in our hope that early intervention against the effect of bias mechanisms during clinical training may alter counselor trainees' clinical inferences and pave the way to a more competence-based approach with clients (Masterpasqua, 1989).

Still, one may ask: Can dispositional bias be deconstructed? Deconstruction is a paradigm that originated in literary criticism. In literary criticism, deconstruction is a means toward dismantling the fixed meaning in literary texts to bring forth previously submerged alternative meanings (Hare-Mustin & Marecek, 1988; Rosen, 1996). Within counseling, theorists have applied the paradigm of deconstruction to confront various issues in therapeutic discourse (Freedman & Combs, 1996; White, 1993). It seems reasonable to assume that such deconstructive effort can be extended to clinical inference processes. Specifically, the process of deconstruction would involve rendering hidden assumptions visible (Kearney, 1984) and overthrowing taken-for-granted practices (White, 1993). In the context of clinical judgment, this means that the mechanisms of dispositional bias would first need to be made visible. Next, the bias would need to be substituted with judgments that are more congruent with clients' experiences.

To meet these conditions, we used two intervention strategies: instruction in attribution processes (Warner, Parker, & Calhoun, 1984) and practice in empathic perspective taking (Storms, 1973). We anticipated that instruction in attribution processes would influence trainees' sensitivity to pitfalls in clinical inference making and increase their awareness of inferential processes. The bias mechanisms would be made visible and deposed, making counselors more willing to consider alternative judgments. Furthermore, we believed that practice in empathic perspective taking (in which the observers assume the role of actors) would result in counselor trainees understanding the clients' experiential reality better. That is, when actor–observer effect is eliminated through empathic perspective taking, observers (counselors) will be more likely to appreciate clients' perspectives and attend to salient environmental contingencies.

On the basis of these reasonings, we designed a study to demonstrate that inferential biases embedded in social perception mechanisms can be deconstructed. More specifically, we tested the following hypotheses: (a) Counselor trainees receiving training in attribution processes will demonstrate significantly fewer dispositional attributions when responding to videotape case scenarios than will participants assigned to a placebo condition; (b) counselor trainees receiving treatment in empathic perspective taking will make significantly fewer dispositional attributions than will participants in a placebo condition; and (c) participants in the two treatment conditions will not differ significantly in the number of dispositional attributions they make.

METHOD

Participants

The participants were counselor trainees enrolled in a master's degree program at a large Midwestern university. Of the 63 trainees who volunteered for the study, 56 completed all of the procedures. Of these 56 trainees, 16 were men and 40 were women. The sample was predominately Caucasian ($n = 54$), with 1 African American and 1 Asian American. Age of participants ranged between 22 and 60 years ($M = 27, SD = 7$). Level of training in counseling ranged from 3 to 57 semester credit hours with a mean of 28 and a standard deviation of 15.

Instruments

Clinical Attribution Scale. The Clinical Attribution Scale (CAS) was constructed to measure the dependent variable, dispositional bias. The original scale consisted of 33 five-point Likert-scaled items, many of which were generated from the open-ended questions used by Storms (1973), Russell (1982), and Batson et al. (1979). The scale was further reduced to 18 items in a separate study in which 83 participants responded to a written stimulus case. Examples of CAS items include "The cause of the person's difficulty is primarily related to what was going on around him," "Deficiencies in the person's personality should be the target of treatment," and "The person's behavior might be different if the situation were different." Item analysis performed on the revised CAS yielded a Cronbach alpha reliability coefficient of .87.

To assess construct validity, we used rater judgment to determine where each item fell along the dispositional–situational continuum. Three judges who were unaware of the purpose of the study were trained to rate items on a 7-point rating scale. Analysis of interrater agreement using ±1 interval resulted in an average correlation coefficient of .96 and an average interrater agreement of .93, indicating strong rater agreement.

Total CAS scores suggest participants' inclination toward dispositional or situational attribution. The CAS was designed so that higher scores reflect a more situational inclination in clinical attribution and lower scores a more dispositional inclination.

Stimulus videotaped cases. To provide stimuli for responding to the CAS, we developed five 7- to 12-minute videotaped cases. All five cases were constructed following guidelines from Kelly's (1967, 1972) covariation model for presenting problems. This was done to ensure that the clients' presenting problems were primarily situational in nature. The tapes depicted clients whose problems made two points clear to the viewers. First, many individuals would behave in similar ways as did the client under the same circumstances (high consensus across people). Second, the client's self-report clearly indicated that she or he behaved differently in other similar situations (low consistency across situations). The combination of these conditions made the problems presented in these cases predominantly situational in nature. For example, a young man, Craig, was suffering from a depression that began to tax his relationship with his girlfriend. Craig related his depression to his father's prolonged hospitalization. Craig also indicated that he had never felt this way before and that he had known other people who felt similarly depressed when going through this kind of stress.

Raters' judgments were used to assess the extent to which each coached client demonstrated situational problems in the stimulus case. Three raters who were unaware of the purpose of the study independently rated each of the five cases. The judges rated the cases of Bill, Craig, Terry, and Linda to be primarily situational in emphasis and the case of John to be dispositional. The four cases that effectively displayed situational problems were used for assessment purposes.

Training Interventions

The first intervention involved instruction in attribution processes modeled after the work of Warner et al. (1984) and operationalized with attribution processes drawn from Fiske and Taylor (1984). Participants in this condition reviewed an instructional videotape specifically developed for this intervention. The instructional videotape discussed correspondent inference theory, fundamental attribution error, the actor–observer effect, its relationship to clinicians' observer and helper roles, and Kelley's (1967, 1972) normative attribution model. Printed handouts featuring an outline of instructional content were also provided. A facilitated discussion followed in which participants shared examples from their own lives relevant to attribution processes and then considered possible applications to counseling practice.

The second treatment consisted of practice in empathic perspective taking. This treatment approach, also inspired by the work of Warner et al. (1984), included a set of carefully structured role-reversal procedures. Participants were first instructed in the "imagine-self" procedure originally developed by Stotland (1969). The videotaped case of "John" was then shown. While watching the case, participants were asked to practice the imagine-self exercise in which they imagine how they would feel if they were the client. The intent was for each participant to mentally retreat from his or her role as observer and to become the actor in the presented scenario. In the second phase, participants were directed actually to take on the client's role. They were to put themselves in John's position, to see the event through John's eyes, and to verbalize John's possible feelings and experiences. Each pair took up to 14 minutes for role playing, with each participant having approximately 7 minutes of role reversal. The intervention concluded with a facilitated discussion focused on the participants' experience in role playing the client and the participants' perception of differences between playing the role of the client and simply observing the client.

The attention placebo condition involved instruction in self-processes and behavioral problems. For the placebo control condition to serve its purpose, it was important that the material presented to the participants not directly affect their original bias mechanisms. Achieving balance between dispositional and situational bias in the presentation of materials was, therefore, an important objective in assembling materials. To increase the likelihood of achieving this balance, we modeled materials after those used with placebo control conditions in previous research. The participants were shown an instructional video presenting concepts of self-awareness, self-esteem maintenance, and self-defeating behaviors extracted from Leary and Miller (1986). The content of the instructional video was intended to be similar to other content received in their counseling training, thus keeping participants in their current attributional position. Once again, printed handouts were provided followed by a facilitated discussion. Participants shared personal examples illustrating related concepts.

Three research assistants were trained with double-blind procedures (Borg & Gall, 1989) to conduct each of the three treatments. Precautions were taken to standardize treatment content, ensure treatment integrity, and promote procedural consistency. To achieve content standardization, we developed scripts for each of the treatment conditions in creating training videos. This precaution served to minimize experimenter effects. To increase treatment integrity and procedural consistency across sessions, we developed training manuals for research assistants. To further reinforce adherence to experimental procedures, research assistants audiotaped each of their sessions.

Procedure

Participants were recruited through announcements made to graduate-level counseling classes and through advertisements sent via electronic mail networks. Prospective participants were informed that the purpose of the study was to investigate the way counselor trainees perceive the problems clients bring to counseling. They were also informed that 2.5 hours would be needed to complete the two phases of the study; that participation would be voluntary, anonymous, and confidential; and that a token payment of $15 would be given to each participant on completion of the experiment. Volunteers were asked to read and sign an informed consent form.

Three steps were taken to stratify participants across experimental conditions. First, participants were divided into male and female subgroups. Second, within each subgroup, participants were randomly assigned to one of three groups. Third, each group was randomly assigned to one of the three experimental conditions. Random assignment positioned 19 participants in the attribution processes condition, 18 in the empathic perspective taking condition, and 19 in the placebo control condition.

Personal data were collected in a pretreatment session 2 weeks before the treatments. Participants were asked to use an anonymous code for personal identification. Then the stimulus case of "Bill" was shown and the CAS was administered. The same procedures were repeated for the video case of "Craig." Experimental treatments took place in mini classrooms equipped with a VCR, television monitor, desks, and chairs. During the treatment sessions, no reference was made to the video scenarios used in the pre- or posttreatment assessment. Immediately following each treatment, participants were first shown the videotaped case of "Terry" and directed to respond to the CAS using their anonymous personal codes. The same procedures were repeated for the videotaped case of "Linda." To ensure confinement of treatment effects, we reminded participants to refrain from discussing any of their experiences until they received debriefing notification.

Following the completion of the entire experiment, a debriefing statement was sent to all participants. The debriefing statement discussed the construct of dispositional bias and its relation to clinical inferences, the research questions, the design, and the three experimental conditions. Participants were encouraged to communicate with the researchers if they had further questions or concerns.

RESULTS

Preliminary Analyses

Although random assignment was used, possible pretreatment differences among groups necessitated several procedural checks. The chi-square procedure revealed no significant differences across treatment levels with regard to gender, marital status, degree of specialization in counseling, undergraduate major, or primary theoretical orientation ($p > .05$). These findings indicated that the participants' nominal demographic characteristics, particularly their theoretical orientation, were equivalent across groups and not likely to mediate treatment effects.

Second, we used one-way analyses of variance (ANOVAs) to detect possible between-group differences on interval demographic characteristics. ANOVA results indicated that groups did not differ significantly with respect to counseling credit hours earned or semesters of supervised clinical experiences ($p > .05$). However, ANOVA results did reveal a significant between-group difference in participants' age, $F(2, 55) = 6.438$, $p < .01$. To ensure that age did not confound the treatment effects, we conducted a correlation analysis to evaluate the need for statistical control. Results indicated no significant relationships between age and the CAS premeasure ($r = .034$, $p > .05$) or between age and the CAS postmeasure ($r = .082$, $p > .05$). Thus, age was not used as a covariate.

Next, to test the assumption that group differences in dispositional attribution did not preexist, we conducted a one-way ANOVA on the pretreatment CAS scores. Results confirmed that there were no significant group differences in the pretest, $F(2, 55) = .756$, $p > .05$. Although significant differences across groups were not observed, it should be noted that counselor trainees in the placebo condition ($M = 60.08$) displayed more pretreatment situational attribution than either the empathic perspective taking group ($M = 57.08$) or the attribution processes group ($M = 57.97$). To control for this potential problem, we decided to use the pretreatment CAS score as a covariate.

Treatment Effect

A test of homogeneity of the slope was conducted before testing the treatment effect. Results showed no significant differences across treatment conditions in slope of regression for the covariate, $F(2, 50) = .05$, $p > .05$, indicating no interaction effect between the treatment and the covariate. A one-way analysis of covariance (ANCOVA) then followed. Table 1 displays means, standard deviations, adjusted means, and adjusted standard deviations for the posttreatment measures. After adjustment for pretreatment variation in CAS scores, ANCOVA results revealed a significant difference in CAS mean scores among treatment groups $F(2, 52) = 6.54$, $p < .01$. These results indicated a treatment main effect. Multiple comparison tests followed to determine which contrasts contributed to the significant main effect. The three hypotheses, each involving an a priori nonorthogonal contrast, were tested using the Dunn-Šidák procedure. Results of the multiple comparison indicated that the adjusted means for both the attribution process group ($M = 63.88$) and the empathic perspective taking group ($M = 62.39$) were significantly different ($p < .01$) from the placebo control group ($M = 56.48$). However, the adjusted means for the two groups receiving treatment were not significantly different from each other ($p > .05$).

These results provided support for all three hypotheses. As predicted, participants who practiced empathic perspective taking responded with significantly higher CAS mean scores as compared with participants in the placebo control group. This higher mean score indicated a lower dispositional attribution. Also, as predicted, participants receiving instruction in attribution processes responded with significantly higher CAS scores, indicating significantly lower dispositional attribution tendencies. Finally, as predicted, participants in the group receiving instruction in the attribution processes did not respond differently from participants in the empathic perspective taking group.

To establish an index of clinical significance, we used Cohen's (1977) method to estimate the strength of the study's interventions. Results showed an effect size of .884 for the instruction in attribution processes treatment and .621 for the practice in empathic perspective taking treatment. These results indicate that the relative strength of both interventions was medium to large.

DISCUSSION

In this study, we examined the effectiveness of instruction in attribution processes and practice in empathic perspective taking in reducing dispositional bias of counselor trainees. Results suggest that dispositional bias can be deconstructed with well-planned interventions. These findings are consistent with results from studies with nonclinician participants reported by Regan and Totten (1975), Sherrod and Farber (1975), and Warner et al. (1984). By becoming cognizant of the mechanisms contributing to fallacies in clinical judgment and being reminded of appropriate inferential principles, counselor trainees' dispositional bias can be shown to decrease (Fiske & Taylor, 1984). Furthermore, the findings support the importance of empathic experiencing where counselors (observers) assume the role of the clients (actors). When the observer-actor role is switched, the counselor's point of view is reversed. This allows the counselor to espouse clients' phenomenological perspectives. As they attend to clients' salient environment contingencies, counselors make fewer biased clinical attributions and judgments. Thus, clients' situational realities are more accurately reflected.

Implications for Clinical Training

Results of this study suggest that instruction in attribution processes is potentially useful for improving clinical judgment. Counselor education has been criticized for lacking training in clinical critical thinking (Gambrill, 1990). Training in statistics is the primary component for critical thinking. Counselor trainees are encouraged to differentiate correlation from causation and to avoid sources of error that influence reliability and validity. Still, they remain uninformed of various formal and informal fallacies in clinical inference. This lack of critical thinking against clinical inference fallacies "makes it likely that their influence on clinical decisions will slip by unnoticed" (Gambrill, 1990, p. 7). Because insight into one's own faulty cognitive processes is limited (Fiske & Taylor, 1984), systematic efforts are needed to alter prospective counselors' error and bias. The results of this study suggest that counselor educators must first familiarize themselves with sources of attribution errors and biases. With this knowledge, counselor educators can create more open educational environments where critical thinking is encouraged and errors in judgment can be dis-

TABLE 1

Means, Standard Deviations, Adjusted Means, and Adjusted Standard Deviations for Posttreatment Scores

Group	n	M	SD	Adjusted M	Adjusted SD
Attribution training	19	63.68	7.86	63.88	1.51
Empathy training	18	61.77	7.14	62.39	1.56
Placebo	19	57.26	7.26	56.48	1.52

cussed openly. With this kind of training, clinical judgments reflecting clients' actual experiences are more likely to enter trainees' everyday inference making.

Another implication of this study concerns the merit of incorporating empathic experiencing into counselor training. Empathy has been shown to be a potent factor in facilitating client growth (Rogers, 1975). A high degree of empathy enables prospective counselors to make fewer judgmental or oppressive clinical attributions. Therefore, educating trainees to become genuinely and deeply empathic is a principal goal of counselor training. However, empathy is often treated as a communication process comprising a set of words and techniques (Miller, 1989). It tends to be taught as an assortment of response patterns rather than an attitude (Winslade, 1996). Consequently, trainees are ill-equipped to recognize the intricacy of multiple realities in clients' experiences. To attenuate this discrepancy, counselor training could provide trainees with empathic perspective taking experience as a part of regular training. Empathic experiencing would enable trainees to espouse clients' perspective and thereby recognize the intricacy of clients' multiple realities.

Implications for Counseling Practice

This study points to the need for a paradigm shift from a person-focused to an interaction-focused clinical attribution for counseling practice. All too often, client difficulties are attributed to deficits and pathologies inside the individual, whereas factors and structures external to the individual are deemed of little consequence (Gergen, 1985; Lax, 1995; McNamee, 1996). The locus of change is, therefore, predominantly within the individual client. As theorists point out, counseling and psychological practices have often been influenced by positivism and organism that emphasize decontextualized human behaviors (Hayes, 1996; Thomas, 1996). To respond to the call for contextualizing clinical inference, counselors may need to consider redrafting some of these perspectives by including ideas from postmodernism.

The postmodern era is defined by pluralism and multiple realities (O'Hara & Anderson, 1991). Counselors in this era may benefit by understanding that "the person and the system affect each other in an ongoing, circular and multidirectional manner" (Thomas, 1996, p. 532). This recursiveness suggests a paradigm shift in counseling practice, a shift from a person-focused to a system-focused clinical attribution. To pave the way for this paradigm shift, counselors may first need to become cognizant of the influences and mechanisms encouraging dispositional attribution. Making a conscientious effort to deconstruct these attribution errors and biases would more effectively serve clients.

The results of this study also suggest several ways for practicing counselors to deconstruct clinical bias through empathic perspective taking. When a counselor's perspective changes, the observed reality shifts. As Freedman and Combs (1996) asserted, "changing a point of view almost always brings out different details, different emotions, or different meanings" (p. 95). Experiencing the effects of changing one's perspective enables counselors to appreciate reality as multifaceted and contextual rather than singular and objective (Dunne, 1992; Parry & Doan, 1994). Empathic perspective taking can be practiced daily in counseling by looking through clients' eyes, looking from a reflecting position, or looking forward in anticipation of the preferred outcome. Through this empathic lens, counselors enable themselves to recognize each client's multiple layers of reality. The counselor's capacity for helping clients generate alternative meanings and pathways to change is also enhanced.

Limitations and Suggestions for Future Research

Certain limitations should be considered when drawing conclusions from this study. First, because there was no follow-up assessment on the extended effects of treatment, we do not know how long treatment effects would be sustained. Second, although the CAS showed a high reliability, support for its validity is limited. Third, clinical inferences about clients' problems may have been influenced by our use of simulated cases. Participants may have responded differently in actual clinical judgment contexts. Fourth, we have attempted to align the attention placebo content with what trainees received in their typical counseling training. Still, the significant differences observed between the treatment conditions and the attention placebo condition might be attributed to the fact that trainees in the placebo condition were exposed to more dispositional content compared with those in the other two groups. Finally, it is also possible that participation in the two treatment conditions invited participants to make more socially desirable responses on the CAS posttest. These possibilities should be considered when drawing conclusions from these findings.

Bias deconstruction deserves continuing research attention if we hope to ensure counseling effectiveness. The findings of this study indicate that dispositional bias can be deconstructed through learning about attribution processes and experiencing empathic perspective taking. It is important for future researchers to explore additional strategies that may hold promise in deconstructing clinical biases.

A number of ways exist for extending this line of research. First, given the complexity of the clinical inferencing process, it is necessary to increase the complexity of the measurement instrument. As Murdock and Fremont (1989) suggested, dispositional attribution may involve more dimensions than just the internal–external. Stability or globality may be subtly involved in dispositional bias. Therefore, future instrumentation may require a multidimensional approach using multiple scales and including both quantitative and qualitative probes. Second, future studies should include follow-up assessment for examining durability of treatment over time. Third, inclusion of a pure control group as a fourth experimental condition should be used to control for and examine possible effects of the attention placebo condition. Fourth, future research should examine the role that cognitive complexity plays in mediating dispositional bias. Results reported by Spengler and Strohmer (1994) indicate that counselors with lower cognitive complexity are more likely to demonstrate diagnostic overshadowing bias in clinical judgment than are counselors who demonstrate higher cognitive complexity. Future research may inform us how counselor cognitive complexity can be used to both deconstruct and mitigate dispositional bias.

Finally, although this study emphasizes contextualizing clinical inference and practice, the methods used in this study are quantitative in nature. The empirical methods are appropriate when evaluating the effects of interventions, yet qualitative methods may be more adequate for in-depth exploration. Therefore, we encourage future investigators to conduct qualitative research in this area. We believe that qualitative inquiry may provide us with rich data and insight into the complex phenomena of attribution errors and biases in clinical judgment. These insights may guide us toward new directions for deconstructive intervention.

REFERENCES

Albee, G. W. (1986). Toward a just society. *American Psychologist, 41,* 891–898.

Aubrey, R. F., & Lewis, J. (1983). Social issues and the counseling profession in the 1980s and 1990s. *Counseling and Human Development, 15,* 1–15.

Batson, C. D. (1975). Attribution as a mediator of bias in helping. *Journal of Personality and Social Psychology, 32,* 455–466.

Batson, C. D., Jones, C. J., & Cochran, P. (1979). Attributional bias in counselors' diagnoses: The effect of resources. *Journal of Applied Social Psychology, 9,* 377–393.

Batson, C. D., O'Quin, K., & Pych, V. (1982). An attribution theory analysis of trained helpers' inferences about clients' needs. In T. A. Wills (Ed.), *Basic processes in helping relationships* (pp. 59–80). New York: Academic Press.

Borg, W. R., & Gall, M. D. (1989). *Educational research: An introduction.* New York: Longman.

Cassel, J. (1976). The contribution of the social environment to host resistance. *American Journal of Epidemiology, 104,* 107–123.

Cohen, J. (1977). *Statistical power analysis for the behavioral sciences* (Rev. ed.). New York: Academic Press.

Dumont, F., & Lecomte, C. (1987). Inferential processes in clinical work: Inquiry into logical errors that affect diagnostic judgments. *Professional Psychology: Research and Practice, 18,* 433–438.

Dunne, P. B. (1992). *The narrative therapist and the art.* Los Angeles: Drama Therapy Institute of Los Angeles.

Fiske, S. T., & Taylor, S. E. (1984). *Social cognition.* New York: Random House.

Freedman, J., & Combs, G. (1996). *Narrative therapy: The social construction of preferred realities.* New York: Norton.

Furman, B., & Ahola, T. (1989). Adverse effects of psychotherapeutic beliefs: An application of attribution theory to the critical study of psychotherapy. *Family Systems Medicine, 7,* 183–195.

Gambrill, E. (1990). *Critical thinking in clinical practice.* San Francisco: Jossey-Bass.

Gergen, K. J. (1985). The social constructionist movement in modern psychology. *American Psychologist, 40,* 266–275.

Gergen, K. J. (1990). Therapeutic professions and the diffusion of deficit. *Journal of Mind and Behaviors, 11,* 353–368.

Gergen, K. J. (1994). *Reality and relationships: Soundings in social construction.* Cambridge, MA: Harvard University Press.

Gergen, K. J., & Kaye, J. (1992). Beyond narrative in the negotiation of therapeutic meaning. In S. McNamee & K. J. Gergen (Eds.), *Therapy as social construction* (pp. 166–185). Newbury Park, CA: Sage.

Hare-Mustin, R. T., & Marecek, J. (1988). The meaning of difference: Gender theory, postmodernism, and psychology. *American Psychologist, 43,* 455–464.

Hayes, R. (1996, April). *Constructivism: Reality is what you make it.* Paper presented at the annual conference of the American Counseling Association, Pittsburgh, PA.

Jones, E. E., & Davis, K. E. (1965). From acts to dispositions: The attribution process in person perception. In L. Berkowitz (Ed.), *Advances in experimental social psychology* (Vol. 2, pp. 219–266). New York: Academic Press.

Jones, E. E., & Nisbett, V. A. (1971). *The actor and the observer: Divergent perceptions of the causes of behavior.* Morristown, NJ: General Learning Press.

Kearney, R. (1984). *Dialogues with contemporary continental thinkers.* New York: St. Martin's Press.

Kelly, H. H. (1967). Attribution theory in social psychology. In D. Levine (Ed.), *Nebraska symposium on motivation* (Vol. 15, pp. 192–238). Lincoln: University of Nebraska Press.

Kelly, H. H. (1972). *Causal schemata and the attribution process.* New York: General Learning Press.

Langer, R. D., & Abelson, R. P. (1974). A patient by any other name: Clinician group differences in labeling bias. *Journal of Consulting and Clinical Psychology, 42,* 456–461.

Lax, W. D. (1995). Offering reflections: Some theoretical and practical considerations. In S. Friedman (Ed.) *The reflecting team in action* (pp. 145–166). New York: Guilford Press.

Leary, M. R., & Miller, R. S. (1986). *Social psychology and dysfunctional behavior.* New York: Springer-Verlag.

Masterpasqua, F. (1989). A competence paradigm for psychological practice. *American Psychologist, 44,* 1366–1371.

McArthur, L. (1972). The how and what of why: Some determinants and consequences of causal attribution. *Journal of Personality and Social Psychology, 22,* 171–193.

McNamee, S. (1996). Psychotherapy as a social construction. In H. Rosen & K. T. Kuehlwein (Eds.), *Constructing realities: Meaning-making perspective for psychotherapists* (pp. 115–137). San Francisco: Jossey-Bass.

Miller, M. J. (1989). A few thoughts on the relationship between counseling techniques and empathy. *Journal of Counseling and Development, 67,* 350–351.

Murdock, N. L., & Fremont, S. K. (1989). Attributional influences in counselor decision making. *Journal of Counseling Psychology, 36,* 417–422.

Nisbett, R. E., Caputo, C., Legant, P., & Marecek, J. (1973). Behavior as seen by the actor and as seen by the observer. *Journal of Personality and Social Psychology, 27,* 154–164.

O'Hara, M., & Anderson, W. T. (1991, September–October). Welcome to the postmodern world. *Networker,* 19–25.

Parry, A. & Doan, R. E. (1994). *Story re-visions: Narrative therapy in the postmodern world.* New York: Guilford Press.

Regan, D. T., & Totten, J. (1975). Empathy and attribution: Turning observers into actors. *Journal of Personality and Social Psychology, 32,* 850–856.

Rogers, C. R. (1975). Empathic: An unappreciated way of being. *The Counseling Psychologist, 5,* 850–856.

Rosen, H. (1996). Meaning-making narratives: Foundations for constructivist and social constructionist psychotherapies. In H. Rosen & K. T. Kuehlwein (Eds.), *Constructing realities* (pp. 3–51). San Francisco: Jossey-Bass.

Ross, L. (1977). The intuitive psychologist and his shortcomings: Distortions in attribution process. In L. Berkowitz (Ed.), *Advances in experimental social psychology* (Vol. 10, pp. 173–220). New York: Academic Press.

Ross, L., Lepper, M. R., & Habbrad, J. (1975). Perseverance in self perception and social perception: Biased attributional processes in the debriefing paradigm. *Journal of Personality and Social Psychology, 32,* 880–892.

Russell, D. (1982). The Causal Dimension Scale: A measure of how individuals perceive causes. *Journal of Personality and Social Psychology, 42*, 1137–1145.

Sherrod, D. S., & Farber, J. (1975). The effect of previous actor/observer role experience on attribution of responsibility for failure. *Journal of Personality, 43*, 231–247.

Snyder, C. R., Shenkel, R. J., & Schmidt, A. (1976). Effects of role perspective and client psychiatric history on locus of problem. *Journal of Consulting and Clinical Psychology, 44*, 467–472.

Spengler, P. M., & Strohmer, D. C. (1994). Clinical judgmental biases: The moderating roles of counselor cognitive complexity and counselor client preferences. *Journal of Counseling Psychology, 41*, 8–17.

Storms, M. D. (1973). Videotape and the attribution process: Reversing actor's and observers' points of view. *Journal of Personality and Social Psychology, 27*, 165–175.

Stotland, E. (1969). Exploratory investigations of empathy. In L. Berkowitz (Ed.), *Advances in experimental social psychology* (Vol. 4, pp. 271–313). New York: Academic Press.

Sue, D. W. (1990). Culture-specific strategies in counseling: A conceptual framework. *Professional Psychology: Research and Practice, 21*, 424–433.

Thomas, S. C. (1996). A sociological perspective on contextualism. *Journal of Counseling & Development, 74*, 529–536.

Tomm, K. (1989). Externalizing the problem and internalizing personal agency. *Journal of Strategic and Systemic Therapies, 8*, 54–59.

Tomm, K. (1990). A critique of the *DSM*. *Dulwich Centre Newsletter, 3*, 5–8.

Warner, M. H., Parker, J. B., & Calhoun, J. F. (1984). Inducing person-perception change in a spouse-abuse situation. *Family Therapy, 11*, 123–138.

White, M. (1989). *Selected paper*. Adelaide, Australia: Dulwich Centre.

White, M. (1993). Deconstruction and therapy. In S. Gilligan & R. Price (Eds.) *Therapeutic conversations* (pp. 22–61). New York: Norton.

Wills, T. A. (1978). Perceptions of clients by professional helpers. *Psychological Bulletin, 85*, 968–1000.

Winslade, J. (1996, October). *Sharpening the critical edge: A social constructionist approach in counselor education*. Paper presented at the national conference of the Association of Counselor Education and Supervision, Portland, OR.

Witkin, S. L. (1982). Cognitive processes in clinical practice. *Social Work, 27*, 389–395.

Qualitative Evaluation Methods Applied to a High School Counseling Center

PAUL V. MURRAY, JUSTIN E. LEVITOV, LOUIS CASTENELL, and J. HENRY JOUBERT

The authors present a case study demonstrating how qualitative techniques can be used to evaluate a high school counseling and guidance program.

Determining the effectiveness of service delivery is a pressing concern of all educational practitioners in charge of program evaluation. Evaluation models traditionally have relied on standardized criteria that purport to measure quality or effectiveness numerically. For example, Bardo and Cody (1975) proposed that "guidance evaluation, in part, be a study of student responses to items on a questionnaire" (p. 178). Using the conventions of criterion-referenced measurement, Robie, Gansneder, and Van Hoose (1979) developed a list of goals, objectives, and measurements, ostensibly as a step toward standardizing measures of guidance and counseling program outcomes.

Although standardized instruments can produce useful statistics, thoughtful social scientists and researchers have raised significant questions about the limitations of quantitative data on which programmatic changes will be based (Lincoln & Guba, 1985; Patton, 1980). Similarly, counseling researchers have begun to look at alternative methods of inquiry. These methods, relatively new to evaluation theory and practice, are grounded in a phenomenological paradigm centered on how individuals construct or make sense of their surroundings:

> Understanding the meanings given by individuals to particular situations allows a researcher to appreciate the impact an event has had upon the subject, the way the individual interprets the events, and therefore, the predictability of certain behaviors in subsequent similar situations. While messy, this type of data "is apt to be superior to quantitative data in the density of information, vividness, and clarity of meaning." (Neimeyer & Resnikoff, 1982, p. 77)

This perspective is particularly useful in the evaluation of a program whose success, or effectiveness is embedded in the organizational "culture of the school" (Sarason, 1982, p. 7). Typically, administrators and teachers judge the quality of a counseling program by how it affects their organizational domains. Therefore, Shertzer and Stone (1981) suggested that the relationship between a counseling staff and administrators and teachers is often characterized by mutual misperception and mistrust, which may vary in amount and intensity from school to school. It follows, then, that to the degree that the counseling staff and what they do within a school are misperceived, the articulated or implicit definition of the purpose and effectiveness of counseling will vary from school to school.

The purpose of this article is to report on the evaluation of a secondary school guidance and counseling program through the use of nonstandard methods for determining program effectiveness. These methods focus on the limitations of standardized measurements and take into account issues of intra-organizational perception and trust. This article was written with several audiences in mind, primarily but not exclusively counselors and counselor administrators responsible for evaluating the effectiveness of counseling programs, professional program evaluators, and researchers in general.

In the case described here, the head of the counseling staff at an all-male, private, religiously affiliated high school located in a southern metropolitan area contracted for the evaluation of the counseling program, which served 1,100 students. Financed by the school administration, the evaluation was conducted to determine how well the staff members, all qualified counselors (a priest, two teaching brothers, and a lay person), were carrying out the objectives of the program. Recommendations for improvement were made following the evaluation. The evaluator's final report was distributed to administrators and counselors and was made available to faculty members.

At the time of the project, the four counselors divided the counseling responsibilities according to grade level. Because the school prided itself on its academic excellence, much of the counseling revolved around student academic credits, grades, and planning for postsecondary education. Because of the school's religious affiliation, however, there was an emphasis on the individual's affective and spiritual domains. That these two goals could be in conflict, and that this conflict would in all probability have a significant effect on the validity and reliability of standardized measures, strongly suggested that other measures would be more appropriate. In addition, taking into consideration Shertzer and Stone's (1981) contentions noted above, the project director determined that in this particular setting, a qualitative evaluation methodology would provide a richer and more comprehensive data base from which recommendations could be generated.

METHOD

The research methodology chosen for this project has been labeled *ethnographic* (Fetterman, 1984), *qualitative* (Cook & Reichardt, 1979; Miles & Huberman, 1984; Patton, 1980; Van Mannen, 1983; Van Mannen, Dabbs, & Faulkner, 1982), or both (Goetz & LeCompte, 1984). Under the general qualitative rubric, a variety of evaluation designs are available. Patton's (1980) definition of *process evaluation* is most appropriate for the purposes and contextual conditions found in the setting in question:

> Process evaluations are aimed at elucidating and understanding the internal dynamics of program operations, [focusing] on the following kinds of questions: What are the

factors that come together to make this program what it is? What are the strengths and weaknesses of the program?

> Such descriptions [of program operations] may be based on observations and/or interviews with staff, clients, and program administrators. Many process evaluations focus on how the program is perceived by participants and staff. The mandate to generate an accurate and detailed description of program operations particularly lends itself to . . . qualitative methods. (Patton, 1980, p. 62).

Whereas the trustworthiness of quantitative data relies on factors such as validity and reliability, qualitative data is verified through the process of triangulation. When there are no external measures of verification (e.g., in a statistical test), multiple internal measures or sources of information about the same program or phenomenon provide what Miles and Huberman (1984) called *convergent evidence*. From the four types of triangulation (data, investigator, theory, and methodological) described by Denzin (1978), a combination of the first two was chosen: (a) a convergence of data from three sources, and (b) independent verification of consistency or disparity in responses to interview questions by two separate research teams.

The four members of the evaluation team were a professor of counselor education, a doctoral candidate in administration with private school teaching experience, and two professors of education with experience in teaching and administration in both private and public schools. The latter two served as interviewers.

The primary source of data was a series of semistructured interviews with (a) the counseling staff, (b) a group of seven volunteer teachers, and (c) the five members of the administrative staff. Data triangulation from these three groups provided cross-verification of conclusions. Before visiting the school, the interviewers prepared a list of questions to elicit information regarding (a) the purpose of the counseling program; (b) the extent to which the program's services were used by the school's administrators, teachers, and students; and (c) the program's strengths and shortcomings. It was agreed that the interviewers would pursue relevant lines of questioning outside the list of questions if these activities seemed to have promise of providing useful information.

The individual interviews were conducted in 9 hours over 2 days. Although the sample of teachers was small given the total teacher population ($N = 80$), there was sufficient variety in the group regarding the length of service at the school (2-15 years), grade level taught, and subject area expertise to safely assume that the group was a reliable cross-section of the faculty.

Responses of the interview subjects were first analyzed by the two interviewers. They began by locating similarities and discrepancies in responses to the questions *within* groups (all teachers, counselors, and administrators) and then did the same *across* groups (teachers and counselors, teachers and administrators, administrators and counselors). On the basis of these patterned similarities and discrepancies, recurring themes were identified and categorized as tentative conclusions regarding the effectiveness or value of the program. The data were then analyzed in the same manner by the other two members of the evaluation team (who were not aware of the interviewers' conclusions). The final conclusions were based on the consensus among all four members. The entire procedure involved approximately 12 to 15 hours.

DISCUSSION

On the basis of the information generated by the interviews and the documentary evidence, the evaluation team made the following conclusions.

Perceptions of Program Purpose: Practically all of the people who chose to comment on the program's purpose admitted that the program was supported to provide the students with personal counseling and academic guidance, although there was some confusion regarding the school's perceived assignment of priority. Some interviewees simply did not know which function (if any) the school considered most important.

Some of the teachers, as well as two of the administrators, perceived a conflict in the school's being committed equally to academics and to the personal growth of the students. Similarly, there did not seem to be any unanimity among the counselors regarding the relative importance of academic versus personal counseling. One counselor implied that there should be more emphasis on personal counseling. Another admitted engaging in personal counseling only when "pressed" to do so, explaining that he "doesn't like to pry." Still another was curiously evasive when asked anything regarding his perceptions of the purpose of the program.

Perceptions of Guidance Center Use: The administrators and teachers admitted not making much use of the guidance center for student referral. Members of all three groups said that they thought the students made relatively little use of the center except when they had to do so for academic reasons (e.g., class changes, college admissions). One counselor summed up the interviewees' perception of the extent of the center's use by saying that the center "is not a force in the school," implying that it should be.

Perceived Program Strengths and Weaknesses: There was general consensus among the three groups that what the staff of the center did best (and apparently did quite well) was record keeping. One counselor believed that perhaps too much time was spent performing that function. Some of the teachers and at least one counselor believed that teachers would make more personal use of the center if there were more office space for them to sit down and peruse the records.

There was little criticism among any of the groups about the competence or industriousness of the counselors individually, and none about the counselors as a group.

Some administrators and teachers hinted that the counselors were coddling students who could profit more from a firm hand. A related criticism, generally offered by the same people, was that an unspecified number of students used the center to avoid classes they did not like or to keep from taking tests.

As a result of these conclusions, four major recommendations were made. First, the members of the counseling center should participate in an off-campus, in-service retreat so as to redefine objectives, clarify the program's relationship to the school's mission, and clarify the role(s) each counselor would play.

Second, the evaluators suggested that once the counselors agreed on the program's objectives and their own related professional roles, these objectives and roles would have to be "marketed" to the administrators and teachers. Third, that there was insufficient space in the guidance center for teachers to have easy access to student records should be further verified and the problem remedied. Finally, should the principal and counselors believe that additional information was needed about the perceived effectiveness of the guidance and counseling program, the next step would be to study student perceptions of it.

LIMITATIONS OF THE RESEARCH

Interviewing students during this project may have encroached on their confidentiality, for which permission, and perhaps security from liability, would have been necessary because all were minors. Regardless, a second phase of the evaluation including program clients had originally been planned but was not pursued by the administration. This is noted as a limitation because such responses could have supported or disconfirmed data collected from the three groups identified above.

Other forms of triangulation were not used. Although we are confident that the recommendations were of value to the program staff, other, longer-term strategies would have enhanced the evaluation. For example, counselors could have been asked to keep logs over a specified period of time to detail what was done with individual students and the rationale. These data could then have been analyzed and critiqued for technical competence, and feedback could have been given to counselors individually.

Some quantitative measures may have helped indicate program use by students and teachers. There were no records requested regarding the number of students served over a specified period of time, relative to the entire school population, nor how many of these were walk-ins, referrals from teachers, and so forth. Although these data alone would not have been conclusive, they may have provided valuable information for the staff.

CONCLUSION

Shertzer and Stone (1981) suggested that relationships among counselors and teachers and administrators in schools tend to be strained, and that these relationships are often complicated by misperceptions. The data reported in this article were consistent with the results of Shertzer and Stone.

This case study suggests that process methods, such as the one reported here, can be useful techniques for the evaluation of counseling centers, especially when these organizations are located within larger organizational structures. Specifically, data were obtained, evaluated, and synthesized so that a series of conclusions could be drawn about the activities and operation of the counseling center while honoring the complexity of the center's connections with the rest of the school. Also, because this process involved personnel from different disciplines within the school, we believe it generated more interest in the evaluation and, ultimately, a greater commitment to act on the recommendations for change.

Could a particular counseling staff conduct its own program evaluation from the method described in this article? If interviewing is going to be among the tools of choice, interviewee candor is critical. We question whether co-workers and colleagues in schools, generally speaking, trust each other sufficiently to engage in an interview whose success depends on the articulation of genuine and authentic personal meanings that may require criticism and praise of self and others. The usefulness of the data generated by qualitative methods, rooted in anthropological paradigms, depends on the outsider's perspective, which allows identification of patterns in the data from a relative (and safe) distance. It is easier to draw a city map from the air than from the middle of Main Street.

Given these limitations, it seems that if those responsible for evaluating counseling centers see value in these strategies, they need to seek out professionals in program evaluation versed in their use. In our opinion the trade-off between expedience and the usefulness and richness of information generated by qualitative evaluations is worth the time and resources expended. We hope our contribution, if not to evaluation theory and research, has been to encourage practitioners to consider using qualitative methodologies in the development of school guidance and counseling programs in the future.

REFERENCES

Bardo, H., & Cody, J. (1975). Minimizing measurement concerns in guidance evaluation. *Measurement and Evaluation in Guidance, 8*, 163-168.

Cook, T., & Reichardt, C. (Eds.). (1979). *Qualitative and quantitative methods in evaluation research*. Beverly Hills, CA: Sage.

Denzin, N. (1978). The logic of naturalistic inquiry. In N. Denzin (Ed.), *Sociological methods: A sourcebook*. New York: McGraw-Hill.

Fetterman, D. (1984). *Ethnography in educational evaluation*. Beverly Hills, CA: Sage.

Goetz, J., & LeCompte, M. (1984). *Ethnography and qualitative design in educational research*. New York: Academic Press.

Hills, J. (1981). *Measurement and evaluation in the classroom*. Columbus, OH: Merrill.

Lincoln, Y., & Guba, E. (1985). *Naturalistic inquiry*. Beverly Hills, CA: Sage.

Miles, M., & Huberman, A. (1984). *Qualitative data analysis*. Beverly Hills, CA: Sage.

Neimeyer, G., & Resnikoff, A. (1982). Qualitative strategies in counseling research. *Counseling Psychologist 10*(4), 75-89.

Patton, M. (1980). *Qualitative evaluation methods*. Beverly Hills, CA: Sage.

Robie, B., Gansneder, B., & Van Hoose, W. (1979). School guidance and counseling program outcomes and measures for their assessment. *Measurement and Evaluation in Guidance, 12*, 147-166.

Sarason, S. (1982). *The culture of the school and the problem of change*. Boston: Allyn & Bacon.

Shertzer, B., & Stone, S. (1981). *Fundamentals of guidance*. Boston: Houghton Mifflin.

Van Mannen, J. (Ed.). (1983). *Qualitative methodology*. Beverly Hills, CA: Sage.

Van Mannen, J., Dabbs, J., & Faulkner, R. (1982). *Varieties of qualitative research*. Beverly Hills, CA: Sage.

Paul V. Murray is an assistant professor and Justin E. Levitov is an associate professor, Department of Education, Loyola University, New Orleans, Louisiana. Louis Castenell is an associate professor, Department of Education, Xavier University, New Orleans. J. Henry Joubert is coordinator, Information and Community Services, New Orleans Public Schools.

Mellinee Lesley

Exploring the links between critical literacy and developmental reading

Restructuring the curriculum of a remedial reading course to incorporate a critical literacy pedagogy led to skill improvements for the students.

Through all my experiences with people struggling to learn, the one thing that strikes me most is the ease with which we misperceive failed performance and the degree to which this misperception both reflects and reinforces the social order. Class and culture erect boundaries that hinder our vision...and encourage the designation of otherness, difference, deficiency... [S]ome of our basic orientations toward the teaching and testing of literacy contribute to our inability to see. To truly educate in America, then, to reach the full sweep of our citizenry, we need to question received perception, shift continually from the standard lens. (Rose, 1989, p. 205)

Mike Rose speaks to my experiences both as a student and as a teacher. I think first of the ways I have failed students in my hurried evaluations of their literacy, but I realize that even my failures have taught me an immense amount as a teacher. To keep learning, I must keep assessing myself. I must have "failures" to be able to recognize and know success. I must misperceive in order to perceive. I like this passage because it reminds me to think differently about literacy, how I teach it, and how to recognize it in its most nascent forms.

The story recorded here is one of students' successful formulation of literacy as measured in test scores, reading interest inventories, and written artifacts. It's also one of success for me as a teacher, taking a huge risk to revamp an entire developmental reading program for my university. It took a great deal of risk to try to sell a pedagogy of critical literacy to instructors and graduate assistants with minimal amounts of training in literacy in general and absolutely no comprehension of constructivist approaches to literacy (Atwell, 1998; Johnston, 1992; Noguchi, 1991) let alone any understanding of the domain of critical literacy (Bee, 1993; Brady. 1995; Ellsworth, 1992; Freire, 1995; Giroux, 1993; Lankshear & McLaren, 1993; Shor, 1996).

The other risk occurred in the classroom with my own students. Attempting to evoke a pedagogy of questions (Freire, 1995), bring students out of "intellectual Siberia" (Shor.. 1996), and deal with resistance (Bigelow, 1990; Ellsworth, 1992; Lather, 1992) was not easy. In some ways these actions paralleled the professional development work I undertook with the other instructors and graduate assistants. Unlike some of the other instructors, my students were able to navigate the process of critical literacy and come to a measured level of "conscientization" (Freire, 1995), working through false consciousness (Lather, 1992) and resistance (Ellsworth, 1992; Lather, 1992) to obtain a new degree of control over their literacy development, histories, and futures. To say the least, learning more about the possibilities in enacting critical literacy with a "remediated" population of students was an important experience for me as a teacher.

Local and national trends in developmental studies

The current status of basic skills, "remediated" courses in English, reading, and mathematics has reached a critical juncture in die history of developmental studies programs in higher education across the U.S. Every year enrollment in such noncredit courses in-creases along with student attrition and academic failure rates (The Institute for Higher Education Policy, 1998). This increase in remedial student population is concomitant with an overall increase in the number of students attending college, thanks to open enrollment admission standards (The Institute for Higher Education Policy, 1998).

While attention to developmental studies programs tends to be nonexistent in institutions of higher education, remediation constitutes a core function of these programs (Brittain, 1982; The Institute for Higher Education Policy, 1998). A 1995 survey conducted by the National Center for Education Statistics (NCES) found that 78% of higher education institutions offered at least one remedial reading, writing, or mathematics course. All too often, pedagogy in developmental studies courses is "hit or miss" with little, if any, oversight of the curriculum and staff responsible for teaching these courses. In such courses, our most academically at-risk students are subjected to part-time adjunct instructors and teaching assistants with very little institutional efficacy or permanency. Another concern with developmental studies courses lies with the fact that there are no national criteria to determine placement in such courses. In other words, there are no standards for what constitutes "college-level" work and consequently what constitutes remedial college work. This phenomenon peculiar to developmental studies further alienates these courses from the intellectual rigor that is heralded in the academy proper.

At my university, we offer developmental courses in mathematics, English, and reading to provide students with prerequisite skills for entry into college-level coursework. From the fall 1994 semester to the fall 1998 semester, the average percentage of first-year students enrolled in English 100 was 49.3%. In the same period, the average percentage of first-year students in Reading 100 was 27.5%. Despite the numbers of students enrolling in developmental studies courses, the status of these courses has remained low. The developmental reading course, for instance, had been moved from the Reading Education program to administration by-Student Academic Services in the early 1980s. Locating Reading 100 in a service program heightened the nonacademic reputation of the course. With this shift in administrative placement, Reading 100 suffered from little administrative oversight and no curricular attention. As a result of my preliminary research on the developmental reading program a year prior to conducting this study, Reading 100 was returned to the oversight of the Reading Education Program in the Department of Curriculum and Instruction. This simple yet important shift signaled the transition of this course from marginalized to a status of more import, recognizing the relationship of this course to subsequent credit courses offered in the institution.

In an effort to ameliorate the current status of developmental studies courses. I was appointed to chair a committee to study the problems afflicting these courses. While the committee addressed many issues related to the problems troubling our developmental studies courses, the greatest concern was over the pedagogy of these courses. I was appointed as the Coordinator for Reading 100 and permitted to teach one section of the class during the fall 1999 semester.

Prior to my appointment as the coordinator, Reading 100 consisted of weekly vocabulary drills, basic comprehension of brief texts (paragraphs), and eye exercises to increase students' reading rates (speed reading). The course concluded with a full-blown research paper. The course did not ask students to do any reading of the sort that would be required of them in a university-level academic setting. Furthermore, Reading 100 was predicated on a restrictive philosophy of remediation that taught basic skills with repetitive drills. Another glaring problem with the design of this course was the fact that the curriculum followed an illogical practice of teaching lower level drill activities and then expecting students to write a research paper. Little emphasis was placed on reading "real" texts or the interconnectedness of reading and writing, and certainly no attempt was made at reflexive practice or evoking a pedagogy of critical literacy. These identified weaknesses in the pedagogy of Reading 100 led to my research and restructuring of the course to reflect constructivist notions of literacy as well as a pedagogy of critical literacy.

Collecting the data

Broadly stated, the objective for this research was to design an alternative pedagogy for a developmental studies reading course offered at an open enrollment state university. In an attempt to foster the successful literacy acquisition required to survive in a university setting, I examined the effects of enacting a critical literacy pedagogy within the course. The curriculum developed in this study emphasizes the interrelatedness of processes of reading and writing as well as critical reading and writing within an academic discourse community. Consequently, the pedagogy presented in the new-course incorporated research from the domains of critical literacy, adult literacy, emergent literacy, and developmental studies in order to shed light on developmental reading programs in higher education.

The following research questions guided my study:

1. What happens when students enrolled in a basic skills reading course experience critical literacy (reading and writing conscientization) as an entrance into academic modes of discourse?

2. To what extent do the students enrolled in this course construct or begin to construct themselves as readers and writers through the means of critical reflection and critical literacy pedagogy?

To answer these questions I first had to design a literacy program where critical literacy was a curricular goal. Consequently, I began by restructuring the course around the following tenets that I would require of all Reading 100 instructors:

- Writing will be used primarily as a tool for strengthening processes of reading/thinking/learning.
- Texts will consist of Mike Rose's (1989) book *Lives on the Boundary,* readings chosen from the Freshman Seminar Reader, and selections chosen by the instructor.
- "Basic skills" in reading (e.g., summarizing, synthesizing, developing inference, developing vocabulary) will be embedded in the processes of reading "real" texts and explicitly taught as mini-lessons that are to be applied to immediate experiences with reading and responding to reading.
- Themes for the course will emphasize translation into academic modes of discourse (especially critical and analytical reading), "territories" for reading (Atwell, 1998) (how people read or learn to read in authentic venues), and literacy narratives.

Goals for the students included the following:

- Reconstruct their identities as readers and writers,
- Develop fluency in using writing as a tool for thinking,
- Develop skills to foster critical and analytical reading ability, and
- Develop metacognitive awareness about their reading processes.

With these tenets and goals, I grounded the course in a constructivist philosophy (Vygotsky, 1978). Through the texts chosen for the course,

FIGURE 1

Nelson-Denny Reading Test result

Year	Section number	Beginning*	Ending*
Fall 1998	104	11.5	10.5
Fall 1998	101	9.0	8.4
Fall 1998	102	8.6	9.1
Fall 1998	103	10.9	9.9
Fall 1999	101	9.1	9.8
Fall 1999	102	9.9	12.0
Fall 1999	103	10.0	10.9
Fall 1999	104	8.8	9.1
Fall 1999	105	9.1	10.2

*Average grade equivalency as scored on the Nelson-Denny Reading Test

the reflective assignments, and the first student goal, I also set the stage for establishing a pedagogy of critical literacy in the course.

I collected data through qualitative interpretive (Erickson, 1986) methods. However, I also collected quantitative data from norm-referenced test scores and surveys. My stance was primarily that of a teacher-researcher (Cochran-Smith & Lytle, 1993, 1999). There were 22 students enrolled in my course. As recent graduates from high school, all of the students in the course could be categorized as "traditional" students. Fourteen of the students were female, and eight were male. Eight of the students were Hispanic, two were African American, and one was Native American.

Data sources for the study consisted of pre- and poststudy Nelson-Denny Test scores, interest inventories, and responses to literature; writing samples; transcripts from focus group interviews and class discussions; archives of student writing; and a reflective journal of my experiences as a teacher. I analyzed each source of qualitative data through linguistic coding according to Fairclough's (1995) work on critical discourse analysis and Vine and Faust's (1993) work on situated reading. With these tools for analysis, I looked specifically for trends in students' reflection and self-ascribed literacy labels. I also coded the data for personal connections students were making in reading, intertextual connections in their reading and writing, and instances of critical observations about developmental studies. Through all of this analysis, I was looking for trends in students' abilities to read the texts analytically as well as position themselves as readers in the broader contexts for literacy the institution entails (e.g., developmental studies). As revealing as the qualitative data was, the most compelling data were the increases made in students' reading scores on the Nelson-Denny Test. (See Figure 1.)

Developmental reading

Focusing as it does on a lack of vocabulary and comprehension skills, research on developmental reading methods is almost exclusively predicated on a deficit model of learning. Developmental reading courses are similarly constructed as "college success" courses with a great deal of emphasis placed on study skills and content area reading strategies (Barksdale-Ladd & Rose. 1997). Nearly two decades ago, Brittain (1982) found that college reading instruction invariably fell into one of the following two categories: (a) courses where reading was constructed as a series of study skills, and (b) courses where reading was constructed in relation to a combined content area course. While Laine, Laine, and Bullock (1999) found that successful developmental reading instaiction is contingent upon innovative teaching and learning strategies, little research to date has been conducted on evoking critical literacy pedagogy in either of Brittain's two categories within the framework of a developmental reading course (see McFarland, Dowdey, & Davis, 1999 for an exception). This study fills a gap in the research on developmental reading programs, where basic skills in reading are reconceptualized through the lens of critical literacy.

In my study, basic skills of reading (e.g., comprehension, vocabulary development, inference, synthesis) were subsumed into a larger framework of critical literacy. Critical literacy is defined by researchers such as Lankshear and McLaren (1993), Giroux (1993), Bee (1993), Brady (1994), and others as literacy that begins with a rising consciousness of not merely the functionality of print but also the power of language to both silence and give voice to instances of oppression in issues of socially determined disparities. In this vein of consciousness, Paulo Freire (1995) wrote that students first had to read the world before they could read the word. Emergent literacy research (Avery, 1993; Calkins, 1994; Cooper, 1993; Morrow, 1997) espouses a similar philosophy, that children read their environment long before they begin to decode print. In other words, literacy at all levels always begins with the impetus of the context for reading, writing, and speaking. The impetus of the context for students in developmental reading courses exists within a system of social stratification. The construction of developmental studies courses by the larger academic community as subacademic courses teaching subacademic skills creates a relevant context for developmental studies students to delve into issues of power and language from a personal, experiential vantage point.

Students in basic skills courses need to read the world of the academy before they can read and write for an academic community. Critical pedagogues (e.g., Shor, 1996) would argue that we cannot successfully invite students into the world of academic reading by drilling them in a series of disconnected subskills in literacy. Rather, we must give them complete, contextualized reading and writing experiences first and then work on skills through student-driven assessment and instruction. Similarly, we must redefine the concept of "basic skills" in reading through the stance of critical literacy. While this is a seemingly compelling argument in favor of critical literacy in a developmental reading course, fully realizing critical literacy in such a context is problematic. The definition and experience of critical literacy is so utterly dependent upon the students' relationships with the texts of their lives that the story of critical literacy within the population of "remedial" students is always, necessarily, delicately contingent upon these relationships.

In the section of Reading 100 that I taught, critical literacy began with a pedagogy of questions (Freire, 1995) pertaining to discussions surrounding the nature of a developmental studies course in reading. These initial dialogues were pivotal in establishing a culture conducive to critical literacy. The dialogues were difficult for me as a teacher because some students expressed open hostility to being placed in the course based on an arbitrary score on the ACT test, receiving no credit toward graduation, and being required to pay for it.

Rose's (1989) account of remediation, tracking, and the academy in *Lives on the Boundary* served as the core text for the course. This text further fueled class discussions about the perceived unfair placement of students into the course. From this text, students read, wrote, and talked about the larger system of developmental studies across the U.S. as well as their own experiences. The assignments I gave students to keep a dialogue journal, write in-class reflective essays, compile a reader's resource notebook, and write a literacy narrative facilitated their learning and growth from skill development to critical reflection and questioning.

Bound by university guidelines and expectations for developmental studies coursework, I wasn't able to negotiate course assignments to the extent that Shor (1996) did. I did, however, seek to provide assignments that were student-driven. The assignments for the class began with an in-class dialogue journal. This journal consisted of students first responding to class readings and discussions and then responding to their classmates' responses. I also participated in this weekly activity. I included this assignment as a mechanism to give each student a chance to voice ideas and receive feedback on these ideas. The journals also gave students less structured opportunities for writing practice. Over time, students began to generate more in-depth responses and questions with their audience in mind. The following exchange from a dialogue journal exemplifies the beginning of student reflection on their educational experiences.

> Student 1- If I was designing a reading developmental class I would do pretty much the same things that we are doing in here

but I would have prepared students for things like this in earlier grades so they wouldn't have to take these courses in college. I think reading should be taught by understanding what you are reading along with how to read a certain word.

Student 2: I agree they should prepare students in earlier grades and maybe they wouldn't fall behind in college. Understanding what you read might make the reading more interesting.

Mellinee: What happened in your earlier school experiences that led to your having to take a developmental studies course in reading? What were you not taught.

Student 1: I don't think that there really is anything that I haven't learned, that maybe I should've learned. Maybe I don't comprehend all the time but I don't think that it is to the point where I should have to take a basic reading class in college, but that's what the test proved. (Dialogue journal, September, 1999)

In addition to modeling writing and responding for my students, I was also participating in learning through joining this activity.

Students also kept a reader's resource notebook. The purpose of this assignment was for students to create an archive to assist them in their reading and literacy skills. The notebook provided students with an opportunity to personalize skill aspects of their learning in a contextualized and systematic fashion. The reader's resource notebook was a compilation of vocabulary encountered in course readings, notes from class discussions on the readings, and reading strategies that worked for the student. I presented this assignment largely as an investigative tool for students to explore the mechanics of their literacy development. As such, it served the purposes of both skill exploration and metacognitive awareness development.

Every class period, we concluded with a summary of what we did on one side of an index card and what we learned on the other side. These cards not only helped students distill key ideas and recall class events, but also served as data for me. With the cards, my students were able to give me continual and instant feedback on each class. I was also able to monitor my students' literacy development (e.g., questioning, reflection, analysis, rising consciousness) through their observations of the class. The following are examples of responses to one class:

What did we do?

- Today we read pp. 111-114 and got into groups and discussed what went on and how Mike Rose is dealing with what is going on. We responded in our journals about our literacy lessons.
- We read out of *Lives on the Boundary* and David gave his presentation on a soccer player.
- Article presentation: went over Monday dialogue journals; read 111—114 in *Lives on the Boundary*, discussion in small groups about what we read; Nov. 1 class feedback.
- Discussed our journal topic, heard David's presentation. Read pgs. 111-114, got in small groups.
- We did dialogue journals and students volunteered to read from pg. 111-114 in *Lives on the Boundary*. We read 11/1/99 What did we do/ What did we learn and I explained the info I got from it.

What did we learn?

- I learned how Mike Rose feels about students. I learned what other students are learning about Mike Rose.
- I learned what *tracking, resistance,* and *remediation* meant.
- Mike Rose really cares about the kids.
- What I learned was that the children Mike Rose taught live in very harsh environments.
- How others felt about *Lives on the Boundary,* the literacy words *tracking, resistance,* and *remediation.*
- Everybody will have trouble in some subject, but you can't let it take you down. Never give up.
- We learned different people's ideas in their journal and what Mike Rose's students' lives are like.
- I learned what Dr. Lesley does with these cards. I realized that remediation will help in the long run.

(Class archive, November 3, 1999)

From these statements, I could tell how many of my students were developing reading skills such as inference (e.g., how Mike Rose *really* felt about his students), empathy (e.g., how my students felt about the students in the book), and critical analysis (e.g., how concepts of tracking, remediation, and resistance figured into the book). Another assignment in the course consisted of in-class reader response essays written about excerpts from *Lives on the Boundary*. On one occasion toward the end of the semester, I asked students to revise essays written in the previous class to include five vocabulary words from their reader's resource notebooks. I used this revision request to demonstrate for the students Noguchi's (1991) notion of the ways writing signifies class distinctions. By incorporating and applying the academic vocabulary students were encountering in their writing, they were able to begin to emulate the discourse patterns of the academy. This assignment demonstrated the students' growing control of academic discourse. By couching the assignment in terms of social class markers in discourse, I was attempting to move students toward a critical literacy insight on the ways language intertwines with societal power.

The final assignment was to write a literacy narrative (Soliday, 1994) of the story of how students acquired literacy. Through this assignment students noted social and emotional "disconnects" in their education and their lives at times when they were supposed to be developing literacy. For instance, one student wrote the following:

> Reading out loud in front of the class was always a challenge for me. My problem was that I would get nervous because I wouldn't want to mess up in front of my friends. But, of course I would get really nervous and mess up or I couldn't pronounce a word correctly. Sometimes the other students would giggle when I would read or make fun of me. So, therefore, I didn't have a strong self-confidence and I wouldn't push myself to do better because I thought I couldn't be as smart as them. (December, 1999)

Another student wrote about similar disconnects in his literacy narrative:

> From first grade to the fifth grade it got harder and easier at the same time if that makes sense. Reading was the easy part; it was the whole English part that through me off. I understood what a noun and a verb was but I didn't know how to use them. So I was screwed so to speak. Teachers at my elementary school had other things to worry about or they just didn't care. A teacher later on in the sixth grade stumbled across my disability and I was placed in a chapter one class where I was basically taught everything over again. To my disbelief it help. I was teased and picked on for being in the class. The teasing took a toll on my self-esteem. I felt really small and stupid and that caused me to drop the whole idea of reading except in school. My reading skill dropped once again and I didn't care. (December, 1999)

One of the most powerful literacy narratives was written by a student who through our discussions of expanding literacy beyond written texts, realized her literacy was disconnected at home long before she learned to decode print. This student wrote:

> As I was growing up I learn many ways of reading. I learn how to read my father's attitude, I learn to read books from school and on my own, I learn to take care of my younger brothers and sister by reading my mother, I also read feeling and objects to write my poetry.
>
> Since I can remember my father has had a drinking problem. I always knew what to do and how to act after reading him for a few years. Some days my dad would come home smelling weird and had blood shot eyes. I never understood what that was all about, I just knew he was going to be a different person from hours before. At first I would see that my dad's walk was weak and he wore a wicked smile. I would walk by him to see if he had that strong bitter smell on him. Once I smelled that ugly odor I had to think fast, I had to think of ways to tell my mom without him knowing. By reading his actions I learn to act fast and think quickly. As I watched him speak to my mother his words were mixed, his voice was very sharp and deep. Each time he would start talking, he would talk about all the happy and good times they had. Then he moves on to all the bad things that happen between them, after that he gets very angry and he would take his anger out on my mother. As I was reading him I knew that I had to do something once he started to raise his voice. (December, 1999)

These examples of students' writing and reflection about their literacy development mark the beginning of a journey of self-awareness within a larger social and academic structure facilitated by critical literacy. My approach to critical literacy was to bring critical reflection on constructions of literacy into the course content. The themes of the course initiated from this point as we explored concepts of being present, place, silence, play, teachers, community, justice,

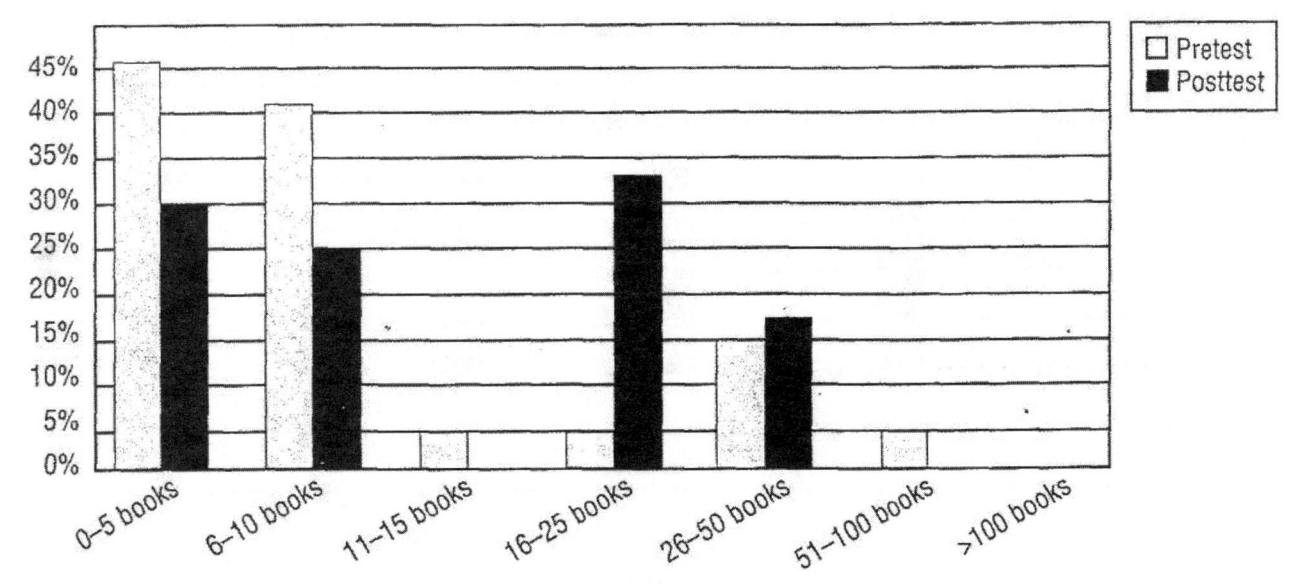

FIGURE 2
How many books do you own?

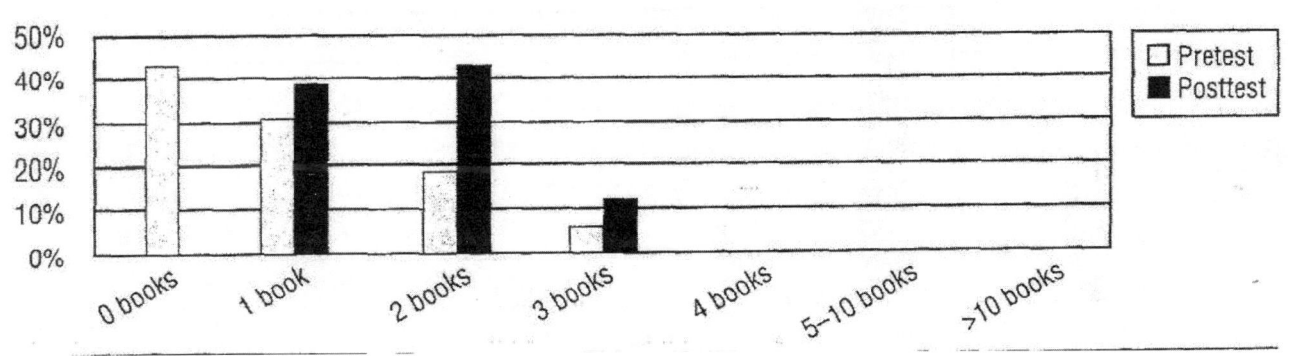

FIGURE 3
How many books have you read in the last four months?

and transformation. We found that what's transformative for one student within a critical literacy context may not be for the next. Also, simply approaching literacy in relationship to critical reflection about the status of language and placement of courses within a university leads to critical literacy.

Critical literacy fosters academic success

I want to conclude with some of the compelling statistics collected on the pre- and poststudy inventories. In each of these measures, students made significant gains, and students' attitudes toward reading and practices with reading improved. (Please see Figures 2-5 for a breakdown of these results.) Perhaps even more impressive was the increase in average reading level of students in all sections of Reading 100. In previous years, students' reading scores had actually decreased upon completion of the course. The section I taught, with an explicit focus on critical literacy (section 102), made the most dramatic

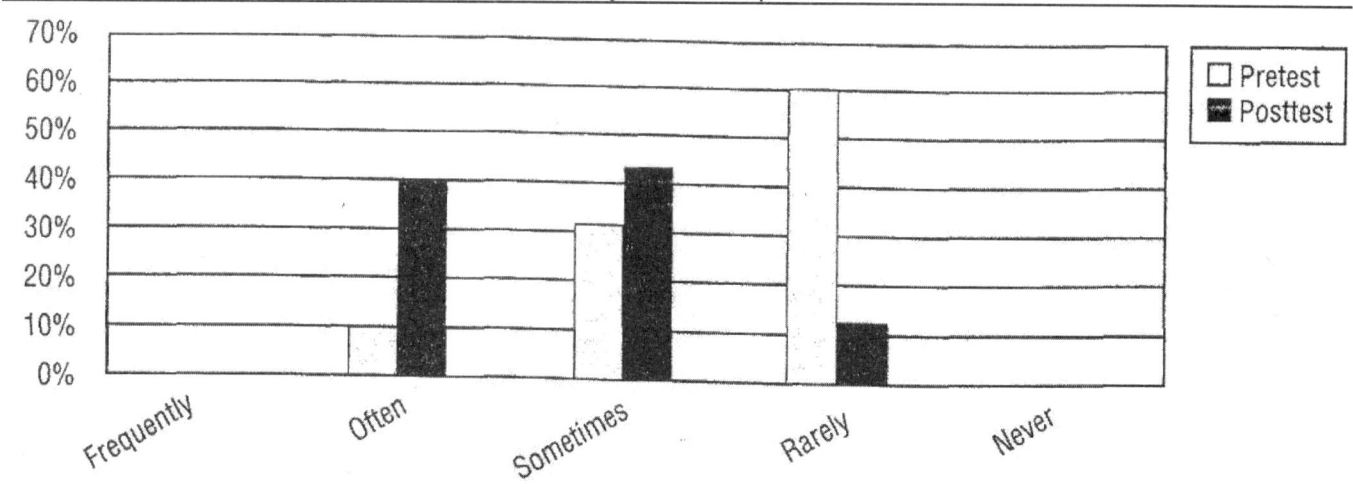

FIGURE 4
How often do you read for pleasure?

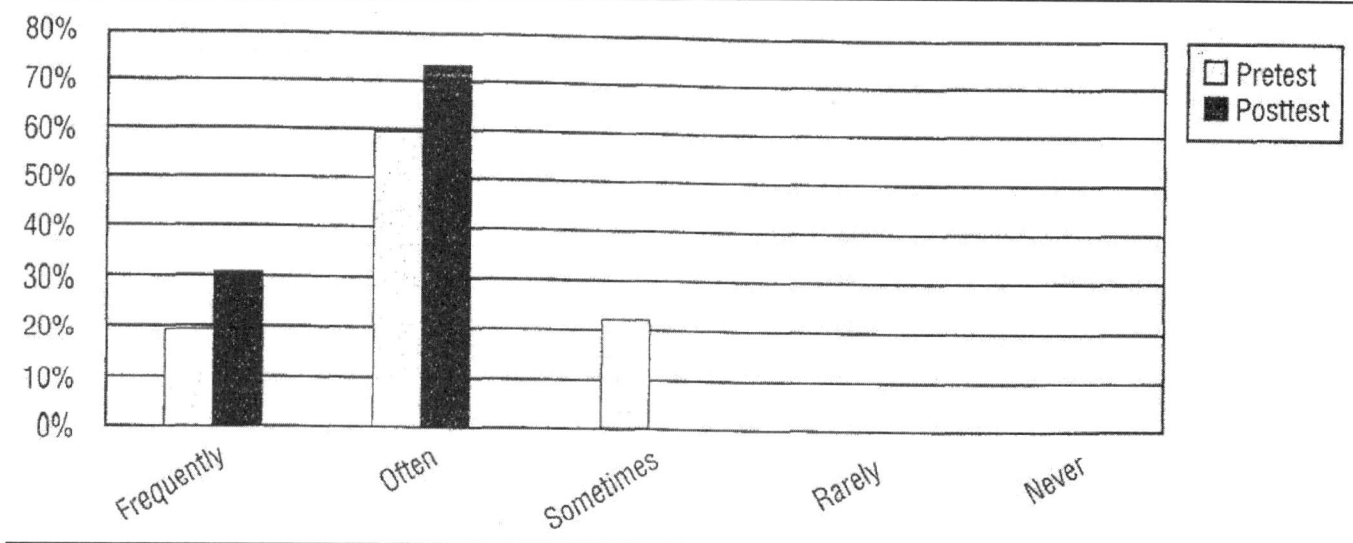

FIGURE 5
How often do you read for school purposes?

gains moving from an average ninth-grade reading level equivalency to a twelfth-grade equivalency. (Please see Figure 1.)

The instructors for the other sections followed some of the assignments for the course and did not complete Rose's *Lives on the Boundary* with their classes. These instructors similarly did not attempt pedagogy of critical literacy in their sections. The results support the previously cited research in favor of critical literacy. If we can learn anything from this study it's the fact that it's critical for students enrolled in developmental reading courses to experience the level of reading—reflection and analysis—that critical literacy fosters.

Critical literacy is a problematic philosophy to translate into practice (Ellsworth, 1992; Lesley, 1997). Yet the ideals of equity- that shape critical literacy make the philosophy particularly compelling for developmental course work. This research suggests that teaching reading as a complex analysis even to "remediated" populations of students yields positive gains in students' literacy skills. The study also highlights the fact that critical literacy occurs in practice as a process. In effect, critical literacy is its own content area for students to master before they can enact a pedagogy of action. Introducing critical literacy to "developmental" readers begins students' successful introduction to academia where complex questions and analysis of answers drive inquiry in every discipline. If "remedial" students are to survive in the world of the academy, they cannot do so through lower level drill practice. They must learn to read analytically, beginning with their own circumstances of tracking, social stratification, and marginalization.

From this experience, I have come to believe that critical literacy fosters critical questioning and thinking and thus enhances students' comprehension skills in reading. Certainly, this study warrants further longitudinal investigation into the potential of academic success that critical literacy pedagogy fosters for developmental students. Finally, my attempt in this study to enact critical literacy hinged on my ability to create an environment where students could develop their own understanding of the concepts of critical reading and writing in the academy. Eminent purposes for literacy compel us all to engage more deeply.

Lesley teaches at Eastern New Mexico University. She may be contacted there at Reading/Literacy Education, Station 25, ENMU, Portals, NM 88130, USA. She may be reached by e-mail at melline8.lesley@enmu.edu.

REFERENCES

Atwell, N. (1998). *In the middle: New understandings about writing reading, and learning.* Portsmouth. NH: Heinemann.

Avery, C. (1993). *And with a light touch: Learning about reading, writing, and teaching with first graders.* Portsmouth, NH: Heinemann.

Barksdale-Ladd, M., & Rose, M. (1997). Qualitative assessments in developmental reading. *Journal of College Reading and Learning, 26*(1). 34-55.

Bee, B. (1993). Critical literacy and the politics of gender. In C. Lankshear & P. McLaren (Eds.). *Critical literacy: Politics, praxis, and the postmodern.* Albany, NY: State University of New York Press.

Bigelow, W. (1990). Inside the classroom: Social vision and critical pedagogy. *Teachers College Record, 91,* 437-448.

Brady, J. (1995). *Schooling young children: A feminist pedagogy for liberatory learning.* Albany, NY: State University of New York Press.

Brittain, M. (1982). *Developmental and remedial reading instruction for college students.* Paper presented at the 9th World Congress on Reading, Dublin, Ireland.

Calkins, L. (1994). *The art of teaching writing.* Portsmouth, NH: Heinemann.

Cochran-Smith, M. & Lytle, S. (1993). *Inside/outside: Teacher research and knowledge.* New York: Teachers College Press.

Cochran-Smith, M., & Lytle, S. (1999). The teacher research Movement: A decade later. *Educational Researcher, 28,* 13-25.

Cooper, P. (1993) *When stones come to school.* New York: Teachers and Writers Collaborative.

Ellsworth, E. (1992). Why doesn't this feel empowering? Working through the repressive myths of critical pedagogy. In C. Luke & J. Gore (Eds.), *Feminisms and critical pedagogy* (pp. 90-119). New York: Routledge.

Erickson, F. (1986). Qualitative methods in research on teaching. In M.C. Wittrock (Ed.), *Handbook of research on teaching* (3rd ed., pp. 119-161). New York: Macmillan.

Fairclough, N. (1995). *Critical discourse analysis: The critical study of language.* New York: Longman.

Freire, P. (1995). *Pedagogy of hope: Reliving* Pedagogy of the Oppressed. New York: Continuum.

Giroux, H. (1993). Literacy and the politics of difference. In C. Lankshear & P. McLaren (Eds.), *Critical literacy: Politics, praxis, and the postmodern* (pp. 367-377). Albany, NY: State University of New York Press.

The Institute for Higher Education Policy. (1998, December). *College remediation: What it is, what it costs, what's at stake.* Washington, DC: Author.

Johnston, P. (1992). *Constructive evaluation of literate activity.* New York: Longman.

Laine, M., Laine, C., & Bullock, T. (1999). Developmental reading in the United States: One decade later. *Research and Teaching in Developmental Education, 15*(2), 5-17.

Lankshear, C., & McLaren, P. (1993). *Critical literacy: Politics, praxis, and the postmodern.* Albany. NY: State University of New York Press.

Lather, P. (1992). Critical frames in educational research: Feminist and poststructural perspectives. *Theory Into Practice, 35*(2), 70-71.

Lesley, M. (1997). The difficult dance of critical literacy. *Journal of Adolescent & Adult Literacy, 40,* 420-424.

McFarland, K.P., Dowdey, D., & Davis, K. (1999). *A search for non traditional pedagogies in teaching developmental reading and writing.* (ERIC Document Reproduction Service No. ED 432 784)

Morrow, L.M. (1997). *Literacy development in the early years: Helping children read and write.* Boston: Allyn & Bacon.

Noguchi, R. (1991). *Grammar and the teaching of writing: Limits and possibilities.* Urbana, IL: National Council of Teachers of English.

Rose. M. (1989). *Lives on the boundary.* New York: The Free Press.

Shor, I. (1996). *When students have power: Negotiating authority in a critical pedagogy.* Chicago: University of Chicago Press.

Soliday. M. (1994). Translating self and difference through literacy narratives. *College English, 56,* 511-526.

Vine, H.. & Faust, M. (1993). *Situating readers: Students making meaning of literature.* Urbana, IL: National Council of Teachers of English.

Vygotsky, L.S. (1978). *Mind in society.* Cambridge, MA: MIT Press.